The Noir Western

ALSO BY DAVID MEUEL

Women in the Films of John Ford (McFarland, 2014)

The Noir Western
Darkness on the Range, 1943–1962

DAVID MEUEL

McFarland & Company, Inc., Publishers
Jefferson, North Carolina

LIBRARY OF CONGRESS CATALOGUING-IN-PUBLICATION DATA

Meuel, David, 1950–
    The noir western : darkness on the range, 1943–1962 / David Meuel.
        p.   cm
    Includes bibliographical references and index.

    ISBN 978-0-7864-9452-1 (softcover : acid free paper) ∞
    ISBN 978-1-4766-1974-3 (ebook)

    1. Western films—United States—History and criticism. 2. Film noir—United States—History and criticism. 3. Motion pictures—20th century—History and criticism. I. Title.
    PN1995.9.W4M45 2015
    791.43'65878—dc23   2014049546

BRITISH LIBRARY CATALOGUING DATA ARE AVAILABLE

© 2015 David Meuel. All rights reserved

No part of this book may be reproduced or transmitted in any form or by any means, electronic or mechanical, including photocopying or recording, or by any information storage and retrieval system, without permission in writing from the publisher.

Cover image: *Blood on the Moon*, 1948 © RKO

Printed in the United States of America

McFarland & Company, Inc., Publishers
  Box 611, Jefferson, North Carolina 28640
    www.mcfarlandpub.com

To Kathryn

Table of Contents

Preface	1
Introduction: The Dark Cowboy Rides into Town	5
1. The Darkening West: Conscience and Cruelty Collide in William Wellman's *The Ox-Bow Incident*, *Yellow Sky* and *Track of the Cat*	21
2. The Tyranny of Troubled Pasts: Escape and the Futility of It in Raoul Walsh's *Pursued* and *Colorado Territory*	38
3. Where Treachery Springs Eternal: Staying Human in the Harsh Worlds of André de Toth's *Ramrod* and *Day of the Outlaw*	55
4. "The topography of menace": Painting the Western Black in Robert Wise's *Blood on the Moon*	70
5. Westerns Shaken and Stirred: Sam Fuller Upends Genre Conventions in *I Shot Jesse James* and *Forty Guns*	81
6. Delving Deeper into the Dark Side: Gregory Peck's Noir-ish Heroes in Henry King's *The Gunfighter* and *The Bravados*	97
7. Deliverance on a Down Note: The Tortured, Grimly Determined Heroes of Anthony Mann's *Devil's Doorway*, *The Naked Spur* and *Man of the West*	115
8. Nightmare in Broad Daylight: Evil Poses as the Law in Allan Dwan's *Silver Lode*	140

9. Helping the Western to Grow Up: The Complex, Shaded Characters in Delmer Daves' *3:10 to Yuma* and *The Hanging Tree*   150

10. "They're going to kill us, Mrs. Mims": Horror and Absurdity Ride Together in Budd Boetticher's *The Tall T* and *Ride Lonesome*   168

11. Darkness in Shinbone: Noir Is Busting Out All Over in John Ford's *The Man Who Shot Liberty Valance*   185

Conclusion: Ride On, Dark Cowboy   197

Fifty Additional Noir-ish Postwar Westerns Worth Seeing   199

Chapter Notes   205

Bibliography   209

Index   211

Preface

"The noir western"—the very term is oxymoronic. On one hand, we have the bright, expansive, colorful landscapes; upright heroes; and nation-building exuberance we associate with most film westerns. On the other, we have the dark, claustrophobic, black-and-white (mostly black) cityscapes; flawed, compromised heroes; and bitter disillusionment of the classic noir crime dramas of the 1940s and 1950s. Then, like slapping raw bacon onto a hot griddle, we put these elements together and voila! Something new is sizzling: a budding film form (or maybe we'd rather call it a "sub-genre") that is distinctive and remarkable in its own right and that—for decades to come—will influence not only the western but also other film genres.

That's essentially what happened in Hollywood in the mid–1940s. Influenced not only by the noir crime drama but also by numerous factors from the horrors of World War II, to 1920s German expressionistic cinema, to 1930s "hard-boiled" pulp crime fiction, these "new" westerns incorporated many of the classic noir elements into their stories. Just a few include greater moral ambiguity, greater psychological complexity, greater use of noir-style lighting effects to enhance mood and feeling, and more frequent use of standard noir storytelling techniques such as voiceovers and flashbacks. Now the "Wild West" of the movies was a darker, moodier, more complicated place—a place that more closely mirrored the bleaker, more uncertain mood of the post-war period.

The creative forces behind these darker westerns were a diverse, eccentric, and extremely talented lot. They included—among many others—noted noir directors such as Budd Boetticher, Delmer Daves, André de Toth, Anthony Mann, and Robert Wise; bold, idiosyncratic newcomers such as Sam Fuller; and old Hollywood masters such as Allan Dwan, John Ford, Henry King, Raoul Walsh, and William Wellman.

Together, these directors and their collaborators brought about a major shift in popular cinematic storytelling. This shift didn't mark an end to the traditional westerns that dated all the way back to the beginnings of cinema. Rather than eclipsing those films, these darker counterparts co-existed with them, the two western forms complementing (and enriching) one another throughout the 1950s—often cited as the "Golden Age of Westerns."

The number, variety, and quality of these noir-ish westerns are quite impressive. This is especially true when we adopt (as I have done) a fairly flexible definition of "noir" to an analysis of them. There are literally hundreds of deserving films to choose from. Narrowing my focus to a mere 21 for this book was no small task, and I am certain that readers will wonder why I have left out many that could easily have been included. These films also range from textbook noir storylines such as Raoul Walsh's powerful *Colorado Territory* (1949), itself a remake of Walsh's early crime noir *High Sierra* (1941), to Budd Boetticher's idiosyncratic minimalist films such as *The Tall T* (1957) and *Ride Lonesome* (1959), to Sam Fuller's eccentric, in-your-face iconoclasm in *Forty Guns* (1957). And the quality—even among relatively obscure films such as Mann's *Man of the West* (1958) and de Toth's *Day of the Outlaw* (1959)—is surprisingly high. It's a shame the Academy of Motion Picture Arts and Sciences and other awards organizations have long had a prejudice against westerns and other "lowly" genre films, because many of them should have received much more attention and recognition in their day than they did.

While an enormous amount has been written about both film noir and the western, there is little in-depth examination about the strong and vital connection that exists between them. The subject is briefly discussed in numerous articles and blogs, in sections from two books about Anthony Mann, in an appendix from *The Film Noir Encyclopedia* by Alain Silver, and in sections from books on the western that span much longer periods of time. Jim Kitses' *Horizons West: Directing the Western from John Ford to Clint Eastwood* (2004), for example, has insightful chapters on Ford, Mann, and Boetticher, but its principal focus is much broader, namely the western genre from Ford's first features in the 1910s, to Clint Eastwood's various efforts up to the 1990s. Another and more recent example is Mary Lea Bandy and Kevin Stoehr's excellent *Ride, Boldly Ride: The Evolution of the American Western* (2012). Again, this covers the western genre as a whole and includes a section on the more noir-ish, psychologically complex post-war period westerns. But again, the focus of the book is relatively broad, and the subject of the noir western is not explored as fully as it could have been.

My hope is that this book strikes a responsive chord among people who enjoy westerns, classic noir crime dramas, or both. I have organized the chapters around individual directors rather than individual films for a specific reason. Each of these directors, I believe, looked at the western (and, by extension, life) in a very personal way, and, as a result, made worthy (and very distinctive) contributions to the noir western form. In turn, each of their contributions added to the form in some way, blazing a trail for other filmmakers to follow or depart from according to their preferences. For those who would like to continue their exploration of this subject after they finish this book, I have also included a list of 50 additional noir-ish westerns made between 1946 and 1962 they might find worthwhile.

―⚎―

The initial inspiration for this book came from a course I took several years ago through Stanford University's Continuing Studies Program. It focused on the western from 1939 to 1959, and, while the emphasis wasn't western noir, I was struck by how much noir influence had seeped into to the venerable western genre. The idea for a book-length study of this phenomenon grew from there.

The teacher of the course was Elliot Lavine, a longtime film programmer and instructor in the San Francisco Bay Area who has received wide-ranging praise for his efforts to connect modern audiences with excellent vintage films that—for various reasons—have been unfairly dismissed or simply forgotten. As well as providing me with wonderful ideas and insights, Elliot has always supplied ample enthusiasm and support. I could not have written this book without him.

I also want to thank my trusted "kitchen cabinet" of friends and family members who have generously offered their ideas and insights as I have gone through the book development process. These include James Meuel, Annette Hulbert, Bob and Melanie Ferrando, Peter Nelson, Natalie Varney, Scotty Martinson, Jim Daniels, and Paul Bendix. As always, I've appreciated their good ideas, patience (as they've listened to me ramble on about this subject *ad nauseum*), and unflagging support. Much of the credit for this book belongs to them as well.

Finally, photographs are always a critical part of any book on film, and I would like to thank the people at the New York-based photo archive Photofest, who supplied all the photographs for this book. Their knowledge, professionalism, and enthusiasm were very impressive.

―⚎―

As I went through the process of building this book chapter by chapter, I made many intriguing and some startling discoveries not only about noir westerns but also about the 11 film directors I singled out as significant contributors to the phenomenon. While some of these directors, such as John Ford and perhaps Raoul Walsh, William Wellman, and Robert Wise, are familiar names to many classic film aficionados, others—such as Allan Dwan, Henry King, and André de Toth —are probably not. Yet, despite their relative anonymity, their contributions both to western noir and to other kinds of films are notable and their personal stories fascinating. It's a shame that—as each passing day puts more distance between us and the great achievements of Hollywood's classic era—their names are fading from the ongoing conversation. With luck, though, this book might spark renewed interest in them and in their better films, some of which were fine noir westerns.

Introduction: The Dark Cowboy Rides into Town

On September 2, 1945, the American battleship the USS *Missouri* was only one of more than 250 U.S. warships anchored in Japan's Tokyo Bay, but, for a short while that day, it commanded the full attention of the world. At about 9:00 a.m. Tokyo time, representatives from the Japanese, American, and several other governments met on its deck and, with stiff but gracious formality, signed what was known simply as the "Japanese Instrument of Surrender." As they wrote their names in the designated places on the documents, the deadliest and, in many respects, the most hideous war in all of human history officially came to a quiet, unassuming end.

The size, scope, and horror of World War II are difficult for most people today to grasp. According to the more conservative estimates, the war took somewhere between 60 and 65 million lives, about 2.5 percent of the world's entire population at the time and about three times the number of people who had died in the deadliest conflict up until that time, World War I. About two-thirds of these people were civilians, and the death tolls in some countries were staggering. The Soviet Union lost about 14 percent of its entire population. Poland lost about 17 percent, a great many of its dead being among the six million people killed at Auschwitz, Dachau, and the other Nazi extermination camps that dotted Central and Eastern Europe.[1]

Also difficult to grasp is the impact the war had on those who survived. Not only were their lives changed in ways they could scarcely imagine just a few years before, but many had also changed fundamentally as human beings. Millions were wounded and many of these disabled for life. An untold number also suffered from emotional wounds, various psychological conditions including the one we now call post-traumatic stress disorder, or PTSD. These people saw the human experience very differently now, and they often decided to take their lives in entirely different directions.

Among these survivors was a celebrated U.S. film director named George Stevens. Born in 1904, Stevens broke into films in 1930 as a cameraman on Laurel and Hardy comedy shorts and within a half dozen years was directing both the Katharine Hepburn romantic comedy *Alice Adams* (1935) and the Fred Astaire and Ginger Rogers musical gem *Swingtime* (1936). In the early 1940s, he continued to work in the same vein, directing such classic comedies as 1942's *Woman of the Year* and *Talk of the Town*, and 1943's *The More the Merrier*. Anxious to contribute to the war effort, he joined the U.S. Army Signal Corps and headed a film unit in Europe. His group photographed inspiring moments such as the liberation of Paris in 1944, but it also documented the war's horrors on the beaches of Normandy on D-Day in 1944 and at the liberation of Dachau in 1945. His team's work proved invaluable. In fact, its footage of Dachau was used at the Nuremberg Trials in 1945 and 1946 to show the extent and brutality of the Nazi extermination practices.

Afterwards, Stevens returned to Hollywood and to directing films—the workplace and the work he had known before the war. For him, however, things would never be the same. After just one semi-comic effort, 1948's *I Remember Mama* (and despite efforts by Katharine Hepburn and others to get him to do so), he never directed another comedy or even another film with comic scenes in it. While some of his post-war films were superbly done, they are all very somber in tone. As his widow, Yvonne, remarked years later, "He just never dreamed, I'm sure, what he was getting into when he enlisted."[2]

While Stevens' story is a poignant example of the war's impact, it is certainly not unique among filmmakers in the 1940s. We can see the war's influence on the work of just about everyone who participated in the war from John Ford (who was wounded at the Battle of Midway and who also led a photographic unit on D-Day) to Frank Capra, John Huston, William Wyler, Sam Fuller, and thousands of others involved not only in directing but with every aspect of filmmaking. In addition, the war's impact was felt—often just as keenly—by filmmakers who weren't on the front lines but who followed what was happening to people both in Europe and throughout Asia and the Pacific. Sometimes the war's influence brought a greater humanism, a greater empathy, to the stories they brought to the big screen. We certainly see this in the work of Stevens and Ford. Sometimes, though, it brought greater bitterness and cynicism as we often see in the films of Billy Wilder and Fritz Lang, two of Hollywood's other major post-war directors. But whether a film was infused with Stevens or Ford's humanism or Wilder or Lang's cynicism, it usually expressed a greater wariness about human nature, a darker view of the world and the people in it.

As the war had changed these filmmakers, it had also changed filmgoers, who increasingly wanted to see something that more closely reflected the new view of things. As a result, the movies went in a variety of new directions, and one of these led into one of the medium's oldest, most beloved, and relentlessly optimistic genres—the western. Audiences didn't quite know it when the war officially ended in Tokyo Bay on September 2, 1945, but the dark cowboy would soon be riding into town.

For many of the filmmakers returning from the war, Hollywood appeared to be a very different place from the one they had left. Gone were such major stars as Leslie Howard and Carole Lombard, both victims of the war (Howard killed when the German Luftwaffe shot down his plane; Lombard killed in a plane crash after a rally promoting war bonds). Gone were Shirley Temple's childhood years and golden locks. Gone was the entire, largely upbeat filmmaking era that had culminated in 1939, the so-called "greatest year of the movies," a year highlighted by such enduring classics as *The Wizard of Oz* and, yes, *Gone with the Wind*.

Yet much of the old Hollywood—including most of the moguls, directors, stars, writers, cinematographers, designers, technicians, and others who made up its fabled studio system—remained. Although it was showing cracks and would soon be threatened by the new entertainment medium of television, the studio system would stay dominant and vibrant for another decade as well.

What was decidedly different was the *tone* of more and more of the films now being made. Stories—especially in the crime and suspense genres—were darker, harsher, and more fatalistic. Screen violence (though mild by today's standards) had become more intense, visceral, and graphic. Heroes could be weak and corruptible. Leading ladies, while still beautiful, were often manipulative and just pure evil, eventually earning themselves the unflattering label femme fatales. Happy endings were by no means a foregone conclusion. Characters were often more complex and contradictory, more nuanced psychologically, and more at the mercy of personal demons. To ratchet up audience anxiety, these films were also photographed in very different ways from the films people were used to seeing. Most were darkly lit, with scenes frequently taking place at night and on ominous (and sometimes rainy) city streets. Shadows were prominent and usually meant to suggest menace or something (or

Heavily influenced by the German expressionist cinema of the 1920s and 1930s, Boris Ingster's *Stranger on the Third Floor* (1940) is a fascinating early example of American film noir. Here, the stranger (Peter Lorre at his creepy best) makes things very uncomfortable for young Jane (Margaret Tallichet).

someone) sinister. Cameras frequently captured scenes from extremely high and low angles, putting audiences off-balance and adding to their general discomfort and uneasiness. There were a few color films of this kind, of course. John Stahl's *Leave Her to Heaven* (1945) starring Gene Tierney is a good example. But the form thrived in—in fact, it seemed tailor made for—the more abstract, otherworldly, and emotionally detached medium of black and white, still dominant in the 1940s.

These kinds of films had actually been in evidence during and, in a few cases, before the U.S. entered the war. One early example is Boris Ingster's *Stranger on the Third Floor* (1940) with Peter Lorre, John McGuire, and Margaret Tallichet, a low-budget thriller that involves a man haunted by unsettling nightmares who's also wrongly accused of murder. This darker tone of filmmaking went more mainstream the following year. One major milestone was the release of Orson Welles' seminal *Citizen Kane*, which—with its extreme camera angles, boldly innovative use of shadow and light, complex flashback structure, and morally ambiguous hero—had an enormous influence not only on this new kind of film style but on filmmaking for decades to come. Another was John Huston's film of Dashiell Hammett's classic detective novel *The Maltese Falcon*, a film noted for its hard-edged dialogue, harsh tone, and treacherous femme fatale, Mary Astor's Brigit O'Shaughnessy. Films such as Billy Wilder's *Double Indemnity* (1944), Fritz Lang's *Scarlett Street* (1945), and others offered steadily darker and bleaker takes on human beings and their relationships. More and more, too—as in *Double Indemnity* and *Scarlett Street*—the obligatory Hollywood happy ending went by the wayside.

While American audiences usually referred to these kinds of films as crime stories or melodramas, French filmgoers, who had been denied U.S. films throughout the war and were anxious to catch up, were seeing something else—something new. In particular, they felt, American wartime films exhibited a different worldview, or sensibility, than they had experienced in pre-war American films (even in hard-edged 1930s gangster movies), and this worldview was being expressed in a very different cinematic style. In 1946, the French film critic Nino Frank coined a name for this new kind of film. He called it "film noir," or "the black film."[3]

Although World War II was certainly a driving force behind changed attitudes in the world and the emergence of new film forms to express those attitudes such as film noir, it by no means did the job single-handedly. The roots of film noir are many and varied. In literature, they go back to the "hard-boiled" school of crime fiction that includes work by Ernest Hemingway, Hammett, Raymond Chandler, James M. Cain, Cornell Woolrich, and many, many other writers. In fact, classic noirs have been made from Hemingway's *The Killers* (1946), Chandler's *The Big Sleep* (1946), Cain's *Mildred Pierce* (1945) and *The Postman Always Rings Twice* (1946), and Woolrich's *The Black Angel* (1946) as well as Hammett's *The Maltese Falcon* and Cain's *Double Indemnity*. In film, we can find the roots of noir in films dating back to the German expressionist efforts of the 1920s and early 1930s such as Robert Wiene's *The Cabinet of Dr. Caligari* (1920), F.W. Murnau's *Nosferatu* (1922), and Fritz Lang's *M* (1931). Highlighted by both desperate economic conditions and political unrest, the pre-war climate in Europe during the 1930s also had an enormous influence. As a result, many of Europe's most talented filmmakers—opposed to Nazism and fearing that another European war was inevitable—emigrated to the U.S. A number of these—including Lang, Wilder, Robert Siodmak, Edgar G. Ulmer, and André de Toth —brought their talents, their experience with expressionism, and their dark takes on life (the seeds of noir) with them.

While film historians love to quibble and quarrel, there is more or less a consensus that the classic era of U.S. noir existed from the early 1940s until the late 1950s or early 1960s. There is also widespread agreement that noir is still very much with us. In the 1970s, for example, the term "neo-noir" first appeared in an attempt to describe contemporary films that possessed a distinct noir sensibility. A few of many, many examples over the years include *Mean Streets* (1973), *Taxi Driver* (1976), *Body Heat* (1981), *The Grifters* (1990), *The Last Seduction* (1994), *Pulp Fiction* (1994), *American Psycho* (2000), and *Dead Man Down* (2013).

In addition to remaining a mainstay in the crime and suspense genres, the noir style and sensibility have become prominent in numerous other genres from science fiction to superhero films. Some noteworthy examples include such dystopian futuristic thrillers such as Ridley Scott's *Blade Runner* (1982) and John Carpenter's *Escape from New York* (1981) and *Escape from L.A.* (1996) as well as the three superhero films that make up Christopher Nolan's brilliant Batman trilogy: *Batman Begins* (2005), *The Dark Knight* (2008), and *The Dark Knight Rises* (2012).

Long before this noir style and sensibility began to seep into science fiction and superhero films, however, it was exerting an enormous influence on one of the oldest and most optimistic film genres of them all—the western. Spurred by the horrors of a world war and the styling of the noir crime drama during the mid 1940s, Hollywood's filmmakers—many now veterans of noir films as well as the war—began to look at the venerable western form in a new way, one that more closely reflected their current attitudes and preoccupations. The result was the birth of a new kind of western. Darker in tone and more nuanced psychologically than its usually sunnier and more simplistic predecessors, this "noir western" would soon make a major impact on this hallowed genre. Not only would it help to trigger a Golden Age of westerns from the late 1940s to the early 1960s (a period, which, incidentally, maps very closely to the classic period of noir), but it would also change the western forever.

—⚎—

Tracing its origins to the very beginnings of projected motion pictures in the 1890s, a time when the "Wild West" was still very much a reality, the film western is—in much the same way as jazz, baseball, or national parks—a distinctly American creation. In part, of course, these stories of the American West, usually in the late 1800s, are based on reality. People such as Wyatt Earp, Doc Holliday, Jesse and Frank James, Calamity Jane, George Armstrong

Custer, Sitting Bull, Wild Bill Hickok, Billy the Kid, Annie Oakley, Geronimo, and numerous other legendary figures actually did live during this time and did do many of the things we've seen them do in films. Wagon trains also crossed the Great Plains, ranchers fought range wars, and lonely U.S. Cavalry outposts dotted the Southwest. In part, too, these stories are pure invention. The exploits of real figures were often exaggerated and romanticized in the dime novels of the time, and writers—to satisfy a public that seemed to find the subject endlessly fascinating—eagerly created new characters and stories as well. Probably the first modern western novel and one of the most influential of the era is Owen Wister's *The Virginian* (1902). Another enormous influence was the prolific Zane Gray, whose more than 60 novels, the most popular of which is *Riders of the Purple Sage* (1912), inspired dozens of films. Whether mostly real, somewhat real, or totally concocted, western stories took hold in the public imagination. Almost instantaneously, they became (as they largely remain today) our nation's founding myths—the heroic tales of how those who came before us crossed and tamed the vast continent and prepared the way for us—our equivalent of ancient Greece's Trojan War stories or England's Arthurian legends.

This transition from reality to myth came quickly, so quickly, in fact, that many real western figures went on to live (at least in part) off their myths. The Lakota Sioux chief Sitting Bull, for example, became a star attraction at Buffalo Bill Cody's Wild West Show, earning $50 a week for simply riding a horse once around an arena during each performance. And Wyatt Earp, who lived until 1929, became a consultant on Hollywood silent westerns, sharing his knowledge of the "Wild West" with such directors as the young John Ford.

The transition of these mythic stories to film happened nearly as quickly. Some of the very first westerns came from Thomas Edison's budding filmmaking company in the 1890s. Although short and crudely made, they feature some elements that soon became fixtures of the genre. One of these films is the one-minute-long *Cripple Creek Bar Room Scene* (1899), which shows a prototypical western bar room scene complete with a barmaid (played in this film, incidentally, by a man). Another, *Poker at Dawson City* (also 1899), depicts a crooked poker game, which leads to a bar-room fight.

A major breakthrough came just a few years later with the release of Edison protégée Edwin S. Porter's *The Great Train Robbery* (1903). Often called the first narrative western, this 10-minute-long film was a major step forward in cinematic storytelling and included many of the elements that soon became standard in the genre such as good guys versus bad guys, a robbery or other wrongdoing, a chase on horseback, and natural outdoor settings.

By the 1910s, both "two-reelers" (films about 20 minutes in length) and feature-length westerns were appearing in droves, and by now most of the conventions of the genre were firmly established: bright sunlight; vast desert or mountain landscapes; brave, resourceful heroes; sweet young heroines; colorful, often comical sidekicks; clearly delineated bad guys; and happy endings. These efforts included suspense, lurking danger, and occasional violence, of course, but a rough-and-tumble exuberance and optimism usually abounds. These were stories, after all, of a young, restless, energetic nation that was ceaselessly building and expanding. The features soon gave way to epic silent westerns such as James Cruze's *The Covered Wagon* (1923) and John Ford's *The Iron Horse* (1924), both stories that continued to celebrate America's "Manifest Destiny."

To support their usually optimistic sensibilities, most traditional westerns—not just during the silent era but also well into the 1930s, 1940s, 1950s, and 1960s—were filmed in a direct, unpretentious way. They begin with establishing shots of wide-open country, and audiences look their heroes straight in the eye. As color became more economically feasible for productions in the 1950s, these films also highlight the dramatic and often beautiful color location shooting in Wyoming, Oregon, Utah, Arizona, and half a dozen other scenic western states. The warm, rich hues of color cinematography and westerns go well together, and sometimes they take on a pristine, travelogue quality. As we watch many of these films, it's sometimes natural to start planning a visit to Wyoming's Grand Tetons, Oregon's Cascade Mountains, or numerous other gorgeous locales.

In just about every respect, of course, all of these western trappings seem incongruous with noir films with their disconcerting dark shadows and extreme camera angles meant to heighten audience anxiety; stark, stifling, present-day urban locales; psychologically haunted men; and dangerous, manipulative women. In fact, it seems inconceivable that these two film types—one overwhelmingly optimistic and the other intrinsically pessimistic (and occasionally even nihilistic) in sensibility and style—should cross-pollinate in a big way.

Yet that's exactly what began to occur during the mid–1940s. Slowly at first but then with increasing frequency, audiences began to experience "new" westerns that told stories much darker in substance and tone than their usually sunnier predecessors and often conveyed in much the same way a noir crime drama might be.

John Ford's *The Iron Horse* (1924) was one of the large-scale western epics that raised the bar for the genre in the last years of the silent era. Here, the film reenacts the 1869 ceremony at Promontory Summit, Utah, where the golden spike, signifying the completion of the Transcontinental Railroad, was driven into place.

Over the years, critics and scholars have given these films many names. In addition to the "noir western" or "western noir," they have been called "the psychological western," "the existential western," "the Freudian western," and (a favorite) "sagebrush noir." In noting the trend to change and enhance the traditional western by incorporating new elements into these films in the 1950s, critic Andre Bazin went as far as to invent the term "superwestern." This, he wrote, "is a western what would be ashamed to be just itself, and looks for some additional interest to justify its existence—an aesthetic, sociological, moral, psychological, political, or erotic interest—in short some quality extrinsic to the genre and which is supposed to enrich it."[4] Bazin's point is well taken. Although traditional westerns would continue to be made for decades after the mid–1940s, he suggests that, by the mid–1940s, filmmakers had already sensed that audience tastes were evolving and that, if venerable genres such as the western were going to survive, they needed to evolve as well.

Rather than corrupting or polluting the western as some purists might have assumed, these changes had a decidedly different impact. Because they were so antithetical to the norms of the traditional western, they gave the genre added dimension, complexity, and dramatic tension—an enormous creative spark, if you will. The result was a synthesis of sorts, and, from the late 1940s to the early 1960s, the genre enjoyed a period of popularity and inspired creativity unequaled at any other time in its long, rich history. An enormous number of fine to great westerns were made, and tens of millions of appreciative filmgoers flocked to them.

—◊—

Although many film historians cite 1947 as the official birthdate of western noir, we can, if we like, go back to some westerns made several years earlier to see noir influences already at work on the genre. One example of what we might call a "proto-noir western" is William Wellman's *The Ox-Bow Incident* (1943), which superbly tells the story of a frontier lynching with the help of Arthur C. Miller's disturbingly dark and bleak cinematography. A second is John Ford's *My Darling Clementine* (1946). While not nearly as dark in tone as *The Ox-Bow Incident*, it does include a few noir-ish elements new to Ford films. One is the film's characterization of the doomed and deeply troubled Doc Holliday (one of Victor Mature's best roles). Another—which is quite under-appreciated—is the characterization of Pa Clanton (portrayed brilliantly by Walter Brennan), which conveys a depth of evil very rarely seen in Ford's work up to that time.

Despite these and other efforts, however, 1947 is most often cited as the official birthdate because of two films, which premiered exactly two months apart that year—Raoul Walsh's *Pursued* (released on March 2) and André de Toth's *Ramrod* (released on May 2). Usually designated as the first of the new breed, both films runneth over with noir-ish elements. *Pursued*, for example, is drenched in them from its stark, eerie, black-and-white cinematography by James Wong Howe to its flashback story structure, to its voice-over narration (by noir icon Robert Mitchum, no less), to its hero's nightmares and psychological torment. *Ramrod*, which features a traumatized hero and plenty of unsettling noir-ish camera angles and lighting as well, is a rare example of a western that also features a scheming femme fatale (played by noir siren Veronica Lake).

Soon to follow in the late 1940s are a number of very intriguing westerns with a decided noir edge to them. One fine and little-known example is Wellman's *Yellow Sky* (1948), in which a bank robber (Gregory Peck) struggles between a growing desire to "go good" and intensifying pressures from others in his gang to stay bad. *Yellow Sky* also makes great use of cinematographer Joe McDonald's fine camera and composition work to visually reinforce this struggle in one of the bleakest of natural landscapes, California's Death Valley. The next year, Sam Fuller's *I Shot Jesse James* shows a man (John Ireland's Robert Ford) who murders his friend for money and (as one must in noir) meets an ignominious end.

Then, throughout the 1950s, noir westerns came fast and furiously. Many of them were the work of veteran Hollywood masters such as Wellman, Walsh, and Henry King. Many more were from directors who had first distinguished themselves in 1940s noir crime dramas such as Anthony Mann, André de Toth, and Budd Boetticher. As these directors transitioned from noir to the western, bringing both their personal worldviews and filmmaking styles with them, so did many of the actors, writers, cinematographers, and others who had been major contributors to noir. Among the actors, just a handful of notable names include Mitchum, Barbara Stanwyck, Robert Ryan, Susan Hayward, Kirk Douglas, Burt Lancaster, Gregory Peck, Glenn Ford, Richard Widmark, Dick Powell, Jane Greer, John Payne, Van Heflin, and Dan Duryea.

Of all the noir-ish elements, however, perhaps the one that appears to be most dominant in these films is the hero, a character who is often much darker in spirit than his pre-war cowboy predecessors. Frequently, this dark view is the result of a severe psychological trauma experienced in the past— the kind of trauma many people would either recognize or directly identify with in the years immediately after World War II. Usually, the hero continues to struggle with this trauma (many times the violent death of a loved one), and often the action of the film centers around "settling a score" so the hero can (he hopes) put the past behind him and move forward. Sometimes the reason for this dark view is not as clearly spelled out in exposition. The hero may have experienced a traumatic event or events, or he simply could be someone who has been hardened by the world or is, by nature, dark and difficult. The lonely life is a frequent theme, too. Many of these heroes may want to find love and community, but they ultimately find that, however hard they try, they don't—and will never—fit in. Again, this echoes the sense of not belonging, of displacement, common among many war veterans. How these heroes manage their demons also varies widely. Some, such as the characters actor Randolph Scott often played, are stoic and persevering. They bear their grief quietly and with dignity. Others can't help but bring their rage and pain to the surface, expressing their dark sides in every way from bouts with the bottle to outbursts of violence.

Perhaps the best-known examples of the quintessential "dark cowboys" are the James Stewart roles in a series of five westerns he did for director Anthony Mann between 1950 and 1955. Among these, the two clear standouts are two of the darkest, *Winchester 73* (1950) and *The Naked Spur* (1953). Stewart, at mid-career, was anxious to shed the wholesome, "Aw, shucks" image he had honed in his films of the 1930s and 1940s and take on darker, more complex, more troubled characters. Mann proved to be an excellent partner in that process. In all five of these films, the Stewart character must contend not only with immediate problems but also face serious unresolved personal issues. In *Winchester 73*, this literally reaches the level of Greek tragedy when he hunts down and kills his brother because the brother had earlier killed their father. It's hard to imagine life getting darker than that.

As with Mann and Stewart, many of the most successful ventures into this territory during this time were the results of director-actor collaborations that lasted for several films. Just a handful of these collaborations include Henry King and Gregory Peck (1950's *The Gunfighter* and 1958's *The Bravados*); Delmer Daves and Glenn Ford (1956's *Jubal* and 1957's *3:10 to Yuma*); Budd Boetticher and Randolph Scott (1956's *7 Men from Now*, 1957's *The Tall T*, 1959's *Ride Lonesome*, and 1960's *Comanche Station*); and, lest we forget, John Ford and John Wayne (1956's *The Searchers* and 1962's *The Man Who Shot Liberty Valance*).

Some film historians might roll their eyes in exasperation at the idea of lumping directors such as Ford and King in with anything noir, but, to a greater or lesser extent, several of their post-war films do have a distinct noir look and sensibility about them. John Wayne's Ethan Edwards in Ford's *The Searchers*, for example, is rarely discussed as a noir-ish character, but, if we were to dress him in city clothes and place him in post–World War II America, he bears an amazing similarity to classic noir racists played by Robert Ryan in such films as *Crossfire* (1947) and *Odds Against Tomorrow* (1959). Ethan is also one of the screen's seminal loners, a person who never quite fits into any kind of communal setting. And, with its pessimistic tone, flashback story structure, and dark, ominous visual design, Ford's other great western during this period, 1962's *The Man Who Shot Liberty Valance* is filled with noir-ish elements. Gregory Peck's characters in two of the fine films he did with King, *The Gunfighter* and *The Bravados*, are just as noir-ish in their conception. In *The Gunfighter*, Peck plays a world-weary gunfighter tired of fending off challenges from young upstarts who eventually is bested and dies bitterly. In *The Bravados*, he is a vengeful rancher, so consumed with hatred for the men who may have killed his wife that he is often thoughtlessly and foolishly violent.

Choosing the year 1962 to end this book's examination of western noir is purely arbitrary. The noir western, while not as prevalent as it was during its own Golden Age from the late 1940s to the early 1960s, is still very much with us. In fact, if it weren't for all the dark cowboys who rode across movie theater screens during this time, many films from directors such as Sam Peckinpah, Sergio Leone, Robert Altman, and Clint Eastwood as well as from much younger directors such as James Mangold, Paul Thomas Anderson, Andrew Dominik, and Christopher Nolan would probably have turned out quite differently. In the 21st century alone, the impact of the early noir western continues strong in films ranging from Mangold's remake of *3:10 to Yuma* (2007), to Anderson's *There Will Be Blood* (2007), to Dominik's *The Assassination of Jesse James by the Coward Robert Ford* (2007), to the Coen Brothers' remake of *True Grit* (2010). On the small screen, we've also seen a major impact in cable series such as HBO and David Milch's *Deadwood* (2004–6), perhaps the darkest western of them all. Yes, as Americans continue to reevaluate and revise our nation's foundation myths to more closely align with our current attitudes and preoccupations, the dark cowboy continues to ride and, in all likelihood, will continue to evolve.

That said, the year 1962 proved to be a good stopping point for several reasons. First, it was a watershed year when two of the finest American westerns, Ford's *The Man Who Shot Liberty Valance* and Peckinpah's *Ride the High Country*, were released. While high-water marks for the western, they were both—ironically—stories about the end of the West. Second (and there's an irony here, too) is that these two great films about the end of the West also ushered in an era of decline for the western genre from which it has never fully recovered. Great westerns have been made from time to time since 1962, of course, but this was roughly the time when the seemingly fanatical interest audiences had in the western and the Golden Age of film westerns began to wane. Third, about the same time, many of the grandmasters of the genre were also hanging up their professional spurs. By the mid–1960s, the directing careers of Boetticher, Daves, de Toth, Dwan, Ford, King, Mann, Walsh, and Wellman were either over or almost over. In most cases, the timing was right because the old studio system, which had financed and produced the enormous number of westerns made since the 1910s, was riding into the sunset, too. It was, as any cowboy worth his saddlebags would say, the end of the trail.

Keeping all this in mind, this book focuses on the impact of film noir on westerns made during this Golden Age. Just as setting 1962 as a stop date is an arbitrary decision, the choice of the directors and films featured in this book is as well. In some cases, such as Budd Boetticher, Andre deToth, Allan Dwan, Henry King, and Delbert Daves' westerns, the intent is to acknowledge talented and greatly under-appreciated filmmakers and their especially under-appreciated films such as Boetticher's *Ride Lonesome*, de Toth's *Day of the Outlaw* (1959), Dwan's *Silver Lode* (1954), and King's *The Bravados*. In other cases, such as Mann or Ford's westerns, when so much has already been written about them, it's nevertheless impossible to exclude them from the story. And, in every case, the intent is to single out a filmmaker's unique contribution to the development of this fascinating and resilient sub-genre.

Noticeable omissions—such as Henry Hathaway, Joseph H. Lewis, John Sturges, and Howard Hawks' darker westerns, King Vidor's *Duel in the Sun* (1946), Fred Zinnemann's *High Noon* (1952), Nicholas Ray's *Johnny Guitar* (1954), and William Wyler's *The Big Country* (1958)—will be apparent to some readers. The reasons behind these omissions are varied. Generally, these films have already received much attention elsewhere, and there are many other fine and often lesser-known examples that seemed more appropriate for this book's purposes. Overall, hundreds of westerns worth attention and analysis were made during this period, and any writer attempting to cover this "big country" of creative outpouring must drastically pare down material.

In a 2013 article titled "A Darkness on the Plains: 8 Classic Western Noir Films," Jake Hinkson writes (with a bit of tongue in cheek): "Noir is like a disease. Its symptoms are moodiness, despair, guilt, and paranoia…. [And] the tropes of the western—sunlight, open spaces, nature—would seem to be immune to the noir disease. But make no mistake: the western caught the disease. A genre that seemed to be the quintessence of American optimism, a genre that seemed to embody the notion of moral clarity, slowly gave way to darker themes and more neurotic characters."[5]

While seeing noir—even in this lighthearted vein—as a "disease" that the western "caught" has a definite ring of truth to it, this view tells only part of the story. The noir western is merely one manifestation of a new way in which Americans saw things during and after World War II. It is darker and often more neurotic in tone than nearly all the westerns that preceded it, but it is also much more complex, emotionally and psychologically richer, and closer to great art. In essence, the emergence of the noir western was an enormous step forward in the western genre's ongoing evolution. It certainly reflects the loss of some of our nation's innocence and youthful exuberance, but it also suggests our ability to *grow beyond* our innocence, ultimately coming to see more complicated and often darker human realities with greater clarity, insight, and empathy.

This, we can assert, is a major reason why audiences between the late 1940s and early 1960s embraced these new westerns in such numbers and with such enthusiasm.

This, too, is why—in the current film world dominated by science fiction, action, and superhero offerings—the dark cowboy still rides in westerns and variations of him have even ventured into these other genres.

1

The Darkening West

Conscience and Cruelty Collide in William Wellman's *The Ox-Bow Incident, Yellow Sky* and *Track of the Cat*

"[I]t'll be over for me in a little while, but they'll have to go on remembering for the rest of their lives." — *The Ox-Bow Incident*

People have a hard time coming to grips with the work of William Wellman (1896–1975). He made most of his films in an era when directors prided themselves on their versatility, and he loved the fact that he could move from genre to genre as well as from low-budget pictures to prestige projects (and then back again) with the greatest of ease. When he started work on David O. Selznick's big-budget version of *A Star Is Born* (1937), which eventually received seven Academy Award nominations, for example, he had just finished work directing scenes on the much less prestigious *Tarzan Escapes* (1936), which features one of Johnny Weissmuller's many turns as the "King of the Apes." This pattern continued throughout his career as he moved from gangster film to women's drama, to biting comedy, to war film, to aviation adventure, to western as naturally as the rest of us move from one room to another.

This pattern, which was typical of many directors of his era from the 1920s through the 1950s, certainly solidified his reputation for versatility: he could do just about anything a studio wanted him to do and usually do it well. But, as the "auteurist" school began to dominate critical thinking in the 1960s, his reputation began to suffer. Unlike Chaplin, Ford, Hitchcock, Billy Wilder, Fritz Lang, and others, the auteurists contended, Wellman was not considered a filmmaker with a specific worldview or sensibility that exhibits itself over and over again in his films; he was not the true "author" of his works. As a result, many critics consigned him to the lesser tier of solid craftsmen (as opposed to artists) such as Clarence Brown and Victor Fleming—directors who made many good films but whose work overall lacked that distinct and very personal worldview or sensibility.

Yet, while we rarely talk about Clarence Brown or Victor Fleming anymore, Wellman and his films continue to captivate. As part of its high-profile *Forbidden Hollywood* DVD boxed-set series in 2009, for example, Turner Classic Movies released an entire boxed set of six Wellman films (which came, by the way, with two repackaged documentaries about Wellman). In May 2012, Cinemark showed a restored version of Wellman's Academy Award–winning aviation film *Wings* (1927) in a limited re-release in its theaters throughout the U.S. And, at a pre–Code film festival at San Francisco's Roxie Theater in 2013, Wellman's *Safe in Hell* (1931) was—according to the festival's programmer—the hit of the show. Clearly, much of his work still resonates (sometimes very deeply) more than 60, 70, or 80 years after it was first shown.

Two particular facets of Wellman's work may be most responsible for his continuing staying power.

One is his storytelling style. As few people will dispute, he was a superb craftsman. He tells stories with great vitality and urgency, using a fluid camera, suggestive dialogue, and other tools to bring audiences into the heart of the action in a very immediate, visceral, and sometimes just plain in-your-face way. In *Safe in Hell*, for example, we never see the worms we are told are in the drinking water, but, because of the way Wellman conveys this information and the actors' reaction to it, the very notion of it makes us squirm. He was also a master of compression, conveying great amounts of information in very short periods of time. In his 1943 film version of William Van Tilburg Clark's novel *The Ox-Bow Incident*, he and screenwriter Lamar Trotti reduced the book's first 50 pages to just a few minutes of screen time, leaving out many details, of course, but preserving the essence of the themes, the characters, and the action. In addition, he was endlessly inventive in the ways he told the story visually. We see this in how he positions characters in relation to one another, places the camera in relation to characters and action, lights characters' faces, and does much more. Rarely does he become self-conscious or pretentious. Almost always, he makes an artistic choice for a specific storytelling purpose, and often the result is a searing directness.

The other reason for Wellman's staying power is—despite what some of the auteurists have told us—his worldview. It isn't always evident in his films, but he did have one and his better films reflect his views and preoccupations in a variety of ways. First, most have a strong humanist streak— an immense empathy for his characters (bad and seriously flawed as well as good) that rarely descends into sentimentality. This is obvious in such films as several of his other pre–Code gems, *Night Nurse* (1931), *The Purchase Price* (1932), and *Frisco Jenny* (1932), with their very likeable heroines. But it's just as apparent in films such as *The Public Enemy* (1931), where we really do get inside the disturbed soul of James Cagney's Tom Powers, or *A Star Is Born* (1937), where we watch with great sadness as Frederick March's troubled Norman Maine descends into alcoholism. Tom Powers also suggests another of Wellman's preoccupations, the human capacity for evil. What compels some people to act in this way? And what is the effect of such actions on the evildoer as well as the victims? Examples—ranging from Powers to Morgan Wallace's Mr. Bruno in *Safe in Hell*, to Frank Conroy's Major Tetley in *Ox-Bow*—abound in Wellman's work. Finally, a subject Wellman explored repeatedly during his career is justice and judgment. What responsibility, if any, do we as individuals or as a society have in addressing economic and social injustices? We see this idea explored in films such as *Beggars of Life* (1928), *Heroes for Sale* (1932), and *Wild Boys of the Road* (1933). And who decides what's just and what's unjust, and ultimately who is entitled to pass judgment on people accused of crimes or socially unacceptable behavior? Wellman films that make these issues the essence of the action range from *Frisco Jenny* to *Midnight Mary* (1933) to *Ox-Bow*, to *Yellow Sky* (1948).

Between 1943 and 1954, Wellman directed six westerns. As the case often is with groups of Wellman's films, they are a mixed bag, ranging from the light, escapist *Buffalo Bill* (1944) to the much darker and more ambitious *The Ox-Bow Incident*, *Yellow Sky*, and *Track of the Cat* (1954). While these three darker films are quite different from one another, all contain the essential Wellman components—the genuine feeling for people and the preoccupations with both the nature of evil and justice/judgment that characterize much of his more memorable work. These are all elements Wellman brought to the noir western, elements that clearly enriched the subgenre.

Today, many film historians have anointed Raoul Walsh's *Pursued* (1947) and André de Toth's *Ramrod* (1947) as the first official noir westerns. Yet a strong case can also be made for *Ox-Bow*. The film lacks many of the conventions (from exaggerated camera angles to flashback sequences to femme fatales) we've come to associate with the noir style, but—in stark contrast to westerns that preceded it—it is deeply noir in tone and theme. Wellman—who saw the connection between the events in *Ox-Bow* and events taking place in Europe in the late 1930s and early 1940s and who had long explored the human capacity for evil and themes of justice and judgment in films—arrived in dark western territory a full four years before Walsh and De Toth did. As his son, William Wellman, Jr., has noted about the film, "This was a dark western, and all of those dark westerns that started coming after it, I think, are a response to *Ox-Bow*."[1]

If *Ox-Bow* isn't the first true noir western (which is clearly debatable), it is a hugely influential proto-noir, one that left an indelible mark on Walsh, De Toth, Wise, King, Boetticher, and all the other filmmakers who've since traveled to the dark side of the range.

"Wild Bill"

A descendant of Puritans who settled in the Massachusetts Bay Colony in the 1600s, William Augustus Wellman came from highbrow New England stock. But most of the people he came into contact with would have never imagined it. As a teenager, he was expelled from high school for dropping a stink bomb on the principal's head, and in later years he admitted to "borrowing" other people's automobiles without their knowledge so he and his friends could party with fewer constraints. Ironically, his mother, a highly respected probation officer, was once asked to address the U.S. Congress on the subject of juvenile delinquency.

Before the U.S. entered World War I, Wellman, who never lacked a sense of adventure, went overseas as an ambulance driver and soon joined the aviation unit of the French Foreign Legion. As a flier, he proved to be quite a daredevil, shooting down several German planes and earning the nickname he would carry with him for the rest of his life, "Wild Bill."

Soon after the war, he made friends with Hollywood star Douglas Fairbanks, Sr., who—impressed with both Wild Bill's war exploits and youthful good looks—offered to help get him started in the film business as an actor. But, after acting in one role in a 1919 Fairbanks western called *The Knickerbocker Buckaroo*, Wellman was—as he recounted later in life—so distressed watching himself on screen that he immediately left the theater and vomited. With Fairbanks' help, he soon found opportunities in the production side of the business and quickly worked his way up to directing low-budget pictures.

Then, in 1927, Wellman received his big career break. Paramount was mounting a major production of a World War I aviation story called *Wings*, and, although Wellman's directing resume was fairly sparse at that point, he did have both the flying experience and a cocky exuberance that impressed Paramount's executives. He was hired. Before production concluded, he was nearly fired several times, too. But the finished film—which features aerial photography that's still impressive today—was an enormous hit. It won the first Best Picture Academy Award (the only fully silent film to do so), and it catapulted the young Wellman into the front ranks of Hollywood film directors.

Despite his cantankerous image, "Wild Bill" Wellman was one of Hollywood's most respected and versatile directors from the 1920s through the 1950s, excelling in just about everything from pre–Code women's films to aviation adventure stories to darker post-war westerns.

In a career that spanned 36 years (from 1922 to 1958), Wellman directed more than 80 films for a variety of major studios and independent producers. As noted earlier, they spanned the spectrum with regards to genre and quality. Today, some of his best known works in addition to *Wings* are *The Public Enemy*; *A Star Is Born*; the dark comedy *Nothing Sacred* (1937); the Foreign Legion adventure *Beau Geste* (1939); *The Ox-Bow Incident*; two World War II films, *The Story of G.I. Joe* (1945) and *Battleground* (1949); and two later aviation adventures he made for John Wayne's independent production company, *Island in the Sky* (1953) and *The High and the Mighty* (1954). In recent years, several of his pre–Code films such as *Wild Boys of the Road* and *Heroes for Sale* have also received more attention. He was nominated three times for the Best Director

Academy Award, but he won his only Oscar for his writing contribution to *A Star Is Born*.

His personal life stayed wild through three short-lived marriages in the 1920s and early 1930s. Then, in 1933, he met a young Busby Berkeley dancer named Dorothy Coonan, cast her in the female lead in his *Wild Boys of the Road*, married her, and had seven children with her, including actor and film historian William Wellman, Jr. Wellman often credited Coonan with saving his life, and the two remained married until his death in 1975. Coonan died at age 95 in 2009.

Darkness Descends: The Ox-Bow Incident

There's a story the actor Harry Morgan, who had a featured role in *The Ox-Bow Incident*, once told William Wellman, Jr.

Morgan had just come out of a preview showing of the film and was concerned about the audience's response. People were respectful, but they were far from enthusiastic or even pleased. Then, he ran into Orson Welles, also at the preview, and Welles, sensing Morgan's disappointment, said: "They don't realize what they just saw."[2] If anyone knew about the difficulty of communicating something new, perhaps revolutionary, to movie audiences, it was Welles, whose *Citizen Kane* (1941) had problems of its own winning over audiences. And Welles clearly saw something new, perhaps revolutionary, here, too.

While *Ox-Bow* impressed critics and even received a Best Picture Academy Award nomination that year, it was—as both Morgan and Welles sensed it would be—a box-office bomb. And an interesting footnote is that all the key people involved with it—Wellman, 20th Century–Fox production head Darryl Zanuck (who green-lighted the film), writer/producer Lamar Trotti, star Henry Fonda, and others—also knew this going in. But they all believed in the story, they all went ahead with the project anyway, and they all accepted consequences. As part of the bargain to even do the film, Wellman—to help the studio recoup anticipated losses—agreed to do two additional and far more marketable (and forgettable) films for Zanuck. In return, Zanuck and 20th Century–Fox lost a good deal of money on *Ox-Bow*.

The result is not merely the film that would play a major role in revolutionizing the western but also a major work of American cinema. "William Wellman has directed the picture with a realism that is as sharp and cold as a knife," wrote Bosley Crowther in the *New York Times* upon the film's release. "*The Ox-Bow Incident* is not a picture which will brighten or cheer your day.

1. The Darkening West

But it is one which, for sheer, stark drama, is currently hard to beat."[3] Writing more than 60 years later, Japanese film critic Toshi Fujiwara has called it "one of the most important westerns in the history of American cinema."[4] Finally, one of the great practitioners of westerns himself, Clint Eastwood has repeatedly called *Ox-Bow* not just one of his favorite westerns but also one of his favorite films.[5]

The action of *The Ox-Bow Incident* begins in the town of Bridger's Wells, Nevada. Two strangers, Gil Carter (Henry Fonda) and Art Croft (Harry Morgan), ride in and enter the local saloon. There is talk of recent cattle rustling, and, because they are strangers, Gil and Art are immediately suspected.

We hear that a nearby rancher, Larry Kincaid, has been murdered, and people immediately presume that these rustlers are the culprits. A posse is formed, and, with amazing speed, the people in the town break into two camps—those who want the captured suspects brought back for a formal trial and those who want to dispense frontier justice, that is, hanging the culprits on the spot. It's also clear that the voices advocating reason and respect for the legal process are ineffectual when pitted against the voices of vengeance. In fact, it even seems unmanly *not* to be in favor of a lynching.

The posse—which Gil and Art join so they won't be suspected—rides toward the Ox-Bow, an area in the nearby mountains. Along the way, the posse's de-facto leader, Major Tetley (Frank Conroy), conveys to the others that he's heard that there were three rustlers. The posse comes upon three men sleeping by a campfire. Nearby are some head of cattle, which the members of the posse immediately presume to be the ones that have been rustled.

One of the men, Donald Martin (Dana Andrews), claims he's purchased the cattle from Kincaid, but he can't produce a bill of sale. Eventually, too, the posse finds that another of the three men has Kincaid's gun. The posse votes on whether to bring the three men back to town or to hang them then and there. Gil, Art, a storekeeper named Davies (Harry Davenport) and a few others vote to bring the men back. The overwhelming majority, however, is for hanging. Knowing he is doomed, Martin writes a letter to his wife and asks Davies to make sure that she gets it. Davies agrees and reads it. He is so moved that he wants to read it aloud in the hope that it will sway other members of the posse. Martin, because the letter is so personal in nature, refuses to let him. Despite Gil's efforts to try to stop the proceedings, the three men are hanged.

The mob readies for the lynching in this beautifully composed and highly charged moment from Wellman's *The Ox-Bow Incident* (1943). In the Confederate officer's uniform is the head of the mob, Major Tetley (Frank Conroy), who faces the three falsely accused and soon-to-hang men (Dana Andrews, Francis Ford and Anthony Quinn).

On the way back to Bridger's Wells, however, the posse finds out that Kinkaid is not dead and that the three men who shot him have been arrested.

When they return to town, Major Tetley—now disgraced—returns home and shoots himself. Meanwhile, most of the others have gathered at the saloon and drink in silence. Then, as the other men listen, Gil, who has agreed to deliver Martin's letter to his wife, reads it aloud:

> "My dear wife, Mr. Davies will tell you what's happening here tonight. He's a good man and has done everything he can for me. I suppose there are some other good men here, too, only they don't seem to realize what they're doing. They're the ones I feel sorry for. 'Cause it'll be over for me in a little while, but they'll have to go on remembering for the rest of their lives. A man just naturally can't take the law into his own hands and hang people without hurtin' everybody in the world, 'cause then he's just not breaking one law but all laws. Law is a lot more than words you put in a book, or judges or lawyers or sheriffs you hire to carry it out. It's everything people ever have found out about justice and what's right and wrong. It's the very conscience of humanity. There can't be any such thing as civilization unless people have a conscience, because if people touch God anywhere, where is it except through their conscience? And what is anybody's conscience except a little piece of the conscience of all men that ever lived? I guess that's all I've got to say except kiss the babies for me, and God bless you. Your husband, Donald."

Afterwards, Gil and Art ride out of town to deliver the letter.

A great deal of the power of *The Ox-Bow Incident*, of course, is due to Walter Van Tilburg Clark's story, a sobering look at mob psychology and violence. While Gil, Art, Davies, and others plead for the order of law and more reasonable, rational behavior to prevail, the mob has its way. It's as if Clark is saying, and Wellman and Trotti are confirming, that this is not at all unusual but, in fact, the natural state of human behavior. The story's pessimism, whether we read the book or see the film, looms large. Conscience and cruelty collide, and—in this case, at least—cruelty wins out.

While remaining true to the dark spirit of Clark's novel, Wellman adds a great deal to enhance the experience cinematically.

One clear Wellman contribution is the film's visual design. The story begins in the outdoors, on the streets of Bridger's Wells, during the day. After the posse is formed, we see it riding through wide-open country, still in daylight. But, as the posse learns about the three men and rides to the Ox-Bow, night descends and, while the setting is still the outdoors, everything also becomes very dark and constricting, very noir-ish. In part to save money, the heart of the film—the sequence with the three men at their campsite—was shot on a sound stage rather than on location, but the choice also contributes to the film's enormous impact. Arthur C. Miller's eloquent, brooding cinematography makes the setting especially gloomy and ominous, underscoring the darkening direction of the story and the darkening souls of many of those involved. In addition to being dark and ominous, the setting also becomes more confining, even suffocating. Fugiwara offers an interesting comment on this choice, which he sees as being "stunningly present throughout." Specifically, he views it as an attempt to create a kind of "gothic claustrophobia" in order to show a "community entrapped by itself ... so that the feeling [is] that these people are doomed by their own will."[6]

Another Wellman contribution involves the characters and the actors he uses to portray them. In a departure from the novel, one character, Sparks, who offers a Christian perspective, is African American, a clear outsider in this community, both racially and philosophically. Another, which is an inspired example of casting against type, is assigning the actress Jane Darwell to play the one woman who participates in this lynch mob, the bloodthirsty Jenny Grier. Darwell, who is best remembered today as the long-suffering Ma Joad in Ford's *The Grapes of Wrath* (1940) and the bird woman in Disney's *Mary Poppins* (1964), was almost always cast in kindly old woman's roles. To see her here, relishing the prospect of a hanging, suggesting that the men who find the proceedings repugnant are too "feminine," cackling with glee at Donald Martin's suffering, and later on even volunteering to help hang one of the men, is absolutely chilling. It is also, we can assume, exactly the effect Wellman wanted.

The other Wellman contribution is the use of minimalism for artistic effect. Because of budget and other constraints, there were numerous other minimalist westerns made before *Ox-Bow*. But usually they just looked cheap. Rarely (if ever) had minimalism been used to such artistic effect in a western. As he did in many of his best 1930s films, Wellman gets to the essence of his story and stays focused on that essence throughout. When Bosley Crowther said in his 1943 review that Wellman directed with a "realism that is as sharp and cold as a knife," it's irresistible to think of the cutters in a Hollywood studio's editing room. Everything about his film—which compresses a 309-page novel into 75 minutes of screen time—is compact and cut to the bone. In the process, nothing really important is lost and the story is actually enhanced. It's an amazing achievement, and we can see the influence of Wellman's minimalism in many of the dark westerns to follow from such people as André de Toth and Budd Boetticher.

"With *The Ox-Bow Incident*, westerns became a true, autonomous art form," Fugiwara writes. "Perhaps it took a while for the world to really appreciate what it is—a genuine piece of art. But today, when people like Clint Eastwood call it the greatest, most beautiful western ever made, finally its status becomes a justified one, worthy of the efforts and genius poured into it."[7]

The point is duly noted. We might add, too, that whether or not *Ox-Bow* really is the first bona-fide noir western or an important proto-noir doesn't matter as much as the power of its story, the uncompromising honesty of Wellman and others who made the film, the enormous influence the film has had on the western genre, and the enduring appeal it has today. It's one for the ages.

"Plum greediness": Yellow Sky

Five years after Wellman and screenwriter/producer Lamar Trotti worked on *The Ox-Bow Incident*, they teamed up again to make *Yellow Sky*, a little-known but beautifully rendered morality tale that features some spectacular location shooting in California's bleak and beautiful Death Valley. While not as relentlessly dark as *Ox-Bow*, it nevertheless contains a good share noir themes, human behaviors, and storytelling techniques.

The action begins as a gang led by James "Stretch" Dawson (Gregory Peck) robs a bank and, to escape a pursuing posse, decides to ride across 70 miles of brutally hot desert that, as one character remarks, "even a rattlesnake couldn't get across." Exhausted and out of water, the gang chances upon a ghost town named Yellow Sky, where they meet the only remaining residents, a feisty young woman called Mike (Anne Baxter) and her cagey grandfather (James Barton). Although Mike and her grandfather don't want the visitors there, Stretch persuades them to let his men and their horses rest and recover from their hard desert crossing. Several of the men, including Stretch, develop lusty attractions for Mike. But Stretch's most formidable rival in the gang, Dude (Richard Widmark), is more focused on why Mike and her grandfather have remained in this ghost town. He concludes that the reason can only be gold, and soon he and others in the gang confirm this and want "in" on the gold, too. After a confrontation, Mike's grandfather agrees to split the gold with the gang. While Mike doesn't trust the gang, Stretch assures her that the agreement will be honored.

Cinematographer Joe McDonald eloquently conveys the lust for gold in this scene from Wellman's *Yellow Sky* (1948). Kneeling are actors John Russell and Harry Morgan. Standing behind them are Gregory Peck, Robert Arthur, and Charles Kemper.

But Dude doesn't feel that way. Eventually, the gang splits over the issue; several skirmishes occur; and, in a very suspenseful, final three-way shootout, Stretch resolves the dispute, dispatching Dude and the last gang member still loyal to him.

Finally, to prove to Mike (and perhaps himself) that he really is "going straight," Stretch returns the money he and the gang originally stole from the bank and rides back to Mike and her grandfather.

—m—

In many respects, *Yellow Sky* is a more traditional western than *Ox-Bow*. The story of a fundamentally good bad man whose love for a good woman reforms him goes back to the William S. Hart and Harry Carey westerns of the 1910s. The spunky "tom-boy" heroine is yet another familiar fixture harkening to the roles early silent screen actresses such as Molly Malone often played.

But we're in 1948 now, and the world is a very different place. Westerns featuring darker themes, more complex characters, and noir storytelling techniques to reinforce tone and mood are popping up with increasing frequency. And *Yellow Sky* is in tune with the times, incorporating many distinctive noir elements into the proceedings.

One of these elements is its central theme—the quest for earthly vanities, in this case, wealth and sex—a subject that immediately reminds us of *Double Indemnity*, *The Postman Always Rings Twice*, *Decoy* (1946), and countless other noirs. In one way or another, all of the gang members are governed by their lust for gold, Mike, or both. Mike, too, even feels the longing for a man—and one with a checkered past at that. Only by giving up this all-consuming lust (or at least getting beyond it in some way), the film tells us, can the characters find real peace. As Mike's grandfather says about gold: "[It's] a mighty dangerous thing if you want it out of plum greediness. I've seen it ruin many a man." Before the story ends, of course, he'll see it ruin a few more.

A secondary theme that's not quite as apparent in the film—and one that's explored in Fred Zinnemann's *Act of Violence* (1948) and many other noirs—is the effect of war on its survivors. *Yellow Sky*, which came out just three years after the end of World War II, is set in 1867, just two years after the end of America's Civil War. Stretch, we eventually learn, came from "good people," who were forced into violence because of the threatening and perilous times, and this, we assume, contributed to his turning to crime. Again, it is Mike's grandfather who offers the interesting take: "I guess the war's upset a lot of those boys," he says, "set 'em off on the wrong foot."

As this insight also suggests, there's some real complexity to Stretch, who is perhaps the film's most nuanced and—in terms of the change he experiences—most dynamic character. At one point, one of his gang calls him "an honest thief," and the oxymoron points to Stretch's central contradiction. At heart, he seems to be a decent, honorable man, but war and then a short career as a thief have dehumanized him. Controlling his unruly gang sometimes means that he must be brutal, and living with this wild bunch on the run has made him primitive in other ways as well. After telling his men to stay away from Mike, for example, he breaks his own rule, finds her, physically overpowers her, and repeatedly (and violently) kisses her against her will. Not only is Mike shocked and repulsed by his actions but she is also repulsed by his body's "smell."

Her rejection and repulsion, however, serve as a "teachable moment," emphasizing to him how dehumanized he has become. Soon after this, he shaves, cleans himself up, and acts in a much more respectful way toward her.

He also learns that Mike's grandfather is really playing it "square" with him and his gang and feels he has a responsibility to live up to his end of a one-sided deal they made to split the gold with Mike and her grandfather. He, too, wants to play it square—at least, somewhat square.

This leads to additional problems. Becoming a man of conscience puts him on an obvious collision course with Dude and others in his gang. Eventually, there will be a deadly reckoning.

Ultimately, though, conscience also brings him closer to Mike and her grandfather and, perhaps, to the kind of person that he's always wanted to be. In the end—much like the hero in Polonsky's *Force of Evil* (1948) and numerous other noirs—Stretch has emerged from his own personal darkness and found a form of redemption.

Perhaps the most striking element of *Yellow Sky*, however, is its visual look and feel. With cinematography by the very underrated Joe MacDonald, who shot films for John Ford, Elia Kazan, Nicholas Ray, Henry Hathaway and other iconic directors as well as Wellman, the lighting and the compositions are stunning. In addition, Wellman's staging is pure Wellman, oozing with energy and visceral immediacy. We see all of this at work from some of the film's earliest scenes. Soon after the gang robs the bank, for example, there's a wonderfully orchestrated chase scene, with cavalry pursuing with relentless vigor. Then, to escape the cavalry, the gang crosses the 70 miles of desert—mostly salt flats and sand dunes—and we see the small, dark figures dwarfed by the immense landscape and hobbling in the intense heat.

For a western, many key scenes in *Yellow Sky* are also set at night, allowing Wellman and MacDonald to exploit noir composition and lighting to great effect. Faces are photographed in complete shadow or through curtains and often from odd, curious camera angles. Especially during violent, or potentially violent, scenes, we have to look hard to see what's happening in the darkness, which adds to the suspense. And in the dark, the ghost town of *Yellow Sky*, with its fallen sign saying "The Fastest Growing Town in the Territory," seems all the more ghostly and decayed.

Although there are many well-staged scenes, one of the most effective is the final reckoning near the end of the film. It is night, of course. Dude and his one remaining ally in the gang have retreated to the El Dorado, Yellow Sky's broken down saloon. Their horses are tied up outside. Stretch enters in pursuit. A number of shots are fired. Against the saloon's outside wall we see the shadows of the horses bucking in fear. Then, we see a dusty, broken roulette wheel spinning, no doubt suggesting that the people inside will either win or lose their bets, too. The shooting stops. Mike enters into the darkness and stillness. She finds Dude, lying dead on the floor with gold pouring out of a pouch he had on him. Then she finds Dude's ally; he's dead, too. Finally, she sees Stretch. He's lying just as still. She moves toward him and kneels down over him, visibly distraught. Then, she sees his stomach slowly rising and falling; he is breathing. The scene, as they say, is pure cinema. With the exception of the gunshots, everything that needs to be said is expressed visually, and the dark, noir-ish setting serves to intensify the drama and the suspense even more.

In addition to the noir-ish look of *Yellow Sky*, the Lamar Trotti script is peppered with some wonderfully sharp and acerbic dialogue, another important component of good noirs. After Mike knocks Stretch down with a punch soon after they meet, for example, he compliments her on it, saying that it will "come in mighty handy when you get married." Later, before Stretch strikes his deal to split the gold with Mike and her grandfather, he suggests that they return to their house, saying, "You might as well be comfortable while you're getting robbed." Still later, when one gang member senses danger, he says, "We're sure gonna be mighty rich corpses."

Yellow Sky is by no means a perfect film. Its intentionally humorous ending with Stretch simply giving the money back to a shocked banker, for example, is far too easy and pat to be believed. When it comes to exploring the nature of evil or issues related to justice and judgment, *Yellow Sky* doesn't dig as deep as *Ox-Bow* does, either. Its ironies aren't as bitter, and its honesty isn't as brutal.

Still, when weighed against its strengths, *Yellow Sky's* weaknesses are relatively minor. As a stand-alone work, it is a stylish, excellently crafted film that gets better with repeated viewings. And, as film writer Josh Anderson has stressed, its value is enhanced even more when seen within the context of Wellman's substantial body of work. "It's part of a tapestry from an artist whose greatness can't be contained by a single great work," Anderson has noted. "Wellman deals with ethical and aesthetic quandaries so universal and amorphous that they spread out in multiple directions, uncontained and unreconstructed."[8] The point is well taken. Watching *Yellow Sky*, it's impossible for anyone familiar with Wellman not to remember bits and pieces from other Wellman films dating back to the 1920s—the themes, the characters, and the searing, visceral, in-your-face immediacy.

A "fascinating misfire": Track of the Cat

"Sometimes even great directors stumble when they attempt bold experiments," Paul Tatara wrote about Wellman's last dark western, *Track of the Cat*.

It's difficult to disagree. Overall, this is just not a good film. The symbolism is heavy handed, the writing is often tedious, the characters are contrived, and the acting performances are forced and strained. Sometimes, too, there doesn't even seem to be a point to the proceedings. In fact, it has all of the elements of a very bad Eugene O'Neill play. But Tatara also recommends this "fascinating misfire" of a film for one very captivating reason—a "visual scheme" that is both unique and oddly compelling.[9]

For years, Wellman had been intrigued with the very noir-ish idea of making a color film that focused almost solely on black and white images to portray a barren physical environment that, in turn, reflected a cold, harsh human environment. Color would be used sparingly for emphasis. Then, when he read the novel *Track of the Cat* (also by Walter Van Tilburg Clark), he felt he had found the right vehicle. The story—which focuses on a dysfunctional and constantly bickering family stuck together in an isolated, snowbound cabin in the 1880s and the quest to kill a huge, almost mythic mountain lion (that symbolizes the evil in us all)—had the elements he was looking for.

A great deal of talent, energy, and money went into this project. For key roles, Wellman rounded up such top actors as Robert Mitchum, Teresa Wright, and Beulah Bondi. For the costly location shooting, the production team ventured to the snowbound slopes of Washington's Mount Rainier. And, to handle the photography, Wellman also enlisted the very talented cinematographer, William Clothier, who would later receive two Academy Award nominations and the Heritage Award from the Cowboy Hall of Fame for his work on westerns.

While most of the film's other components didn't meet expectations, the visual look is exactly what Wellman had envisioned. Shot in the snow amid dark trees and often depicting darkly clothed riders on black horses, the vast majority of what we see in the film looks black, white, or some shade of gray. In fact, even some props such as food on the dinner table are devoid of color. Perhaps the most stunning exception is a brilliant red coat Mitchum wears when he's outdoors, which suggests his character's hubris. It's all very daring, and for the most part this "haunting luminous look," as film writer Dennis Schwartz calls it,[10] pays off handsomely, visually reinforcing the bleak, noirish themes of the story. "Never have I seen such beauty, a naked kind of beauty," Wellman said years later as he recalled viewing the rushes for the first time. "Bill [Clothier] and I saw the first print back from the lab. We sat there together drooling."[11]

Unfortunately for Jack Warner—whose studio was paying the bills—

these rushes provoked a decidedly different emotion. "I'm spending $500,000 more for color," he reportedly shouted, "and there's no color in this thing!"[12]

"American cinema has always been full of oddballs charging into environs no one else anywhere on the planet would go near," Josh Anderson noted in his article about Wellman's later westerns. "And when 'Wild' Bill Wellman went westward, he made camp where few others of his era dare tread."[13]

While this comment suggesting Wellman's courage—even eagerness—to take cinema in new directions is certainly true, it doesn't fully credit the director for his achievements in these westerns. Despite its shortcomings, *Track of the Cat* certainly shows that—as late as four years before his retirement—Wellman had no desire simply to repeat old formulas. The curious color scheme used to amplify the bleak state of the story's human relationships is—as Jack Warner would clearly agree—odd for 1954. But, when watching more recent, much better known revisionist westerns such as *McCabe and Mrs. Miller* (1971), for example, it's impossible not to wonder how much of an influence can be attributed to *Track of the Cat*. *Yellow Sky* came a year after such other turning-point westerns drenched in the noir shooting style as *Pursued* and *Ramrod*, but it was, in its own way, relentlessly inventive. Today, it remains fresh and vibrant. Finally, *Ox-Bow* was not merely influential, but—in terms of its subject matter, sensibility, and style—nothing short of revolutionary. Not only did it change westerns forever, it changed film. And, in the middle of a bleak war—when nearly everyone in Hollywood was focused on comedies, musicals, or uplifting dramas—it took an oddball called "Wild Bill" to fight to make a film that he knew would fail commercially but that was filled with ideas he wanted to convey.

2

The Tyranny of Troubled Pasts
Escape and the Futility of It in Raoul Walsh's *Pursued* and *Colorado Territory*

> "It means we're a couple of fools in a dead village dreaming about something that'll probably never happen."
> —*Colorado Territory*

Every life has its defining moments, and for filmmaker Raoul Walsh (1887–1980), it was the death of his mother from cancer. It was 1902, she was 42, and he was just 15. "I was quite unprepared for the sudden blow that left me motherless," he wrote more than seven decades later. "Mother passed away in the big master bedroom into which I used to steal and beg for one of her stories about an earlier America.... Where before I had loved it, the place became unbearable."[1]

To cope with his grief, Walsh's father encouraged his son to find escape and solace in travel. The teen took the advice and spent the next several years having adventures that ranged from crisscrossing the U.S., to herding cattle from Mexico to Texas, to transporting rum between Cuba and Florida. Soon he had exotic stories of his own to tell, and soon his rapidly developing storytelling skills led him into the newly created medium of the movies.

Despite a long and largely successful directing career, however, this sense of sadness stayed with Walsh. As his biographer Marilyn Ann Moss has put it: "These two—grief and adventure—locked themselves together in his mind. It would be ironic that the grief he felt at the loss of his mother gave his art great range; he escaped repeatedly because he had to."[2] Echoing Moss's sentiments, film scholar Tag Gallagher has noted: "Living is adventure in Walsh's movies, and usually begins as escape—from shame, crime, or life.... Walsh's heroes incarnate the dreams and miseries of first-generation Irish-Americans like himself, parvenus, with something to escape from."[3]

It's also fascinating that one subject we see again and again in Walsh's films is the noir-ish tension between their heroes' burning desire to escape from a harsh reality and the flawed strategies they use in trying to do it—strategies that often doom their efforts and ultimately them. In fact, even before film noir emerged on the Hollywood scene in the early 1940s, this tension plays out in such Walsh efforts as the hard-hitting gangster film *The Roaring Twenties* (1939). Here, Eddie Bartlett (James Cagney) is lured from a meager existence working in a car shop to the glamorous, easy-money world of Prohibition-era bootlegging only to be killed in a gangland-style shootout and eulogized with the words, "He used to be a big-shot."

When the noir sensibility and filmmaking style became more pervasive, Walsh—whose style always tended to be stark and hard-edged—became a leading pioneer and practitioner of noir films. His efforts *They Drive by Night* (1940) and *High Sierra* (1941) are often cited as two of the earliest full-blooded noir crime dramas, and his film *Pursued* (1947) is widely considered to be the first honest-to-goodness, no-doubt-about-it noir western. In addition, Walsh directed several other fine examples in each genre from the noir crime drama *White Heat* (1949) to the noir westerns *Colorado Territory* (also 1949)—a remake of *High Sierra* that in some ways surpasses the original—and *The Lawless Breed* (1953). As well as being instrumental in creating and defining both the noir crime drama and noir western, Walsh also enriched both genres with films that combine a keen understanding of psychology; an empathy for human aspirations (and sometimes delusions) in a harsh, sad, and often hostile world; and an excellent sense of the noir filmmaking style. A film veteran who had been directing features for 25 years by the time noir hit Hollywood with full force, Walsh proved to be a noir natural.

Between the late 1940s and the mid–1960s, Walsh also directed about a dozen westerns ranging from traditional adventure dramas to the decidedly dark and downbeat. Among these dark efforts, two standouts are *Pursued* and *Colorado Territory*. Like some of Walsh's crime noirs, both focus on heroes with a great deal of personal baggage, two outsiders determined to free themselves from troubled pasts. But, in each film, we have very different heroes and situations. In *Pursued*, the psychologically wounded young rancher Jeb Rand (Robert Mitchum) struggles desperately with both repressed childhood trauma and hostility from others he can't understand. Yet, while he and others carry deep emotional scars with them at the end of the story, the resolution is somewhat hopeful. By finally coming to terms with his past, Jeb has managed to break free from the hold that terrible past events have had over him—to escape it. Like the main character in Hitchcock's noir psychodrama *Spellbound* (1945), the truth enables him to begin the healing process. In *Colorado Territory*, however, Wes McQueen (Joel McCrea) is a criminal on the run who naively longs for a good, proper woman and dreams about a second chance at life without fully seeing (or wanting to see) that his end is only a matter of time. The hard truths of his life and current situation are simply beyond his grasp. He can never escape on his terms, except by dying. In this film, noir fatalism oozes out of every frame.

One of Classic Hollywood's Best-Kept Secrets

"People should know Raoul Walsh," film historian and writer Courtney Joyner has said, "because he is a significant American filmmaker who, quite honestly, has not gotten his due."[4]

Documentary filmmaker and film historian Michael Henry Wilson has taken the issue a step farther, calling Walsh "probably the most underrated" major American filmmaker.[5]

Both points are worth noting.

At a time when we've come to lionize such Walsh contemporaries as Charlie Chaplin, John Ford, Alfred Hitchcock, and Howard Hawks, many people—including some who pride themselves on their knowledge of Hollywood's Golden Age—know little or nothing about a director, who, in many ways, rivaled them all. Walsh's output was Herculean. During more than a half-century, from the 1910s to the 1960s, he directed more than 140 films. His versatility was equally impressive. Like many of his contemporaries, he was adept at moving from genre to genre. While he was most in demand for crime dramas, westerns, and other adventure stories, he also directed fine adaptations of a Maxwell Anderson/Laurence Stallings stage play (1926's *What Price Glory*) and a Somerset Maugham short story (1928's *Sadie Thompson*) along with a Mae West comedy (1936's *Klondike Annie*). He was known mainly as an "action director," which to some suggests that his films lacked psychological and emotional depth. But his heroes are often deceptively complex and shaded, and his stories can be filled with tragic irony and intense feeling. Most important, his work has proven durable. Many of his films—especially the ones he made during his tenure at Warner Brothers from 1939 to 1953—continue to find enthusiastic audiences. In addition to *The Roaring Twenties, They Drive by Night, High Sierra, Pursued, Colorado Territory*, and *White Heat*, these include, among others, *The Strawberry Blonde* (1941), *They Died with Their Boots On* (1941), *Gentleman Jim* (1942), and *Operation, Burma!* (1945).

Throughout his career, Walsh worked with some of the most powerful and influential people in Hollywood, quite simply because they wanted to work with him. His mentor was the "Father of Film," D. W. Griffith, who used Walsh as an assistant director, editor, and actor in his epic *The Birth of a Nation* (1915) and paved the way for Walsh to direct that same year. During his career, Walsh also returned the favor to others, mentoring people who went on to become major stars. He gave John Wayne his first leading role in the epic western *The Big Trail* (1930), for example. A decade later, he helped Humphrey Bogart finally break through to stardom in *High Sierra*. At various times, Walsh also had very productive ongoing collaborations with such major Hollywood players as James Cagney, Errol Flynn, and Clark Gable.

A protégé of D.W. Griffith, Raoul Walsh directed his first feature, *Regeneration*, in 1915; pioneered both the noir crime drama and the noir western; and was still directing in 1964 at age 77.

Like the colorful characters in some of his films, there was also a lot of flash and dash about Walsh. Born Albert Edward Walsh to Irish born immigrants in New York, he changed his name to Raoul about the time he entered show business as a stage actor in 1907. There are different versions of the story, but the most plausible is that he wanted to have a more exotic, romantic-sounding name. He was an actor now, after all. He was a roustabout, too, his numerous infidelities effectively ending his first two marriages. And he reveled in male bravado, loving to tell exciting, larger-than-life stories about himself—stories that kept listeners guessing which details were fact and which were made up.

There are many theories about why Walsh isn't better known today. One is that, during his time, he didn't receive the Academy Award notoriety that many of his contemporaries did. While Ford received a record four directing Oscars and Frank Capra and William Wyler received three each, Walsh was never even nominated. This was at least partly due to a longstanding prejudice the Academy has had against crime, western, and other "action" genre films, and this certainly kept him in the shadows compared to many of his contemporaries. Another theory is that during one of filmmaking's greatest decades, the 1930s, Walsh was—instead of moving his career forward—reeling from the huge financial and critical setback he had experienced with *The Big Trail*. (It literally took him the entire decade to recover his reputation as a reliable, bankable director.) Still another theory is that he was a casualty of the "auteur" school of film criticism, which insists that—for directors to be considered true artists—they have to be the primary authors of their films, leaving, say, a distinctive "Capra-esque" or "Hitchcockian" stamp on them. When we look at the great variety of Walsh's films, that uniquely personal stamp is difficult to find. Walsh isn't the only fine director to suffer at the hands of the auteur school. As noted in the last chapter, the reputations of other major classic-era talents have met similar fates. It's a shame, though, that the auteurists have treated so much of the work of these and other directors so dismissively.

Whatever the reason (or reasons), it's also a shame that Walsh remains one of classic Hollywood's best-kept secrets. Yet, despite his low profile today, the growing interest both in noir crime dramas and the darker post-war westerns is leading more people to learn about the "underrated" master who excelled in these genres, particularly during the 1940s. With their stark, gritty takes on the world, these films are a far cry from the genteel Victorian sensibility of Walsh's mentor, D. W. Griffith, and many of Walsh's contemporaries. But this often searing, unsparing honesty also helps contemporary audiences connect with many of his 1940s films far more easily than they connect with most other films from that decade. They were vital then, and they remain vital today.

Purging the Past: Pursued

When *Pursued* premiered in March 1947, many people didn't know what to make of it. While some critics cautiously praised the film's suspense and effective use of outdoor locales, others were far sterner. Writing in the *New York Times*, for example, Bosley Crowther took *Pursued* to task in a big way.

Some of his criticism was aimed at the film's star Robert Mitchum, who was, in Crowther's mind, "a very rigid gent" who "gives off no more animation than a Frigidaire turned to 'Defrost.'" (Apparently, Crowther hadn't yet learned to appreciate the now-legendary "Mitchum cool.") But his harshest words were reserved for the story and its writer, Niven Busch, who, according to Crowther, "tried to write a psychological mystery in a western setting and bungled the job."[6]

What Crowther and many of his fellow critics didn't get was that *Pursued* was (perhaps along with *The Ox-Bow Incident*) on the leading edge of something new. It wasn't just a psychological mystery but rather a dark, deterministic, and consciously stylized film noir in a western setting. Jeb Rand's struggle to learn about his past is certainly central to the action, but this is also a story about a human landscape as harsh and forbidding as some of the film's wild New Mexico locales. Not only for Jeb but also for every other major character in the story, it's hard to be good. And, even though the story is set in the sunny Southwest, it also strongly suggests that human communities can be very dark, neurotic places.

Pursued begins with a Walsh signature shot: a lone rider on a galloping horse crossing a grand landscape with great urgency. We see that the rider is a woman (Teresa Wright), and soon she arrives at a ramshackle ranch house where she finds Jeb and we learn her name, Thorley. They are in love and apparently in danger. Then, in true noir fashion, Jeb starts bringing us all up to speed through a series of flashbacks accompanied by Mitchum's voice-over narration.

As a boy, Jeb had hidden in a cellar as his family was slaughtered. Jeb doesn't know who the perpetrators were; he only knows that Thorley's mother, Medora Callum (Judith Anderson), brought him to live with her, Thorley, and Thorley's brother, Adam (John Rodney). From the beginning, Jeb felt both a special connection with Thorley and had the sense that he was—and would always be—an outsider in this family. As he grows up with the Callums, Jeb also contends with recurring nightmares of the night his family was killed—nightmares he can't figure out and Medora can't bring herself to explain. Her only advice to him is to leave the past behind and look forward. But Jeb is adamant about learning what happened. Unknown to Jeb, too, another Callum, a one-armed man named Grant (Dean Jagger) wants him dead for reasons we aren't quite sure of, either.

When Jeb grows up, the Spanish-American War breaks out, and he goes to fight, leaving Adam to run the ranch. When he returns, Adam—who's always been uneasy with Jeb's close connection with Thorley—becomes increasingly hostile. Eventually, he tries to gun Jeb down from a distance but Jeb—not knowing it's him—kills him instead. Thorley can't bear this and turns against Jeb.

Eventually, however, she coldly allows Jeb to court her. Her plan, we soon learn, is to get close to him and kill him. But together the two confront her rage, and she realizes that she can't kill him because she's always loved him.

More is brewing as well. After several attempts to kill Jeb, Grant Callum has assembled a group of relatives all intent on doing the young man in. This leads everyone back to the ramshackle ranch where the story began and where we now hear why there's so much festering hatred. Jeb's father and Medora had once been illicit lovers, and, after avenging the wrong by slaughtering Jeb's family, Grant had made it his life's mission to get the last of the Rands, Jeb. Now, at the ranch where we now know that this slaughter took place, Grant and his men take Jeb and prepare him to be hanged. Then, to Grant's utter surprise, Medora, who's arrived on her buckboard, shoots him with her Winchester.

Now, the story is out, the villain has been dispatched, Jeb can begin to heal psychologically, and he and Thorley can start leading a more normal life together.

As this summary suggests, *Pursued* is about much more than one person's experience with a childhood trauma. Busch saw the story as similar to a Greek tragedy. Others have cited Biblical parallels such as Jeb and Adam's Cain-and-Abel rivalry. Still others have called it a "gothic" western[7] and noted its "psychological fatalism."[8]

Whatever the case, there is a lot to digest here. To begin with, all the main characters have neuroses of some kind. Grant Callum avenges forbidden sex by orchestrating a mass killing and then making it his life's work to kill an innocent boy. Medora goes to great lengths to conceal her past shame. Adam's incestuous love for his sister and jealousy toward Jeb drives him to attempt murder. Thorley transforms (for a time) into a noir-ish femme fatale who uses love as a tool to wreak vengeance. Finally, an unhappy, disconnected Jeb spends years desperately trying to piece together scraps of memory—scraps he hopes will give him a clearer picture of why he feels so unhappy and disconnected.

"There's something that keeps us apart," he tells Thorley. "[But] there's an answer—something about me that explains everything."

Clearly, this is a very troubled group of people, a group we're much more likely to see in a noir crime drama than in a typical western of the time. In fact, many of the archetypal noir figures—the traumatized hero, the femme fatale, the person hiding a terrible secret, and the crazed avenger—are all here.

In addition to its undeniable noir sensibility, *Pursued* makes great use of stylistic trappings that are hallmarks of noir—a characteristic that may bring it closer to "pure noir" than *The Ox-Bow Incident*. Perhaps the most obvious noir convention is its flashback structure complete with a character's voice-over narration. Not only is this an excellent device to tell a great deal of back-story very quickly, but it also underscores the story's noir-ish determinism. Just a few minutes into the film, for example, we know that Jeb and Thorley are about to face a very unpleasant, and potentially tragic, reckoning. Another distinctly noir convention is the use (when Jeb and Thorley "court") of the

The just married but intensely unhappy Thorley (Teresa Wright) ponders whether to shoot her new husband Jeb (Robert Mitchum) in Walsh's *Pursued* (1947). The staging of this scene, with the revolver in the foreground and the emphasis on the distance between the two newlyweds, is reminiscent of many crime noirs made during this period.

femme fatale: a smart, manipulative woman who uses her sex appeal to try to achieve an evil end. Still another is the magnificent visual design from the legendary cinematographer James Wong Howe. In *Pursued*, Walsh and Howe worked closely to create the eerie, expressionistic, very noir-ish compositions that give the film an anxious, dreamlike quality and reflect the haunted state of Jeb's mind. The results are often stunning. Characters are occasionally shot in silhouette with their bodies outlined by moonlight, an effect that is both beautiful and chilling. Repeatedly, too, we go inside Jeb's mind to see the scraps of memory he has of the night his parents were killed, especially the memories of mysterious flashing spurs—another beautiful but chilling image. While gunfights in most westerns occur during the day and in open spaces, Jeb's second gunfight occurs at night, largely in darkness, and has the look and the feel of an urban back alley gunfight in a noir thriller where characters stalk each other in black, cramped spaces. Walsh and Howe also reinforce the confined nature of Jeb's life in the ways they photographed him riding into rocky canyons or in front of mountains. Shadows are often reaching out, grabbing hold of him like tentacles.

To further enhance aspects of the story, Walsh also employs some intriguing strategies with actors. Although Bosley Crowther was unimpressed by Robert Mitchum's performance, for example, biographer Marilyn Ann Moss sees Walsh's handling of Mitchum—and the result—quite differently. As she notes: Walsh "opened up Jeb's character by getting Mitchum's facial expressions to mirror a perpetual, natural innocence—thereby making him vulnerable to anything good or evil coming his way."[9] As well as aligning Jeb more closely with well-meaning but often gullible noir leads than with self-assured, highly perceptive western heroes, this approach also helped to make the character more nuanced and interesting.

Pursued is not without its shortcomings. At times, for example, the behavior of the main characters seems forced and contrived. Is Adam's jealousy toward Jeb, for example, so all-consuming that it compels Adam to try to kill Jeb? Or would Thorley really vent her rage at Jeb by playing a femme fatale as part of a plan to kill him? In both cases, it seems like a big stretch.

Yet, despite its imperfections, the film remains quite powerful today. Much of this power comes, of course, from Walsh and Howe's visual design and cinematography, which seem to deepen and broaden every emotion being played out in the film. In addition, several of the actors convey their characters' complex and conflicted states of mind with great skill. Mitchum—an actor who could do just about anything extremely well—is quite effective as the sad, lost, and disconnected Jeb. Another standout is the wonderful Judith Anderson, who ably portrays the complicated Medora, a woman who carries terrible secrets and enormous guilt with her but who also grows to love young Jeb as much as her own children.

Still another—and perhaps the foremost—source of *Pursued's* power is Walsh himself or, more precisely, his ongoing processing of his own traumatic childhood experience. As Moss has perceptively put it: "Walsh's connection to the material ... goes even deeper. The film's overriding concern is loss and grief, natural territory for Walsh, who in one way or another was drawn to these subjects and found his way back to them time and again. That Jeb loses his home is not lost on Walsh, who in the deepest sense lost his home when he was young."[10] Jeb's search, then, reflects Walsh's own, and, we might assume, Jeb's story resonated with the director in a primal, profound way. In turn, we might also assume Walsh turned that intense feeling into intensely felt art.

"You can't bust out of what you are": Colorado Territory

While grappling with personal trauma from one's past as Jeb does in *Pursued* is a popular subject in noir films, even more popular is the futility of trying to escape one's past, especially if some of that past has been spent outside the law. We see this in noir classics from Robert Siodmak's *The Killers* (1946) and Jacques Tourneur's *Out of the Past* (1947) as well as in hundreds of other lesser-known noirs. Suggested in many of these films, too, is the nature of the person or persons involved. Some characters might want to lead an upright life, but there is something about *who* they are (and often why they were attracted to shady dealings in the first place) that ultimately keeps them from keeping to the straight and narrow.

In such films as *The Roaring Twenties* and *High Sierra* Walsh had previously dealt with these subjects, and, in 1948, when Warner Brothers was short on good scripts, he came up with the idea of turning *High Sierra* into a western. According to Walsh, Jack Warner listened, liked what he heard, and simply said, "All right. Start tomorrow."[11]

—⚞—

Colorado Territory really begins as the opening credits roll before the action starts. Behind the names of the people who helped to make the film, we see shots of massive Southwestern rock formations. These are sights we'll see again later on in the story—sights that, in their solemn stillness, also suggest tombstones. In fact, we will eventually learn that the name in the film for one of these sights is *Canyon del Muerto*, the Canyon of Death.

Then—quite abruptly—the film cuts to humorous music and action. A sweet little old lady helps Wes McQueen (Joel McCrea), a notorious bandit who's scheduled to hang, escape from jail. An old friend now living in the Colorado Territory named Dave Rickard (Basil Ruysdael) has engineered the escape and wants Wes to join him to participate in a big train heist. But Wes doesn't seem to have the stomach for such things anymore and says so to one of Dave's operatives. The operative doesn't have much patience for this and offers a bit of foreshadowing. "You wouldn't last long being cut off from the herd, McQueen," he says. "You're branded clear to the bone."

Although he doesn't want to return to a life of crime, Wes does want to thank Dave and travels by stage to Colorado. Along the way, he thwarts a hold-up and befriends two other passengers, Fred Winslow (Henry Hull) and his daughter Julie Ann (Dorothy Malone), who've just bought a ranch in Colorado. It's clear, too, that Wes would like to be more than friends with the pretty and "proper" young Julie Ann.

On instructions from Dave, Wes then rides to the ghost town of Todos Santos, where he meets Reno (John Archer) and Duke (James Mitchell), who will help with the train robbery. With them is Reno's part–Pueblo girlfriend, a former dancehall singer named Colorado (Virginia Mayo). Wes doesn't like the set-up. He doesn't trust either Reno or Duke, and he thinks that a woman in the thick of all this might mean additional trouble. But he decides not to make any immediate changes and meets with Dave, who talks him in to taking the lead in the robbery so they can both retire.

As they wait for the robbery, Colorado falls for Wes and tells him so, but he has dreams of marrying Julie Ann and leading a respectable life with her. Colorado is adamant in her belief that she is the best woman for Wes, but he is not convinced.

In true noir form, the robbery goes awry. A train conductor, who is in on it, betrays the gang for the reward money. Then Duke and Reno try to double-cross Wes. Luckily, Colorado is there with the getaway horses, and, although Wes is wounded in the shoulder, the two escape with the money.

But by now a massive posse is in pursuit. Wes and Colorado first go to the Winslows' house where Fred wants to help them. Colorado removes the bullet from Wes' shoulder, but, as the posse approaches, Julie Ann wants to turn the two outlaws in for the reward money—another betrayal. Fred prevails, however, and Wes and Colorado head for Todos Santos, where Wes—who's had a change of heart about which woman he loves—wants a local cleric to marry them. Since he is a brother and not a priest, he can't. Instead, he suggests a priest just over the border in Mexico. For a moment, both beam with happiness. "We're in the clear now," Wes says. But then they discover that they have been spotted; the posse will arrive soon. Now, Wes insists that they separate. He will head for Mexico, and she will join him later. Reluctantly, she agrees. But, when the posse arrives, she hears part of their strategy and goes to warn Wes. But by now the posse has Wes trapped in a Native American cliff dwelling called the City of the Moon, a dwelling that's been carved into one wall of the Canyon of Death, a box canyon with no way out.

Colorado arrives on the scene, refuses to help the posse trick Wes into coming out, and finally joins him in a desperate attempt to escape, firing away at the men in the posse. Within seconds, though, both are overwhelmed with gunfire and fall to the ground dead. They are still holding hands.

While Walsh relied heavily on key noir storytelling tools such as flashbacks, neurotic characters, and dark, expressionistic cinematography in *Pursued*, he got into the marrow of noir in *Colorado Territory*. In a classic western setting, he told the archetypal noir story—one he had pioneered in film eight years before with *High Sierra*—of a doomed dreamer who cannot escape his flawed past. And, rather than diluting the noir bleakness and emotional power of *High Sierra*, *Colorado Territory*, in several ways, improves upon the original. As film writer Frank Miller notes about Walsh and the latter film, "he even got to top himself."[12] This is not to say that *Colorado Territory* is the better film overall. *High Sierra*, after all, is a widely acknowledged classic with much to its credit. But, as with many of Walsh's efforts, *Colorado Territory* is also a superb film that's been greatly undervalued.

Central to the film's effectiveness is the dynamic between its two main characters, Wes and Colorado. Their world views as well as their takes on the immediate situation are both more clearly differentiated than we see with Roy and Marie, their counterparts in *High Sierra*. In one of *Colorado Territory*'s best scenes, when Colorado tells Wes that she's in love with him, we hear this poignantly expressed.

"You bust out of jails or maybe mud holes like I was in," Colorado says, "but you can't bust out of what you are."

"You can if you're set on it," says Wes.

"Can ya?" Colorado asks. "Me, I was born under a chuck wagon. Never

Colorado (Virginia Mayo) and Wes (Joel McCrea) choose to go down fighting rather than to give themselves up at the end of Walsh's 1949 gem *Colorado Territory*. A remake of Walsh's 1941 noir *High Sierra*, this film in many ways surpasses the very fine original.

got much higher. Anything was a step up. Even getting hit by Reno was all velvet."

"He won't do that again."

"He had a right to. He knew Duke was right when he said it was ... *you* I want."

But Wes isn't pleased to hear this. "It won't work," he says. "I've got plans [to marry Julie Ann]. There's no room in them for you—not for the long pull."

"Maybe there won't be no long pull," she says gravely. "Maybe it all ends Friday on that train."

"Yea, yea, that's where it ends. Everybody takes his own road after that."

Here we see that Colorado has a much better understanding both of who Wes is and of what's really happening with them than Wes does. She knows that, despite his sincere efforts, he will never "bust out." In fact, he might not even live beyond the train robbery that's planned for Friday. Yet, despite his naïve dreams (one of which is that he will marry Julie Ann), she loves him.

She is attracted to his real qualities—his strength, courage, and integrity. He's head and shoulders above Reno and most likely the other bleak romantic options she's had in her life. She's keenly aware that there probably won't be a "long pull," but, because she loves Wes's good qualities, she'll stick with him as long as she can.

After the two survive several close scrapes, he proposes marriage, and the two plan to go to Mexico, she has a few brief moments of hope in Todos Santos. "This time, Wes, we can really bust out," she says.

But, a moment later, they see a smoke signal that signifies that they've been spotted.

"What does it mean?" she asks.

"It means we're a couple of fools in a dead village dreaming about something that'll probably never happen," Wes says in his moment of epiphany.

With all hope gone, even for Wes, he insists on separating. They do briefly, but, in a major departure from *High Sierra*, Colorado (unlike Marie) stands beside her man in the final gunfight. Rather than live without Wes, she decides, she would rather die with him. It's a shocking ending (even bleaker and more powerful than *High Sierra's*) and one that speaks volumes of the character of Colorado—a character Frank Miller has called "one of the toughest women in film history."[13]

While this is clearly Wes's story, the character of Colorado might be the film's most intriguing component. Racially mixed and not particularly valued by either the white or the Native American worlds, she is, in effect, an outsider in both. In her own way, she is—like Wes—a person without a real place in the present or a desirable past to return to. Unlike Wes, though, she is usually a realist about her (and their) situation. She knows her (and their) life choices are extremely limited at this point. Finally, of course, her name is Colorado, like the territory, which also happens to be the film's title. This suggests many ironic possibilities. Wes comes to the Colorado Territory to start a new life. Instead, he finds a good woman named Colorado, who offers him both love and a new understanding about himself, which prepare him not for his new life but rather his death. Or perhaps the title could also hint at the place where the couple has gone together in death—a place where the two can finally find peace. There is the slight suggestion of this in the film's final line when the brother—not knowing that Wes and Colorado have died—joyously rings church bells and refers to the pair as "a happy couple who passed this way." Whatever the case, it's intriguing to speculate.

Another interesting component is how the script treats both the

Winslows as counterpoints to Colorado. While Colorado is usually a realist, Fred is even more of a naïve dreamer than Wes. He puts his faith in a swindler and buys a worthless ranch sight unseen. And, while Colorado offers Wes real love and loyalty, Julie Ann never loves Wes and is even willing to sell him out for the reward money. She is the true false love. In fact, as Colorado points out to Wes, a major part of Wes's attraction to Julie Ann is her physical resemblance to Wes's long-dead love, Martha—another delusion.

Still another (and very noir-ish) component to the story is the theme of betrayal; it's everywhere. Duke and Reno and then Julie Ann all betray Wes, of course. In addition, the train conductor betrays the entire gang. Then, in a very subtle bit, after the U.S. marshal agrees to go easy on Duke and Reno if they tell him where to find Wes after the train robbery and they cooperate, the marshal immediately hangs them. As he looks at the two dangling corpses, he casually comments: "It's a nice sight for anybody with a train robbing itch." Finally, in an effort to catch Wes, the marshal tricks Colorado into believing that there's a way out of the City of the Moon. Yes, in this harsh, bitter world, even the word of the law cannot be trusted. Treachery abounds, and the trusting and naïve are especially vulnerable.

Colorado Territory also benefits from fine acting, especially by Joel McCrea and Virginia Mayo in the two lead roles. Both had big shoes to fill, stepping into parts originated by two of the best Hollywood actors of the 1940s, Humphrey Bogart and Ida Lupino, and both deliver excellent performances that in some ways surpass the originals.

McCrea, who had a natural integrity and earnestness about him, was always very interesting when he played morally dubious characters, bringing dimension and complexity to the parts that most other actors couldn't match. As Wes, he does a fine job of showing a man who's both a hardened criminal and a childlike and vulnerable dreamer. He breaks out of jail, robs a train, and kills people, but we never lose our sympathy for him. In the end, we know he's doomed, but part of us keeps hoping he'll beat the odds and find a way to Mexico.

While McCrea does a fine job as Wes, Mayo is terrific a Colorado, ably conveying her character's distinctive mix of toughness, intelligence, skepticism, courage, devotion, and passion. Colorado could have easily have descended into an unbelievable ethnic caricature (similar to Linda Darnell's Chihuahua in Ford's *My Darling Clementine*), but Mayo invests a great deal of conviction into the character and never delivers a false note. That we accept her decision to die along with Wes at the end of the film is as much a testament to Mayo's compelling portrayal as it is to her well-conceived character.

In noting Mayo's performance, Frank Miller laments that the actress—often cast in frothy comedies and forgettable action films—had so few opportunities to display her talent. "Walsh was one of the few directors in Hollywood who saw Mayo's potential as a dramatic actress," Miller has written. "Director William Wyler had given a hint of her potential when he cast her as Dana Andrew's unfaithful wife in the postwar classic *The Best Years of Our Lives* (1946). But it was Walsh who gave her her best roles, first in *Colorado Territory*, then as James Cagney's murderous wife in *White Heat* the same year. The rare glimpses he provided of her usually wasted talents were as tragic as anything that happened to the characters in *Colorado Territory*."[14]

Well, maybe not *as* tragic. Mayo was happily married, had a daughter, continued working for decades after *Colorado Territory*, and died in 2005 at age 84 after a long and full life. But Miller's point is well taken. It's a shame Mayo didn't receive more good roles.

More Than the "Action Man"

According to Walsh, actor Jack Pickford (Mary's brother) once told him, "Your idea of light comedy is to burn down a whorehouse." Apparently, the wisecrack delighted the director, and he repeated it often in conversations throughout his life.[15]

Pickford obviously recognized Walsh's natural attraction to action in his films, and Walsh, it appears, took great pride in the characterization. Maybe because it helped to reinforce his image as a man's man and a hell raiser, he liked being the "action man." But lurking beneath all Walsh's personal swagger was always that sadder and more sensitive side—the side that also bubbled up to the surface in his good films.

His time at Warner Brothers during the 1940s when he made many of his best films may represent a grand convergence of sorts. With its hard-boiled sensibilities and break-neck filmmaking style, Warner Brothers was probably the best place for Walsh's talents at the time. In addition, the emergence of the noir sensibility and style in the crime film and then its extension into the western were both serendipitous. Films such as *High Sierra*, *Pursued*, *Colorado Territory*, and *White Heat* allowed Walsh to tap into and unleash different parts of himself in ways he hadn't really done before—to be rough, tough, sensitive, and sad all at the same time. This brought more dynamic tension and greater complexity to his work and—in new and startling ways—enabled him to soar.

3

Where Treachery Springs Eternal
Staying Human in the Harsh Worlds of André de Toth's *Ramrod* and *Day of the Outlaw*

> "You won't find much mercy anywhere in Wyoming."
> —*Day of the Outlaw*

Life is hard in the films of André de Toth (1913–2002). People often betray each other, and in the process they sometimes betray themselves, too. In pursuit of their own survival, they can also do bad things that result in violence and death. The brutality can come quickly, unexpectedly. A chance meeting or a knock on the door and a person's life is radically changed or simply concluded. And, when all is said and done, many of the characters have some dirt on their hands—dirt that will probably never come off. It's not a pretty picture, but that's basically how de Toth saw human beings and the ways they interacted with one another. "I wanted to rub our noses in the mess we have created and how we shy away from our responsibility to clean it up," he said in an interview late in life.[1] He was referring to one of this films, but he could have been referring to most of them. He had a specific worldview and he communicated it in his films with great consistency. In an age when most genre directors just filmed scripts the studios assigned them, his was a distinctive voice.

With this kind of worldview, de Toth also seemed to have the ideal sensibility for film noir and the noir western. Yet this isn't the whole story. While de Toth was the consummate anti-romantic, he was by no means (as some assume) a cynic. In the harsh worlds of his films, heroes are usually flawed but basically decent people fighting for their souls as well as their survival. Life without at least some integrity, he seems to be telling us, is meaningless. Rather than a cynic, de Toth is more of a humanist with a very hard, often pessimistic edge. He cares intensely for his flawed heroes as they travel difficult paths through harsh worlds in attempts to achieve some kind of peace and happiness, but he is not about to make anything easy for them. The journey will be long and hard, and along the way there will be no shortcuts. In the end, however, the difficulty will make the hero's heroism all the more admirable.

Perhaps more than anything else, this very distinctive viewpoint toward the world and the flawed people who try to live honorably in it is de Toth's main contribution to the development of the noir western. He often gets into the struggling souls of his dark cowboys in ways few of his directing peers can match, and, once there, he never flinches. This is also part of what makes his best western characters and films so compelling.

Between 1947 and 1959, de Toth made 11 westerns, ranging in quality from solid to superb. During this period he worked with major stars such as Gary Cooper in 1952's *Springfield Rifle* and Kirk Douglas in 1955's *The Indian Fighter*, a film noted (for the time) both for its frank sexuality and its unusually respectful treatment of Native Americans. His most frequent leading man during the period, however, was Randolph Scott, who worked with de Toth on six well-crafted Columbia Pictures B-unit westerns between 1951 and 1954.

André de Toth came to Hollywood from Hungary by way of England in the 1940s, married actress Veronica Lake, and quickly found jobs directing both noir crime dramas and dark westerns.

While all of de Toth's westerns have noir shadings, the two that are most emphatically noir are his first, 1947's *Ramrod* with Joel McCrea and Veronica Lake, and his last, 1959's *Day of the Outlaw* with Robert Ryan, Burl Ives, and Tina Louise. As well as being two of his darkest westerns, they are also two of his most uncompromising and most powerful.

The Hard-Edged Humanist

For people who enjoy film noir, westerns with a noir bent, or both, André de Toth is a fascinating subject. Virtually unknown today to just about everyone except film historians and a relatively small number of classic film aficionados, he was responsible for about a half dozen (or more depending on your personal preferences) remarkable films. He was also a bona-fide "character." The son of a Hungarian hussar and a protégé of the celebrated Hungarian playwright Ferenc Molnar, he sported a piratical eye patch, had seven wives, reportedly fathered 19 children,[2] and loved to play the provocateur. "Film schools teach you absolutely nothing," he once wrote.[3] "Life is a betrayal.... Let's have the guts to admit it," he proclaimed in one 1990s interview.[4] In his later years, the interviewers loved him: he could always deliver some choice words.

Born Sasvrai Farkasfalvi Tothfalusi Toth Endre Anral Mihaly in Mako, Hungary, de Toth grew up in relative wealth and comfort. His father, who had retired from the Hussars to become a civil engineer, was devastated when his son, who gravitated toward the arts, declared he had no intention of joining his father's elite regiment. While still a teenager, de Toth began writing plays, and through this work connected with Molnar, Hungary's most celebrated playwright, who in turn introduced him to people in the country's leading film circles. By 1938, he was directing films. The following year, with war on the horizon in Europe, he went to England, where he soon began working as a writer and second-unit director with British producer Alexander Korda. Three years later, Korda took de Toth with him to Hollywood.

As was the case in both Hungary and England, de Toth found work quickly. With Korda's help, he was soon making films with respected veteran actors such as Warren William, Merle Oberon, Franchot Tone, and Thomas Mitchell. By 1944, he had completed three projects, including *None Shall Escape*, a World War II drama that received an Academy Award nomination for Best Story. By 1944, de Toth had also married 1940s sex symbol actress Veronica Lake. The couple would work together on *Ramrod* and *Slattery's Hurricane* (1949), have two children, go bankrupt, and then divorce acrimoniously in 1952.

Despite his topsy-turvy personal life (there would be numerous wives and women after Lake), de Toth proved to be a very productive director for the next decade and a half, churning out some 20 films between 1947 and 1960 alone. Fiercely independent, he never signed multi-picture contracts with specific studios, believing that he would have less artistic control over his films. He also turned down the opportunities to work with major stars such as Humphrey

Bogart and Ava Gardner, preferring actors with less box office muscle whom he felt could do a better job of interpreting the characters in his films.

Perhaps de Toth's best known film today is *House of Wax* (1953), a very effective 3-D horror thriller about a madman who dips the people he kills into melted wax and then, when the wax hardens, puts them on display in his wax museum. One of the ironies of the production that historians find irresistible to talk about is that de Toth—who lacked depth perception because he only had one good eye—was able to work in the 3-D medium so ably. He had mastered a visual medium, which he, as a viewer, could not fully appreciate.

Two top candidates for de Toth's best non-westerns are a pair of fine but fairly obscure film noirs. The first is *Pitfall* (1948) with Dick Powell, Lizabeth Scott, Jane Wyatt, and a wonderfully creepy Raymond Burr, the story of a philandering husband whose affair leads to his own personal fall and ultimately murder. The other is *Crime Wave* (1954) with Sterling Hayden, Gene Nelson, and Phyllis Kirk, the story about an ex-con who's trying to go straight, his old friends from prison who won't let him, and a tough, toothpick-chewing cop who wants to believe in him. In many respects, both are typical of de Toth: betrayals are central to the stories, integrity is important to the main characters, and the world is a harsh place, especially when you want to make amends for mistakes you've made.

Unlike Anthony Mann or Budd Boetticher, who both specialized in crime noirs and then moved mainly to westerns, de Toth went back and forth between the two genres from the late 1940s to the late 1950s. As he did, he developed an expertise in each while also bringing his own concerns and preoccupations to both. For him, in fact, genre didn't matter nearly as much as the stories he wanted to tell. As he said in an interview in 2000: "I want to photograph life. Noir, westerns, whatever kind of picture, I wanted real life. What costumes the characters have on doesn't matter. What's coming through the clothes is what counts. I like to show people naked in front of the camera. And this is the reason, the fringed jacket of a cowboy or the business suit of an insurance investigator—they might as well be the same."[5]

"So you don't want it alone. I guess that squares everything"—Ramrod

"My favorite de Toth picture is perhaps *Ramrod*, a grim ... western which remains so surprisingly fresh."
—Martin Scorsese[6]

3. Where Treachery Springs Eternal

As the story goes, de Toth, who had never directed a western but eagerly wanted to, got his big break from none other than John Ford.

Well aware of de Toth's thick Hungarian accent, Ford loved to call him "Tex." And, with de Toth at his side at a meeting in early 1947, Ford told *Ramrod's* producer Harry Sherman that, while he was busy and couldn't direct the film, he would be thrilled to recommend his good friend Tex for the job.[7]

The result is both one of the first fully formed noir westerns and the film that made de Toth a respected Hollywood player.

"Time was when the ladies of western movies were demure damsels who came on the scene perhaps to pour a cup of coffee, teach school, or to ride off into a pristine sunset with an equally pristine hero," began the *New York Times* review of *Ramrod* in 1947. "But things, as has become only too apparent, have changed. The spirited lassies now are in there bussing and generally riding herd on unsuspecting wranglers enough to befuddle even the hardiest cowpoke."[8]

No one was writing about western noir yet, but the *Times* reviewer was on to something. *Ramrod* was different. The main female character, Veronica Lake's Connie Dickason, is a radical departure from the sweet, idealized female leads people were used to seeing in westerns. On top of that, the title character, Joel McCrea's Dave Nash, is often quite passive and gullible—an unwitting dupe in Connie's schemes. Add to that, several of the other men—including Connie's fiancé and her father—are weak and willing to be pushed around. These definitely aren't your typical featured roles in this very manly genre.

The story begins in a traditional enough manner: the leading cattlemen, led by local bully Frank Ivey (Preston Foster) and Connie's father Ben Dickason (Charles Ruggles), want to drive Connie's fiancé Walt Shipley (Ian MacDonald), a rival rancher, out of the area. Instead of fighting, Walt simply leaves, giving his land to Connie, who is infuriated by his lack of backbone. She'll stay and fight no matter who she has to tangle with.

To run her ranch, she recruits Dave, who then hires his friend Bill Schell (Don DeFore), a charmer with the ladies who also hates Frank Ivey, would love to bring Ivey down, and doesn't mind bending the law when it suits his purposes. To add to the romantic mix, both Dave and Bill have feelings for Rose Leland (Arleen Whelan), the town's kind-hearted dressmaker.

Connie, who sees just about everything in terms of herself, will stop at nothing both to keep her ranch and to win over the earnest (and easily manipulated) Dave. Using her womanly wiles, she convinces Bill to stampede her own cattle (because the upright Dave would never do such a thing) to make Ivey look guilty to the law. Dave brings the evidence to the local sheriff, who confronts Ivey and is killed. When Dave hears this, he finally decides that Ivey and his men need to be brought down.

Two of Ivey's men ambush Dave. Wounded, he escapes and hides out at Rose's, where a doctor tends to him and Bill comes to help. Concerned for his safety and Rose's, Dave, with Bill at his side, heads out to hide in a cave. Worried about Dave as well, Connie finds out about the cave and goes there, unwittingly tipping Ivey and his men off about the hiding place. Knowing they must move again, Bill offers to distract their pursuers and is eventually killed—shot in the back by Ivey.

Meanwhile, Dave has returned to town where he learns that Ivey has killed Bill and that Connie was actually responsible for the cattle stampede that led to the sheriff's death. Ivey arrives, and the two confront each other in the street. Dave kills Ivey, and Connie, who is also back in town, rushes into his arms. She is thrilled.

Ranch foreman Dave (Joel McCrea) tries to understand the scheming ways of his boss, Connie (noir icon Veronica Lake), a rare western femme fatale, in de Toth's *Ramrod* (1947). This film was the first of several dark westerns de Toth would make over the next 12 years.

"It could have been you lying there, but it isn't," she says. "This is the way it was meant to be."

"It's all over now," he answers listlessly. "You've got what you've wanted."

"What *we've* wanted," she stresses. "You and I. All this is ours now for the rest of our lives. Don't you see what we've won, Dave?"

But he isn't persuaded, not now.

"What counts now is our happiness, our freedom, the way we want to live," she reaffirms a moment later.

"Not 'we,' Connie," he says, "just you, alone."

"I don't want it alone."

"So, you don't want it alone?" he responds with some irony. "I guess that squares everything."

At this, he walks away from Connie and toward Rose's dress shop, where he locks eyes with the good woman, suggests marriage, and gathers her up into his arms.

Attempting to put *Ramrod* into its rightful context in an excellent 2003 article in *Senses of Cinema*, Rick Thompson notes: "I see it as a turning-point film—a skillful and moving summary of a long tradition ... and a definitive break with that tradition, setting up a new area of possibilities which proceed to change the genre—in the direction of film noir. I also see it as an isolated film, a film unlike others of its type before or after."[9]

His points are well taken. Much like de Toth does in his film noirs, he stays true to a tradition while also making his own distinctive contributions to it. But, in this case, he is also playing the role of trendsetter: *Ramrod* will have an important impact on numerous westerns to follow from Anthony Mann's *The Furies* (1950) to Nicholas Ray's *Johnny Guitar* (1954) to Sam Fuller's *Forty Guns* (1957). Among de Toth's many noir-ish contributions to this western, two are key. One is the introduction of the noir femme fatale in the person of Connie. The other is the gullible, uncertain, and easily manipulated leading man in the person of Dave, in several respects the classic noir dupe. In addition, Thompson calls the film "isolated" in certain ways. This is true, too. While attacking some of the sacred cows of characterization in westerns, it remains very respectful toward western traditions, much more so than many of the avant-garde 1950s westerns soon to follow.

The film's most startling departure from the western norm (especially for fans in 1947) is Connie. As French critic Bertrand Tavernier has written, "long before *Johnny Guitar, Ramrod* made women the real heroines of the story."[10] Blonde, slim, and with no qualms about manipulating men from Dave to Bill with her sexual allure, she is a classic noir vamp. We have several reasons to feel sympathy for her. Both her fiancé and her father are weak and easily intimidated by the evil Frank Ivey. She buckles at the idea—one that her father and Ivey enthusiastically support—that she should even marry Ivey. She is also smitten with Dave, who never seems wildly enthusiastic about her. That said, however, she has no scruples and will stop at nothing to get what she wants— the wherewithal to stand up to (and possibly topple) Ivey. No one, not even Ivey, is going to tell her what to do. Perhaps her most egregious act is convincing Bill (with her womanly wiles, of course) to stampede her own cattle, a decision that leads to several deaths. She seems almost as reprehensible when, after Bill confesses his trespasses to Dave near the end of the film, she remains silent. Again, betrayal is a major driving force in this de Toth film, and Connie, even more than Ivey, is the story's ultimate betrayer.

Like nearly all noir vamps, Connie gets her comeuppance, but in her case it's not a bullet in the heart or a trip to jail. Dave simply sees her for what she is and rejects her for a much more desirable alternative, Rose. Connie's punishment is to be alone. As Dave tells her, "I guess that squares everything." This is a subtler end for her than it is for most noir bad girls, and, in a curious way, it's absolutely fitting: she gets her ranch, power, and everything else she has schemed for—everything, that is, except the most important thing.

One of many fine touches that gives *Ramrod* its particular richness is how the contrast between Connie and Rose is suggested. Throughout the story, Connie deliberately breaks ties, hurts, and destroys. Breaking from her father and Ivey and ordering the stampede are obvious examples. She also destroys inadvertently, even when she tries to help. We see this when she goes to a wounded Dave's side as he hides in the cave and, without knowing it, tips one of Ivey's men off as to Dave's whereabouts. Even when she tries to do a good thing, it doesn't turn out well. Rose, on the other hand, is all about mending, healing, putting things together. We see this when she gets a doctor to tend to the wounded Dave. And, in a fascinating touch, we also see this with the fabric Dave gives her as a gift near the beginning of the story. After hesitating, she accepts it. Then, in several scenes, we see her with bits and pieces of that fabric in her work area. Finally, she is wearing the finished dress, which Dave suggests can be her wedding dress when they are married.

In addition to Connie's character, another major departure from western tradition in *Ramrod* is Dave. Again, we are given reasons to be sympathetic toward him. Before the action begins, his wife and then his young son were killed and he became a drunk. Like many heroes in noir westerns soon to come, he has been traumatized by the death of loved ones. Connie's fiancé Walt gives him a chance to redeem himself, and he feels a certain loyalty to her for this. He also has a sweet spot for Rose, but, in another of the film's ambiguities, he doesn't quite know what to make of the friendship (or relationship?) between Rose and Bill. Still, at his core, Dave is extremely passive and compliant. Usually, he takes Connie's word at face value and does what she tells him to. This certainly gives him similarities to the typical noir "pushover" male such as Fred MacMurray's Walter Neff in *Double Indemnity* or MacMurray's Paul Sheridan in the aptly named *Pushover* (1954). But there is more to Dave than that. Despite his passivity, he always stands firmly on the side of obeying the law and working through legal channels; he is downright upright. In the end—even though Connie has driven most of the action— Dave comes out the hero: the man who confronts and prevails over both the villainous Ivey and the manipulative Connie. Much like de Toth's noir heroes in *Pitfall* and *Crime Wave*, integrity and conscience are critical to him. Connie can live comfortably without these attributes, but Dave can't.

In addition to giving us intriguing noir-ish characters in *Ramrod*, de Toth makes good use of noir visual techniques to reinforce the drama. One excellent example is in the way the director links Connie's treacherous embrace of Bill with the stampede of her cattle. The film doesn't cut from one scene to the next; it slowly dissolves, closely linking (in a very noir-ish way) the illicit passion the two characters share with the violence of the rampaging herd.[11] *Ramrod* also possesses a noir-ish determinism, which harkens back to the bleak title of de Toth's first U.S. film, *None Shall Escape*. One way this determinism is constantly reinforced throughout the film is with visual linkages between seemingly safe inside settings (a hotel, Rose's dress shop, Connie's ranch, a cave, etc.) and the more precarious outside, where characters are far more vulnerable to danger. Even though the characters in *Ramrod* are constantly seeking refuge of some kind, usually in these interior settings, de Toth seems to be saying here (as he says elsewhere), there really is none—that we really can't escape life's dangers and pitfalls.[12]

While *Ramrod* is an essential film in the birth and development of western *noir*, it is also—as Thompson notes—an anomaly, one of a kind. Unlike the better known "psychological" or "Freudian" westerns of the 1950s that feature dominant women and weak men such as *Johnny Guitar*, *Ramrod* is more ambiguous in attitude both toward its characters and toward the traditional western genre it is derived from. While passive and gullible, for example, *Ramrod's* "pushover" good guy comes through in the end, prevailing over evil while not compromising his principles. He is not such a pushover, after all. Also, while *Ramrod* is iconoclastic, it also seems more affectionate toward the traditions of the western rather than mocking them the way Ray does in *Johnny Guitar* or Fritz Lang does in another of these iconoclastic westerns, *Rancho Notorious* (1952). Its attitude toward adhering to western tradition and breaking with it is much more conflicted and, as a result, less condescending and more interesting.

A Hard Day in a Hard World: Day of the Outlaw

Filmed 12 years after *Ramrod*, *Day of the Outlaw* seems light years away from the previous film. The most obvious difference is its environment. While *Ramrod* is set in a warm, sunny southwestern locale, *Day of the Outlaw* (actually filmed in Oregon's Cascade Mountains) is set in high-country Wyoming in the dead of a very white winter. "The coldest movie ever made," one film blogger remarked. "You feel it in your bones."[13] It includes a vastly different assortment of characters—a hard-boiled anti-hero instead of a noir "dupe," an erring wife who wants to be better to her husband instead of a femme fatale, and—instead of a typical western bad guy—an outlaw leader who prides himself both on his integrity and his ability to control his creepy, totally amoral gang members. And its main conflict, rather than ending in a traditional showdown, culminates in a gruesome "death ride" into formidable, snowbound mountains.

At heart, though, it is also very much the work of de Toth. Betrayals abound, a flawed hero comes to grips with the importance of integrity, and the world—as always—is a harsh place.

—⚎—

The story begins as Blaise Starrett (Robert Ryan) and his foreman, Dan (Nehemiah Persoff), ride into the small, isolated, snowbound town of Bitters, Wyoming. Their horses struggle to walk through the snow, and the music suggests great burden and bleakness. We soon learn that Blaise has it in for Hal Crane (Alan Marshal), a rival rancher, for putting up fences and limiting the grazing territory of Blaise's cattle. But Dan suggests that Blaise might also want to put an end to Hal so he can have Hal's "pretty wife Helen" all to himself.

In town Blaise and Helen meet again, and we learn that they have indeed had an affair, the story's first betrayal. While Blaise still wants Helen, she makes it clear that her desire now is to be a good wife. Tensions rise, and a reckoning between Blaise and Hal seems inevitable. The next morning, Blaise comes to face Hal and a couple of others in the bar. He tells Dan to roll a bottle down the bar. When it falls, he declares, they can all start shooting. Dan rolls the bottle, and de Toth's camera conscientiously follows it down the bar.

Before it falls, however, the world changes.

At that moment, a group of outlaws fleeing the U.S. Cavalry and led by disgraced former officer Jack Bruhn (Burl Ives) enters, confiscates everyone else's guns, and literally takes over the town. The conflict between Blaise and Hal must now take a back seat. For a while, at least, there are more urgent problems to address.

Blaise learns that Bruhn has been wounded and that, if he dies, his men—without Bruhn to control them—will go wild, probably killing all the town's men and definitely raping the town's four women. Needless to say, Bruhn's

A gang of brutal outlaws holds the residents of a small snowbound Wyoming town captive in de Toth's hard-hitting *Day of the Outlaw* (1959). Pictured here are actors Robert Ryan, Alan Marshal, Tina Louise, Jack Lambert, and Lance Fuller.

health becomes a major concern for everyone involved. The town's veterinarian removes a bullet from Bruhn but fears he will still die of internal bleeding. Bruhn also knows that the pursuing soldiers will soon arrive, and, in an uncharacteristically noble gesture, Blaise offers to lead Bruhn and his men through the mountains via a trail only he knows about. Bruhn learns this is a lie (another betrayal), but Blaise tells him he will die anyway and that this will be a way "to die clean" without letting his gang destroy the town. Bruhn isn't quite sure what's motivating Blaise but agrees, saying, "I guess every fool has his reason." Without telling his men (still another betrayal), he leaves with Blaise and them, assuming they all will die.

In this "death ride" through the mountains, Bruhn and most of his men do die, and eventually all who remain are Blaise and two of the outlaws. All spend a very cold night, and one of the outlaws freezes to death. Blaise, half-dead himself, mounts his horse to ride back, as the other outlaw, whose hands are now frozen and can't fire his gun, must simply watch helplessly as Blaise rides away.

Finally, Blaise returns to his ranch and his foreman, Dan, to resume his life—without Helen.

While *Day of the Outlaw* was a commercial failure when it was first released, it has since found a small but enthusiastic cult following. Film writer Fred Camper has called it one of de Toth's two "greatest" films[14] (the other being his very dark 1969 war film, *Play Dirty*). Glenn Erickson has called it "excellent," "an unusually uncompromising show for its time," and a film that "hasn't a hint of artsy pretension."[15] And a blogger named Tristan adds, "The film is just an immensely real, visceral experience. It weighs on you, it chills you, and ultimately, it takes the genre deep into territory that even the likes of Anthony Mann and John Ford hadn't dared to do. It's a very primal film.... Bleak, but mighty brilliant."[16]

Most likely, both the film's initial failure with audiences and its growing cult stature have to do with its with this "uncompromising" bleakness. It is not an easy film to watch, but, with repeated viewings, it becomes increasingly compelling. This film pulls no punches. While it doesn't have a "pushover" hero, a manipulative femme fatale, or some other noir trappings, it is about as noir as a western can get.

Key to its effectiveness are its two main characters and the performances of the two superb actors who played them.

Ryan's Blaise is a fascinating amalgam of contradictory characteristics. On one hand, he's a hard man who's used to solving problems with his guns or his fists and used to getting his way. At his core is plenty of anger as well as disdain for others in the town who have relied on him for years to protect their interests as well as his own. He does have a soft spot for Helen, but, during the first part of the film, his only strategy for winning her is to kill her husband. In this respect, he's similar to some of Humphrey Bogart's better noir characters such as Sam Spade in *The Maltese Falcon* and Dixon Steele in Nicholas Ray's fine *In a Lonely Place* (1950). On the other hand, Blaise goes through a growth arc neither of the Bogart characters nor most "hard-boiled" noir heroes ever experience. As events unfold, Blaise realizes that, to save Helen and the town, the only way out is to sacrifice himself by offering to lead the outlaws out of town and into the freezing, impassable mountains. Ironically, it's this uncharacteristically noble gesture that enables Blaise to save himself by reclaiming his integrity and moral core.

In lesser hands, Blaise's transformation would have been far less credible or captivating, but Ryan—by 1959, a widely known noir icon—pulls it off with great aplomb. "Ryan is always good when expressing ambivalence," notes Erickson. "He comes on like the heavy, and even when he's doing the right thing, he never wears a halo."[17]

Blaise's main adversary, Burl Ives' Jack Bruhn, is equally fascinating. Even though he's been booted out of the military and now commands a group made up mainly of sociopaths, he has his code. He prides himself on his ability to keep his word, to keep his men in line, and to respect and protect the townspeople (especially the women) from his men. By western standards, Bruhn is a very principled, reasonable, and high-integrity bad guy. Blaise's offer of a chance to "die clean" appeals to him. He knows the difference between making that choice and allowing his men to destroy the town.

Ives, who was better known in his day as a folk singer than as an actor, does a fine job here, too. Bruhn is, as Erickson says, "a strangely modulated villain."[18] But his intelligence and his sensitivity toward both Blaise and the other townspeople also make him a very appealing one. And Ives conveys all of this quite convincingly.

In addition to these performances, another of the film's impressive assets is its bleak, relentlessly harsh snowbound setting. Most westerns, of course, are about wide-open spaces and geographic possibilities. Stagecoaches can take us through vast deserts, and wagon trains can cross half the continent. Here, however, the natural environment serves as symbol for the more noir-ish world of Bitters: cold, hard, oppressive, isolated, and claustrophobic. Although de

Toth was pressured to film in color (which was certainly more common in westerns by 1959), he insisted on black and white to reinforce the icy noir mood he wanted to establish, and the decision worked. The actors look very cold in some scenes, because, of course, they probably are. The horses seem to be in real pain as they carry their riders on and on through the deep snow, and they, too, probably are. Again, this film could have been titled *None Shall Escape*. There really is no way out of Bitters, not for these people, at least. Bruhn and all but one of his gang die, and, although Blaise lives, his only real choice is to return to his lonely ranch life.

While we can see (and often feel) the noir elements throughout this film, there are two sequences—both very much the work of de Toth—that deserve special mention.

The first is a dance, which Bruhn agrees to in order to keep his men at least somewhat pacified before the gang leaves town. This could very well be unlike any other dance in the whole of cinema. The town's four women are brought to the local bar and told to dance with the different members of Bruhn's gang. These men are, of course, a grotesque lot, and nowhere in the film is this point made more emphatically than in this scene. As one gang member says of the women when the dance is proposed, "We only want to borrow them; we'll give them back."

In filmed dance scenes, one common directorial technique is to keep the camera fluid, as if it is moving with the dancers, throughout a dance. Often, the effect is to approximate a romantic delirium of, say, a young couple reeling in the throes of love. In this film, however, the effect is quite different. Bertrand Tavernier describes this as "a most impressive sequence, where, without cutting away, the camera follows several women who are passed from the arms of one outlaw to another, as they are forced to dance. The long, circular panning shots accentuate the feeling of chaos, imposing a sudden eruption of physical and mental imbalance, and thus creating a tension, an atmosphere of extremely powerful violence."[19]

The second sequence is the long "death ride," which takes up the last 20 minutes of the film. In its way, it reinforces and magnifies everything that has already been suggested in the story: the immense power of nature over people, the futility of craven human quests, and the very deterministic *None Shall Escape* message. We know that Bruhn and others are going to die, but, as Camper has noted, "the very absence of suspense is part of what makes the film's final 20 minutes so powerful, as one by one they do die."[20] They ride through the deep snow, kill one another fighting over money, and the survivors repeat the cycle. The one bit of suspense is Blaise's fate. He may be resourceful enough to find a way out, we wonder, but he may not be. Ultimately, of course, he does find a way back to Bitters. He still has a life, and, while it will be a lonely one, it will at least be honorable.

—⚹—

Today, it's amazing that André de Toth isn't a household name, even to many classic film enthusiasts. In an age that celebrates the bold, intensely personal visions of the "auturist" directors, his work is about as bold and intensely personal as it gets. In an age that's rediscovered film noir, he made several excellent ones, including the superb *Pitfall* and *Crime Wave*. In an age when people are developing a deeper appreciation for the subtleties and complexities of the post–World War II westerns—and especially for the more noir-ish among them—he made a number that are very good. With *Ramrod*, we can credit him both with making a significant contribution to the creation of the noir western sub-genre and with making an engrossing film that pays homage to traditional westerns as it also turns established western conventions on their ears. With *Day of the Outlaw*, his last western, we can praise him for making an utterly uncompromising noir that also serves in much the same way that *The Man Who Shot Liberty Valance* serves Ford—as an eloquent and comprehensive summary of a life's work.

"De Toth is one of those whose films, under-rated for far too long, are appreciated more and more each time one sees them," Bertrand Tavernier has noted. "As the years go by, they have become indispensable companions which stimulate me and restore my confidence."[21]

It's impossible to disagree.

4

"*The topography of menace*"
Painting the Western Black in Robert Wise's *Blood on the Moon*

> "I always wanted to shoot one of you. He was the handiest."
> —*Blood on the Moon*

For many people, a film by Robert Wise (1914–2005) might seem an odd choice to include in a book about westerns. In a storied film career that extended from 1934 to 2000 and included work on more than 60 films as a sound effects editor, assistant editor, editor, producer, and executive producer as well as a director, Wise made only three of them. He's also on record as saying that he didn't even like the genre.[1] Yet as a dutiful studio employee—at least in the early part of his career—he took his assignments as they came. If his studio, RKO, told him he had to do a "horse opera," he nodded and did it.

Although westerns weren't his passion, Wise still approached them with the same levels of professionalism and perfectionism he approached every film project he undertook and for which he has been widely praised. If anything, perhaps his filmmaking passion was for excellence. Whatever kind of film he tackled from war drama to musical, he put all his energies into surrounding himself with the best people he could get and doing the job as well as possible. As a result, Wise played a key role in creating many film classics. He edited Orson Welles' *Citizen Kane* (1941) and *The Magnificent Ambersons* (1942). As a young director, he distinguished himself in both horror and noir with such films as *The Body Snatcher* (1945) with Boris Karloff and Bela Lugosi and *The Set-Up* (1949) with Robert Ryan. In the 1960s, he won four Academy Awards for both producing and directing the musicals *West Side Story* (1961) with Natalie Wood and *The Sound of Music* (1965) with Julie Andrews. Along the way, he also directed highly respected science fiction films, dramas, comedies, and even epics. Any film worth doing, he seemed to believe, was worth doing well, and—while he was not an avid fan of westerns—this belief certainly extended to them.

When Wise began work on *Blood on the Moon* (1948), a western based on the 1941 novel *Gunman's Chance* by Luke Short, his lack of passion for the western genre—combined with his lack of experience making westerns—may have proven to be assets. While he was respectful of the genre's traditions and conventions, he wasn't married to them. He felt obliged be true to the spirit of the western, but he also felt free enough to infuse this film

Best known today for his blockbuster 1960s musicals *West Side Story* and *The Sound of Music*, Robert Wise first excelled as a director of low-budget horror and noir films and brought much of his noir know-how to 1948's *Blood on the Moon*.

with some of the elements of the horror and noir films he had recently done for RKO and which the studio (later nicknamed the "House of Noir") specialized in.

The result was—and remains—something to behold. While many 1940s and 1950s westerns have noir-ish characteristics, few are as drenched in the classic noir look and atmosphere as fully or as deeply as *Blood on the Moon*. In addition to Wise, of course, many people are responsible for this. One is writer Short, whose darkly tinted western stories became the basis not only for *Blood on the Moon* but also for such other western noir films as De Toth's *Ramrod* and Sidney Lanfield's *Station West* (1948). Another is the great Robert Mitchum, an actor whose ability to convey emotional complexity and moral ambiguity made him a noir icon and whose work here is as intriguing as his work in any of his noir crime films. Still another is the music composer Roy Webb, a noir specialist whose credits range from Hitchcock's *Notorious* (1946) to Tourneur's *Out of the Past* (1947) and whose score for *Blood* deftly blends expansive western and anxiety-provoking noir musical styles. And still another is a person few people outside of the small world of noir obsessives know anything about, Nicholas Musuraca. During his prime at RKO in the 1940s, Musuraca was one of a handful of studio cinematographers who was pivotal in creating and cultivating the noir look not only in crime dramas but also in other genres from horror to the western. "With darkness and light as his instruments," film scholar Eric Schaefer has noted, "Musuraca charted the topography of menace with unparalleled consistency and artistry."[2] And perhaps more than anyone else—with the possible exception of Wise—the credit for *Blood on the Moon's* uncompromising noir look and tone goes to him.

A Man for All Genres

Best known today for his two greatest commercial successes, the musicals *West Side Story* and *The Sound of Music*, Robert Wise often doesn't receive the respect that he should among film historians. The auteurists, for example, criticize him for simply being a cinematic "journeyman" without an individual personal style or worldview. There is certainly some truth to this; he's not Chaplin or Hitchcock. But his films frequently explore specific subjects such as racial prejudice and other social issues from a liberal point of view, and his films almost always portray characters with great empathy and sensitivity. While his own emphasis may have been on professionalism and craft, a distinct sensibility does come through in many of his films. His artistic voice may not have been as pronounced or as idiosyncratic as the so-called "auteur" directors, but he nevertheless had a voice.

Perhaps the best way to characterize Wise might be as a man for all film genres. Like many of the directors of his time, he took a wide variety of assignments, transitioning quite naturally from war film to heartwarming family drama, to musical. But, unlike nearly every other Hollywood director of his time, he excelled in just about every major genre, making fine to great horror films, crime noirs, science fiction films, family dramas, social dramas, musicals, comedies, epics, war films, and, yes, westerns. Part of the reason that he excelled in so many areas is that he understood and could work within the individual strictures of each genre extremely well. And, rather than imposing his own sensibility on different genres the way, say, a Howard Hawks did or a Quentin Tarantino does, Wise respectfully added to the sum total of each genre form, effectively extending, nourishing, and enriching it. During his career, he was key to moving many genres forward in significant ways and influencing directors who came after.

Born in Winchester, Indiana, in 1914, Robert Wise was drawn to both movies and writing. The movies were purely for pleasure. He took the writing more seriously, and, after working on his high school newspaper and yearbook as well as participating in his school's poetry society, he considered a career in journalism. But the Depression intervened, and, after a year at Franklin College, a small liberal arts college near Indianapolis, he had to drop out and start working. His older brother David, who had moved to Hollywood and been hired at RKO Pictures, helped get Robert a job in RKO's shipping department, and Robert's career in the film business was launched.

Showing ambition and a strong work ethic, Wise quickly moved from the shipping department to production roles such as a sound and music editor, assistant editor, and editor. Along the way he worked on a succession of famous films from the Astaire and Rogers musicals *The Gay Divorcee* (1934) and *Top Hat* (1935) to John Ford's *The Informer* (1935) to William Dieterle's version of *The Hunchback of Notre Dame* (1939). Then, in 1941, when he was just 26 (and only about a year older than "boy wonder" director/producer/actor Orson Welles), Wise edited *Citizen Kane*, soon receiving his first Academy Award nomination for his work.

By 1944, he received his first directing credit for his work in *The Curse of the Cat People*, which—although advertised as a horror film—is primarily a psychological drama. Produced by cult figure Val Lewton, this film also marked the first time Wise worked with cinematographer Nicholas Musuraca.

Between 1945 and 1959, Wise made 26 films in numerous genres. Among his best during this time are *The Body Snatcher*, which combined the 1930s horror film style with 1940s psychological drama; 1949's *The Set-Up*, a gritty noir about boxing that influenced the work of both Stanley Kubrick and Quentin Tarantino; the 1951 science fiction classic *The Day the Earth Stood Still* with British actor Michael Rennie, which influenced many of the noirish sci-fi films of the 1950s and afterwards; the searing indictment of capital punishment, 1958's *I Want to Live!*, which led to an acting Academy Award for star Susan Hayward; and 1959's *Odds Against Tomorrow* with Robert Ryan and Harry Belafonte, a gripping, albeit downbeat, noir that explores subjects from greed to racial prejudice.

After his two blockbuster musicals in the 1960s, Wise directed an excellent anti-war film, *The Sand Pebbles* (1966), which was widely praised and led to two more Academy Award nominations for producing and directing.

While Wise continued to work regularly throughout the 1970s, his work was generally not as well received. Gradually, he moved into the role of industry statesman, serving, among other positions, as the president of the Directors Guild of America from 1971 to 1975, the chairman of the Center for Advanced Film Studies for the American Film Institute, a member of the National Council of the Arts and Sciences, and a member of the Department of Film at the Museum of Modern Art in New York. From time to time, however, he came out of retirement to mentor younger filmmakers. He supervised Emilio Estevez's directorial debut in *Wisdom* (1986), for example. And very infrequently, he directed. His last credit is *A Storm in Summer* (2000), a made-for-TV film, which aired on Showtime in 2001.

Wise died of a heart attack just four days after turning 91 in 2006.

A Neglected "Painter with light"

If Robert Wise isn't fully appreciated today, his name—at least among classic film enthusiasts—is well known. The same cannot be said for Nicholas Musuraca (1892–1975), a hugely influential cinematographer whose Hollywood career spanned nearly half a century and included work on more than 180 films and many television series. Heavily influenced by the visual style of the German expressionists of the 1920s, Musuraca is—along with Gregg Toland and a handful of other cinematographers—one of the key players in defining many of the visual conventions of film noir.

Born in Riace, Italy, Musuraca emigrated to the U.S. and, as a young man, found work as the chauffer to J. Stuart Blackton, a pioneering silent film producer credited with making the film with the first animated sequences, *The Enchanted Drawing* (1900). Showing a talent for photography, Musuraca began working behind the camera in different capacities before becoming a "lighting cameraman," the early name for a cinematographer. His first credit was for the 1923 Blackton film *The Virgin Queen*. After focusing on low-budget action films in the 1920s, he moved to RKO in the 1930s, where he soon became one of the studio's most respected directors of photography. In fact, one fellow RKO cameraman was so impressed with Musuraca's artistry that he once called him a "painter with light."[3]

The highpoint of Musuraca's tenure at RKO was the 1940s when he created the look for such films as the influential but long-overlooked noirs, Boris Ingster's *The Stranger on the Third Floor* (1940) and John Brahm's *The Locket*

(1946), as well as Jacques Tourneur's thriller *Cat People* (1942) and celebrated noir *Out of the Past*.

In the 1950s, as opportunities in films began to decline and opportunities in television were growing, Musuraca moved from RKO to Desilu Studios, where he worked on numerous television shows from the very noir-ish drama series *The Untouchables* to 1960s comedy series such as *McHale's Navy* and *F Troop*. He retired in 1966 and died nine years later at age 82.

According to Eric Schaefer, Musuraca "remains a neglected master" for a couple of reasons. One is that, during his years at RKO, he regularly moved back and forth between prestige films and very low-budget efforts such as Tim Holt westerns, which made it difficult to get widespread industry respect. The other is that several of his more notable, and quite innovative, films such as *The Stranger on the Third Floor*, *Cat People*, and *The Locket*, have not received their just due until relatively recently.[4] But, although Musuraca worked on a wide variety of films and for a number of different directors, Schaefer also credits him with maintaining a "uniform personal aesthetic" across his work and cites *Blood on the Moon* as an excellent example of his ability to translate this personal style from noir to the western.[5]

In his analysis of Musuraca's style, Schaefer points to five characteristics that, when grouped together, both differentiate the cinematographer's work and serve as pillars of the noir visual style. First is the use of the "full tonal range of black and white," or the ability to include stark blacks, elegant grays, and bright white all within the same frame to create a special "richness and variety of tone." Second is the use of "natural sources to achieve an expressionistic result" such as the low placement of a light source (perhaps a table lamp to enlarge the shadow behind a character to emphasize a character's sense of being trapped, threatened, or even suffocated). Third is the tight lighting of confined spaces such as small objects or human faces in a largely dark field both to point the viewer to that space and to suggest visual tension. Fourth is the "skimming-silhouetting technique," in which characters are lit from the back to create an outline of light around their bodies, giving them an almost ghostly, otherworldly appearance. And fifth is a tendency toward abstraction, sometimes making objects seem to be something else than what they are, another noir characteristic that plays to the dream-like atmosphere in many of these films.[6]

Combined, these elements of Musuraca's classic noir visual style—while quite different from, and almost antithetical to, the vast majority of expansive, sunny westerns made before *Blood on the Moon*—are instrumental to giving this western its special sense of menace, haunting qualities, often claustrophobic feeling, and dream-like allure. Visually at least, this is one dark, moody western.

"I can buy me that kind of friend for $75 a month."
—Blood on the Moon

From the first shots of *Blood on the Moon*, we know we are in for something different. The film begins with a standard western trope—the lone cowboy on horseback riding through wild country. But this man (Robert Mitchum) is riding in the pouring rain. Rather than sunny, warm, and expansive as the setting in a traditional western might be, this setting is wet, cold, and stifling—much like the rain we would see pouring down on a 1940s urban street scene in a noir film.

After losing his horse and blanket when his camp is stampeded by cattle, the man comes to a camp run by a cattleman named John Lufton (Tom Tully), who eyes him suspiciously. We learn that the rider's name is Jim Garry, and Lufton lays the film's basic conflict out. A newcomer to the area, Tate Riling (Robert Preston) has organized a group of homesteaders in an attempt to squeeze Lufton out. Lufton, of course, plans to fight, and Garry foresees trouble ahead.

Garry meets Lufton's two daughters, the spirited Amy (Barbara Bel Geddes) and the more reserved Carol (Phyllis Thaxter), and arrives in the local town where he reconnects—we learn—with Riling, an old friend who has asked him to come. Riling, we find out, has conspired with a shady Indian agent named Pindalest (Frank Faylen) in a complex scheme involving the homesteaders to force Lufton to sell his cattle to Riling cheap, then allowing Riling to sell the cattle to the government for a huge profit. This effectively would make Riling rich while breaking Lufton. Riling wants Garry on his side for one very compelling reason.

"Lufton's tough and my ranchers aren't," Riling says. "You make up the difference."

"I've been mixed up in a lot of things, Tate," Garry tells him, "but up till now I've never been hired for my gun."

"Can you afford to be particular?" Riling counters.

"No, I guess I can't."

"Now, you're talking, Jim."

But, almost immediately after aligning himself with Riling, Garry has misgivings. He doesn't like the plan, Pindalest, or other shady gunmen Riling has brought in to strengthen his position. He also sees the Luftons as decent people and has sympathies for some of the homesteaders Riling is manipulating, especially an old-timer named Kris Barden (Walter Brennan). When a couple of Riling's gunmen attempt to kill Lufton in a showdown, Garry has had enough. He confronts the gunmen, earning the respect of both Lufton and Amy. He and Riling have it out in a harsh, gritty saloon fight after Garry tells him: "I see dogs wouldn't claim you for a son, Tate."

Then it's all-out range war, with Garry siding with the Luftons and, ironically, making "up the difference" by killing Riling and the last of his gunmen in a shootout and turning Pindalest over to the law. Lufton is grateful, and it seems that Amy is now quite smitten with him. The story ends happily, with all the good folks heading in to celebrate the end to hostilities.

—⚬—

While *Blood on the Moon* has many stock elements of a traditional western from its corrupt Indian agent to its spunky female lead, Amy, to its very

Amy (Barbara Bel Geddes) frets over the safety of Jim (Robert Mitchum) in Wise's rare but very effective venture into the western genre, 1948's *Blood on the Moon*. One of the highlights of this film is the gorgeous noir lighting by veteran noir cinematographer Nicholas Musuraca.

conventional happy ending, it is the non-traditional, noir-ish elements that give it its most enticing qualities.

One of these, of course, is the Jim Garry character and the way Robert Mitchum portrays him. Garry isn't the kind of character an actor such as Randolph Scott would play. For much of the film his moral stance is ambiguous. When he first meets Lufton, for example, he is hard for Lufton—and us—to size up. Is he truthful, or isn't he? What's his reason for coming, anyway? When Lufton asks some basic questions, Garry tells a couple of lies. He denies knowing anyone in town, for instance, but (as we soon find out) he does know Riling. It's curious, too, how Lufton calls him a "loose rider," someone "we gotta watch ... these days," someone who is not clearly committed to one side or another and needs to declare an allegiance. Once he meets Riling and hears his plan, he knows it's dirty, but, because he needs the money, he joins up with him. As the homesteader Kris Barden observes as he watches Garry ride away at one point, "I can buy me that kind of a friend for $75 a month and no questions asked."

As the plot thickens and tensions rise, however, we find that there is just so much of Riling that Garry can stand, and now he must change sides in this conflict. The first key turning point for him is the death of Kris' son as a result of one of Riling's raids on Lufton's cattle. When he delivers the news to Kris, he understands the cost of Riling's double-dealing much more deeply. (In this scene, incidentally, Walter Brennan—one of the best character actors of the era—is superb trying to absorb this overwhelmingly sad news, playing the scene with great honesty and understatement.) The second is when Garry keeps Riling's other gunmen from killing Lufton on the town's main street because he sees their actions as nothing more than murder. But, when young Amy thanks him for doing what he did, he shrugs her off with a hint of a noir hero's self-deprecation. "Don't let a man's whim fool you," he says.

Notable, too, is Mitchum's portrayal of Garry. Already a fixture in noir crime dramas, the actor brought both the complexity and moral ambiguity of noir roles such as his Jeff Bailey in *Out of the Past* to the western setting. And he did it in a very convincing manner. As film writer Craig Butler points out: "Fortunately, Robert Mitchum is exactly what Wise and the film needed, and his questionable, shifting sense of morality adds significant layers to *Blood*. Laconic yet capable of becoming a raging bull in half a second, Mitchum perfectly captures the essence of his character—and of the film."[7]

When interviewed for a biography of Mitchum years after this film, director Wise also shared a curious anecdote about the first time other cast members saw Mitchum suited up in cowboy garb. "Walter Brennan was sitting at a table with a couple of pals," Wise said. "And Brennan was very interested in the Old West; it was a hobby of his. And I'll never forget when Bob came on the set, just standing there, with the costume and the whole attitude that he gave to it, and Brennan got a look at him and was terribly impressed. He pointed to Mitchum and said, 'That is the goddamndest realest cowboy I've ever seen.'"[8]

Another clearly noir element in *Blood on the Moon* is the grittiness we see throughout the film. This is clearly not an idealized west but a much starker, darker one. One excellent example is the bar fight between Garry and Riling. As Wise recalled, "I wanted to avoid one of those extremely staged-looking fistfights used in all the movies, where the stuntmen did this elaborate, acrobatic fighting and you saw the real actors only in close-ups. I wanted this to look like a real fight, with that awkward, brutal look of a real fight, and, when it was done, for the winner to look as exhausted as the loser."[9] In this scene, Wise indeed delivers on his promise. Set in semi-darkness, this confrontation is more violent, visceral, and just painful to look at than western audiences were used to seeing in bar fights at the time—more like an urban street or back alley fight they might see in a dark, gritty noir.

While the Garry character, the general grittiness of settings and scenes, and other elements make *Blood on the Moon* a very noir-ish western, the film's dominant noir characteristic is its often dark, eerie, even dreamlike look. And here, much of the credit goes to Musuraca's skills and sensibility.

Many of the indoor scenes, for example, are darkly lit and generate a sense of confinement, of being trapped. One illustration is the scene upstairs from the saloon early in the film when Riling talks Garry into becoming his hired gun. His "Can you afford to be particular?" makes it abundantly clear that he knows Garry has no real options, and the physical confinement of the darkly lit setting strikingly reinforces this. If this scene had taken place outdoors on a bright sunny day, it would not have had nearly the same impact. The two saloons we see in the film serve the story in a similar way. The saloon scenes are often shot from low angles to include low, confining ceilings to reinforce an almost claustrophobic feeling. Like numerous characters in crime noirs, many of the characters here are imprisoned both by circumstances and by their individual limitations. And again, this point is reinforced visually.

Unlike most westerns of the time, many of the outdoor scenes are set at night and, as such, set a noir-ish tone in several ways. The two towns shown in the film appear ominous and, needless to say, uninviting when Garry arrives at night, for example. The streets are dark, and suspicious, eerily lit characters are checking him out. There is also an ethereal, almost dream-like quality to clouds in the day-for-night scenes when characters are riding in open country at night. It's beautiful to look at, but it's also a little odd and off-putting because it looks so unreal.

Finally, Musuraca often isolates the faces of characters—especially Garry and Riling—lighting them against a sea of blackness. As well as visually reinforcing that the main conflict in the story is between these two characters, this effect also underscores the struggle between good and evil that's going on both between Garry and Riling and, for the first half of the film, between Garry and himself. Seen on a big screen, where facial details such as Garry's troubled eyes and Riling's large, creepy-looking teeth become all the more prominent, this effect is quite powerful.

"Ultimately, what happens in *Blood* is less important than how it happens and what it reveals," Craig Butler notes in his article about the film, "and Wise displays an impressive talent for letting actions speak louder than words and for finding the meaning beneath words that help to tell the 'real' tale of the piece."[10]

This is an astute insight both into how the film's production team approached this project and into why the film continues to captivate. One characteristic that often distinguishes excellent films from those that are merely good is the ability to put the visual presentation at odds with the literal story and script. In other words, we see one thing as we hear something that is at odds with it. So what are we to believe? And it is exactly this characteristic that gives *Blood on the Moon* its special power. While well written and peppered with clever plot twists, the story—in the hands of a less talented director/cinematographer team—would have been a typical "horse opera" with a range war, a hero who sees where his loyalties must lie, a spunky heroine, a final shootout, a happy ending, and other standard western elements. In the hands of Wise and Musuraca (and we might add Mitchum), however, it becomes something quite different—a western, yes, but a western filled with many of the psychological shadings, moral ambiguities, existential suggestions, and ominous undertones of the best noir crime dramas. It is one of the great examples of how the noir influence crept into the staid western genre and changed it forever.

5

Westerns Shaken and Stirred
Sam Fuller Upends Genre Conventions in *I Shot Jesse James* and *Forty Guns*

"I've never kissed a gunsmith before."—*Forty Guns*

When Sam Fuller (1912–1997) wasn't shaking things up in his films, he was stirring them up. Sometimes, too, he managed to do both simultaneously. As both a film stylist and a purveyor of ideas, he loved—with his curious blend of realism and sensationalism—to challenge convention, to confuse and disturb audiences, to provoke thought. At a time when Hollywood producers insisted on clean, logical narratives, he developed a messy, contrarian style of filmmaking that reveled in odd, off-putting visual images; abrupt cutting between extreme long shots and "smash mouth" close-ups; occasional bizarre humor; and surprising, sometimes illogical and shocking plot twists. At a time when most filmmakers stayed far away from thorny social issues, he also tackled topics from racism to the exploitation of women, to the brutal treatment of the mentally ill, to child abuse—always with fearless abandon and always in search of some kind of truth. He really was an original, and his films really are something else.

Given all this, it's not surprising that Fuller struggled for much of his career. His heyday was a 15-year period between 1949 and 1964 when he made 17 of his 23 films. During this time, he worked for independent producers/distributors such as Robert Lippert and major studios such as 20th Century–Fox and Warner Brothers, but he clearly preferred things when he was the one in charge. As a result, most of his films were made on shoestring budgets, in brutally short periods of time, and usually without well-known actors. He had some major hits such as *The Steel Helmet* (1951), his ultra-gritty Korean War film, but, even with their low budgets, many of his films either lost or barely made money.

It's also not surprising that Fuller has become an icon for filmmakers who want to speak with original, provocative voices. This began to happen in the 1950s when French New Wave critic/filmmakers such as Jean-Luc Godard and Francois Truffaut saw his unique contributions, praised his films, and even borrowed from him in their work. Sergio Leone, the premiere director of 1960s and 1970s Italian "spaghetti westerns," quickly followed suit. Martin Scorsese is also a fan, calling Fuller's films "cinema at its essence."[1] And younger filmmakers such as Quentin Tarantino and Jim Jarmusch have credited Fuller as a major influence on their work.

During his career, Fuller made films in several genres. His first two efforts were westerns. Then he branched out in a number of directions, including war films, crime dramas, and 60s exploitation films. Often, however, the genre was incidental to him. The story was the thing, and it didn't matter if the story was set in the old west, a battlefield, a submarine, or a modern city. Whatever the case, Fuller approached each project the same way—with a passion to assault conventions, be startlingly different, and strive to present his own, usually ironic, view of human experience.

This is certainly true in his westerns, which are notable both for their noir sensibility and for the influence they've exerted over other filmmakers from the late 1950s on. If it weren't for Sam Fuller, we can confidently say, most revisionist westerns from Peckinpah's *The Wild Bunch* (1969) to Tarantino's *Django Unchained* (2012) would be decidedly different.

Of the four westerns Fuller made, two warrant special attention.

The first is Fuller's very first directorial effort, *I Shot Jesse James* (1949), which, as film writer Glenn Erickson notes, "turned the Hollywood western on its ear."[2] Riding in on the heels of such offbeat westerns as Raoul Walsh's *Pursued*, André de Toth's *Ramrod*, and William Wellman's *Yellow Sky*, *I Shot Jesse James* might be the most offbeat, and the most truly noir-ish, of the lot. With its shortsighted amoral hero who kills for love and money and struggles to come to terms with the inevitable consequences, the associations with such noir classics as *Double Indemnity* and *Out of the Past* are inescapable. In fact, the fatalism and sense of doom that are hallmarks of noir (but virtually nonexistent in westerns up to this time) are apparent even in the film's first minutes. In 1949, this was a startling departure from conventional westerns.

Equally startling in its own way is *Forty Guns* (1957), a western Fuller made from a script 20th Century–Fox chief Darryl Zanuck had rejected as too unconventional—or, as Zanuck put it, "phony"—when Fuller worked at his studio several years earlier.[3] Starring Barbara Stanwyck, the story centers on a hard-as-nails land baroness in Arizona, who tries desperately to keep her no-good kid brother out of trouble while she also treats the local law and most everyone else with disdain. Again, the noir elements are apparent. In some ways, this echoes back to one of Stanwyck's noir triumphs, Lewis Milestone's *The Strange Love of Martha Ivers* (1946), another story of a wealthy and powerful woman who goes to great lengths both to maintain power and to suppress the truth.

Yet, while both these westerns are clearly noir-ish in sensibility, they are also uniquely Fuller. They are examples not mainly of his ability to combine a noir sensibility with the western genre but of his ability to put his own stamp on any genre he was working in and—by doing so—transform it.

The Typewriter, the Rifle and the Movie Camera

Just a year before Fuller's death in 1997, actor and filmmaker Tim Robbins released a documentary about the director titled *The Typewriter, the Rifle, & the Movie Camera*. The tools of a newspaper reporter, a World War II infantryman, and a film director, these items eloquently summarize the three different careers that influenced Fuller's worldview and shaped him as an artist.

Born in Worcester, Massachusetts, to Jewish immigrants from Eastern Europe, Fuller was first attracted to newspapers and began working as a copyboy when he was 12. By age 17, he was a crime reporter working for the *New York Evening Graphic*, a newspaper that stressed sensationalism in its reporting—a style which would later influence Fuller's filmmaking. Within a few more years, Fuller was writing pulp novels and then screenplays for Hollywood.

Then, when World War II broke out, Fuller put away his typewriter, picked up a rifle, and fought as an infantryman in the U.S. Army's First Infantry Division (The Big Red One) for three years in Northern Africa and Europe. He saw extensive action, eventually earning a Bronze Star, a Silver Star, and a Purple Heart. He was also on hand in May 1945 when the Allies liberated the German concentration camp at Sokolov (located in today's Czech Republic). These war experiences affected him deeply, and he would return to war as a subject in his films repeatedly between 1951 and 1980.

After the war, it was back to the typewriter, but Fuller soon became frustrated with what Hollywood directors did with his scripts, found a producer of B-westerns named Robert Lippert who agreed to let Fuller direct (for either no fee or a very low one, depending on the account), and began to make *I Shot Jesse James*. Although this was a hit for a B-western, Fuller's major breakthrough came two years later with *The Steel Helmet*. Based on some of his own war experiences, the film had a ferocious truth to it that captivated critics and audiences alike.

This success led to numerous offers from major Hollywood studios, and, after considering several, Fuller chose 20th Century–Fox because he was impressed with Darryl Zanuck's commitment to developing high-quality films rather than simply making money. Perhaps Fuller's best-known film during his Fox tenure is an excellent noir called *Pick-Up on South Street* with Richard Widmark, Jean Peters, and Thelma Ritter, who received an Academy Award nomination for her fine supporting role.

Finding life within a major studio too confining, however, Fuller completed his contract in the mid-1950s and left for the more liberating and uncertain life as an independent. During the next decade, he made several of his better-known films, including *Forty Guns*; the crime thriller *The Crimson Kimono* (1959); and two socially conscious exploitation films, *Shock Corridor* (1963) and *The Naked Kiss* (1964). After that, he worked infrequently, and, with the exception of *The Big Red One* (1980), his largely autobiographical account of his World War II experiences, his films were unsuccessful commercially.

Ironically, as his marketability as a director waned, the critical community's interest in his work began to soar. By the late 1960s, influential film critics such as Andrew Sarris and Manny Farber had joined Godard and Truffaut in their praise for Fuller's stylistic originality and uncompromising approach to storytelling. Since then, both Fuller's artistic standing and interest in his work have continued to grow. Today, he is frequently the subject of serious film essays, his films are revived and taught in universities, and he is lionized by avant-garde filmmakers and fans alike. The rough-and-tumble Fuller lived to hear much of this adulation and, by most accounts, thoroughly enjoyed the irony of it all.

Along with all this attention, however, has come a widespread view of Fuller as the ultimate American film "primitive" and the quintessential "outsider/maverick"—a view that film historian Lisa Dombrowski has rightfully pointed out as over-simplified and romanticized.[3]

This idea of Fuller as a "primitive," a filmmaker's equivalent to the art world's Grandma Moses, was first presented in the 1960s when critics struggled to describe and define his work, which at first appeared to be so rough, raw, and at odds with classical filmmaking. At a loss for a better word, other critics followed suit and the description stuck. But, Dombrowski contends, "simply because an artist creates a stripped-down, anticlassical, and emotionally raw work does not imply that he or she is working on instinct alone.... Casting Fuller as a primitive simply does not do justice to the complexity and contradictions evident within his work."[4] This point is very important to an understanding of Fuller's films. Even early Fuller efforts such as *I Shot Jesse James*, *The Baron of Arizona* (1950), and *The Steel Helmet* have fairly sophisticated scripts and visual designs. As a newspaper reporter and a scriptwriter, Fuller had been writing professionally for nearly 20 years by the time he started to direct. He knew how to organize

One of Hollywood's great iconoclasts, Sam Fuller offered his distinctive offbeat take to a variety of genre films from the late 1940s to the late 1980s.

and tell a good, compelling story. He also knew how to reinforce his ideas visually. The opening moments of *The Steel Helmet* provide one of many examples in these early films. The credits have just been shown over a close-up of a soldier's helmet with a bullet hole in one side of it. We assume that this is just an empty helmet sitting on the ground. But, as the credits end, the helmet rises just a bit and we see eyes and a grizzled face underneath the helmet. We're looking straight at a dirty, battle-hardened soldier who seems a bit more than a bit crazed. We ask: Did he actually survive a bullet hole in his helmet? If so, how is he still alive and what condition is he in? This is clearly not the work of a filmmaking primitive.

As a hero of the avant-garde, Fuller has also been hailed as a great cinematic "outsider" and "maverick." Again, Dombrowski notes, this is a simplified view, which overlooks both his extensive (and fairly successful) work with 20th Century–Fox and his successful work with independent producers such as Lippert. "Throughout his career, Fuller championed the distinctiveness of the auteur voice and struggled to direct his own scripts his own way," she writes. "In this sense, he was a maverick. But he also recognized that some of the best production circumstances he enjoyed in his five-decade-long career occurred not when he was an independent but while he was working in the studio system."[5] Again, the point is well taken. Although Fuller preferred to make his kind of film his way, he also appreciated the benefits of working within a well-resourced studio and often showed considerable flexibility, directing such conventional studio films as the 20th Century–Fox submarine drama, *Hell and High Water* (1954).

The Villain as Hero: I Shot Jesse James

Recalling his early conversations with producer Robert Lippert, Fuller said late in life that the first idea he proposed for his first film was a retelling of the assassination of Julius Caesar from the point of view of Cassius, the Roman senator who orchestrated it. Fuller liked the idea of focusing on the actual assassin and the betrayal of friendship, but Lippert, whose bread and butter was westerns, was not enthusiastic. Eventually, the two found common ground in the story of Robert Ford's betrayal and killing of the legendary old west outlaw Jesse James. But again, the priority for Fuller was the story, not the genre. "Making just another western wasn't going to give me a hard-on," he said in his distinctive way. "Holdups, revolvers, leather gloves, and galloping horses didn't do anything for me. The real aggression and violence in the film would be happening inside the head of a psychotic, delusional killer."[6]

The result is a psychological western, which, for its time, was truly outside of the box, and which remains noir-ish, creepy, and highly effective.

The film begins in the middle of an action. Jesse James (Reed Hadley) and his gang rob a bank, killing several people who try to stop them. Then, as they escape, Bob Ford (John Ireland), one of Jesse's gang, is wounded and drops the stolen money. Jesse is understanding about the loss of the money, and lets Bob stay with him and his wife until his wound heals.

Bob, we soon learn, is also in love with an actress, Cynthy Waters (Barbara Britton), who wants Bob to quit riding with the James gang and buy a farm. If he does that, she promises, then they can be married. But another man, a prospector named John Kelley (Preston Foster), also has his eyes on Cynthy, and Bob is jealous.

In need of amnesty as well as money, Bob hears that the governor is offering both to the man who brings in Jesse dead or alive. In fact, the reward is the lordly sum of $10,000. So one day, as Jesse straightens some pictures on his wall, Bob shoots him in the back with a gun Jesse had given him as a gift. Bob gets his pardon but receives just $500, which he immediately spends on an engagement ring.

To make money now, he agrees to perform on stage, re-enacting his shooting of Jesse. Audiences boo him, he feels enormous humiliation, and he can't continue.

After this, Bob decides to go to Creede, Colorado—where silver has recently been discovered—to try prospecting. There he teams up with another miner, the two strike it rich, and Bob sends for Cynthy. While in Creede, Bob

As the man who kills the famous Jesse James, Robert Ford (John Ireland) lives in constant fear of being killed by a young gun wanting to make a name for himself in Fuller's 1949 feature film debut, *I Shot Jesse James*. Here, Ford surveys the street just after someone has taken a shot at him.

also sees Kelley again. He, too, is prospecting but hasn't been as lucky. When Cynthy arrives, Bob proposes and she accepts, but she acts out of fear rather than love. She is repelled by what Bob has done and terrified about what he still might be capable of doing. He is, after all, a man who shot his best friend in the back. She confides this to Kelley, with whom she has grown close.

Meanwhile, Jesse's brother, Frank James, who has come to Creede in pursuit of Bob, overhears this conversation and relays the information to Bob to provoke him into a showdown with Kelley, a showdown Frank knows Kelley will win. Bob and Kelley face off, Bob is shot, and, as he dies, he professes his love for Jesse and apologizes for killing him. It is clear, too, that Cynthy and Kelley will now be together.

While *I Shot Jesse James* is full of standard western trappings from galloping horses to a chatty bartender to a good old-fashion showdown, it is, at its core, a film noir. Its focus from the film's first minutes until the very last moment is not John Kelley, a more conventional western hero, but an amoral, not-too-bright coward who shoots his best friend in the back for the reward money and a chance for love. Bob Ford is not particularly proud of what he's done, but he's also clueless about the consequences. We all know he's a goner long before he does, and his road to doom is mainly what the story is about.

Another director might have structured the storyline quite differently, perhaps building up the tension and saving the killing of Jesse until late in the action. But Fuller had something else in mind. For him, this is more a psychological study of a betrayer and an assassin. Robert Ford is to this film what Fred MacMurray's Walter Neff is to *Double Indemnity* or John Garfield's Frank Chambers is to *The Postman Always Rings Twice*. But there is an added dimension here. It's clear that Bob loves his mentor, Jesse, like a father or wise uncle. There's also an unmistakably clear homoerotic suggestion in the scene where Bob pours water into Jesse's bathtub, accepts a new gun as a present, and than responds to Jesse's request to scrub his back. Exactly what is the nature of this love the two men share? Fuller doesn't explore this topic further, because, in the very next scene, Bob kills Jesse, a person he loves. This introduces a theme that Dombrowski sees as one of the "hallmarks" of Fuller's films—the notion that "truth is often contradictory and absurd."[7] In addition to being a hallmark of Fuller films, this idea is at the heart—the essential irony—of many, many noirs.

A major strength of *I Shot Jesse James* is how its story remains engrossing despite its long anti-climax, and here the credit goes both to Fuller's conceptualization of the Robert Ford character and to John Ireland's portrayal.

In most respects, Fuller's Robert Ford is a character right out of numerous noir crime dramas. From the beginning, he has genuine human aspirations we can all identify with—love and enough money to settle down with that one special person. We can see, too, that he has a special bond with Jesse, his friend and mentor. At heart, he's not a hardened person at all, and, even though he may admit to breaking the law, he truly sees himself as a good man worthy of Cynthy's love and hand in marriage. But, from the beginning, he's both a sociopath and someone who doesn't think things through very well. He kills Jesse, for example, without even considering a myriad of consequences. Cynthy becomes both fearful of him and repelled by him. At one point, a boy shoots at him because killing the man who killed Jesse James would make him famous. And nearly everyone else is disgusted with him. Despite all these ominous signs, however, he puts reality aside and continues to hope. Determined to win Cynthy, he goes to Creede to strike it rich and then send for her. If he can provide, he is utterly convinced, she will want to be with him. Like many of his fellow noir losers, he is naïve to the point of being deluded. Ironically, too, it's this profound lack of insight that helps to make him vulnerable—even childlike on occasion—and helps to make us at least somewhat sympathetic to him.

Often overlooked in discussions of this film is John Ireland's very effective portrayal of Bob. Ireland—one of a large group of second- and third-tier Hollywood actors who constantly moved from small roles in big-budget films to larger roles in small-budget genre efforts and who often seemed more comfortable playing thugs than good guys—shines here. He ably conveys that Bob is both a villain and a victim of his own inability to see the obvious—a man monstrous in his ability to betray and kill with such ease who is also deeply hurt when he realizes that people, Cynthy especially, think less of him for what he has done. Usually, Ireland gave fairly routine performances in films, but in *I Shot Jesse James*, he is always in the moment and always credible in showing us (often in Fuller's extreme close-ups) the shallowness, amorality, naiveté, and vulnerability of Robert Ford. This is some of the actor's best work.

In addition to its noir storyline, *I Shot Jesse James* has a decidedly noir look and tone about it, which is designed of course to emphasize Bob Ford's isolation, alienation, and inevitable doom. One of the film's most noir-like—and bizarre—scenes, for example, is when Ford, in need of money, reenacts his killing of Jesse in a theater before an audience that's both repulsed and riveted (something, incidentally, that the historical Robert Ford actually did do in the early 1880s). This degrading and humiliating act is reminiscent of the noir *Nightmare Alley* (1947), in which Tyrone Power's Stan Carlisle—once a star performer—agrees out of desperation to work as a freakish "geek" in a carnival sideshow. And, as in *Nightmare Alley*, Bob's reenactment underscores not only the hero's degradation but also the base nature of human beings in general. This suggests another common noir theme—that, while the hero might not be especially good, he or she's really not all that different from most other people. Still another very noir-ish scene is the film's final showdown between Bob and Kelley. It doesn't take place at high noon or any other time during the day as it would in most westerns. Instead, it's night, and—to emphasize Bob's growing isolation and impending doom—Fuller films Ireland from a distance and alone in the darkness. Rather than standing face to face, Kelley very cleverly turns his back to Bob and taunts him to shoot him in the back as he shot Jesse. Not only does this tactic give Kelley an advantage in the gunfight, but it also reinforces to Bob that—no matter what happens here—he will always be remembered as a coward. It's a hard thought to die with, but, hey, that's noir.

I Shot Jesse James is not Sam Fuller's best film. It has some rough spots that are probably the results of budget constraints as well as Fuller's lack of directorial experience. That said, it is also a remarkable first effort—an engrossing, iconoclastic work that both established the director as a distinctive filmmaking voice and added to the growing list of late 1940s films that were challenging western conventions and, in the process, dramatically transforming the genre. It's difficult to assess this one film's impact on noir-ish westerns to come, but we can assume that—once someone had made a successful western whose hero is a coward who shoots his best friend in the back—more dark cowboys (and perhaps some dark cowgirls) would soon be appearing on the horizon.

"A high-riding woman ... with a whip": Forty Guns

The first scene of Fuller's 1957 western *Forty Guns* is something to behold. As the film opens, we see three men riding slowly in a buckboard along a road that meanders through pleasant, nondescript rolling hills. In the distance, they spot someone on horseback. Then more riders appear. Then more. We see the company of riders in all its glory—40 hired guns all galloping two by two and generating a huge cloud of dust behind them. Atop a majestic white stallion leading them all is a lone rider dressed entirely in black. We notice that this rider is a woman, but it's not just any woman. It's Barbara Stanwyck, and her character rides with intense, almost ferocious, authority. The riders gallop right up to the buckboard, now stopped, and divide, galloping around it and past, totally covering the three men with their dust.

After seeing these scenes on a big screen, it takes a moment or so to regain our composure. But, once we've processed these images a bit, it sinks in that we're in for something different here. This isn't just another western.

If Fuller shook up the traditional western with noir elements in *I Shot Jesse James*, he takes his iconoclasm to a whole new level in *Forty Guns*. Praising the director's "originality of conceit, freewheeling narrative, and sensational visual style," Dombrowski calls this film his "most audacious assault on classical and genre conventions up to this point in his career."[8] Film writer Tony Williams stresses the film's "radical noir sensibility."[9] And film writer Chris Barsanti echoes these sentiments, calling the film "a western that's thoroughly urban in its outlook"; noting Fuller's desire "to shove the camera into jarring angles…, upsetting the normally staid conventions of contemporary westerns"; and commenting on "the cynicism of (the film's) outlook and the dialogue's brazenly sexual overtones."[10] As westerns go, this is definitely noir. And it's a whole lot more.

The story takes place in Arizona, presumably Tombstone, in the late 1800s. After their dusting, the three men in the buckboard arrive in town. We quickly learn that they are the Bonnell brothers, Griff (Barry Sullivan), Wes (Gene Barry), and Chico (Robert Dix), three siblings who bear a strong resemblance to the legendary Earps. Griff is the "Wyatt" of the group, a reformed gunslinger, who now works for the U.S. Attorney General's office and has come to arrest a local sheriff's deputy for mail robbery. The deputy, we also learn, is one of the 40 guns riding behind Jessica Drummond (Stanwyck), the "boss of Cochise County," one tough woman who controls just about everything—and everyone—in the area. Her one soft spot, we also hear, is her kid brother Brockie (John Ericson). He's rotten to the core: drinking, bullying people, getting a local girl pregnant, even shooting the town's half-blind old marshal. But she protects him no matter what.

One day, as Brockie shoots up the town, Griff intervenes, knocking him out and delivering him to the jail. But Jessica—who controls both the sheriff and the judge—makes sure he's released almost immediately, and it's clear that there will be a reckoning between her and Griff.

Soon afterward, Griff and Wes deliver a warrant to Jessica, requiring her to turn over the man they are after. She complies, and it's also clear that she and Griff share an immediate attraction.

Meanwhile, Wes falls for Louvenie Spanger (Eve Brent), who works as a gunsmith in her father's business. They plan to marry, and Wes agrees to become the new town marshal.

Things heat up between Griff and Jessica, too. Caught in a tornado (perhaps a symbol for their uncontrollable passion?), they take refuge in a small cabin on her land. There, in an intimate moment, she shares her life story with him, explaining how and why she has become as tough and powerful as she is. She also wants Griff to "throw in" with her, but he is hesitant.

Then, at Wes and Louvenie's wedding, the conflicts come to a head. Attempting to kill Griff, Brockie kills Wes instead. Griff captures Brockie and

In Fuller's eccentric and entertaining *Forty Guns* (1957), Barbara Stanwyck plays "the high riding woman ... with a whip," Jessica Drummond, a hard-as-nails rancher with a soft spot for Barry Sullivan's Griff (right), a lawman who must bring her errant younger brother to justice.

again has him jailed. But he escapes, using Jessica as his human shield. Griff shoots her, knowing he is only wounding her, and then kills Brockie, venting his anger by pumping shot after shot into his body.

Finally, after some time has passed, Griff—assuming that Jessica hates him for killing her brother—rides out of town on his buckboard. Seeing him leave, Jessica, now recovered, chases after him. He stops, she climbs on to his buckboard, and it appears that they will wind up together after all.

Forty Guns has sometimes been grouped with other irreverent, noir-ish "diva westerns" of the 1950s such as Anthony Mann's *The Furies* (1950), also with Stanwyck; Fritz Lang's *Rancho Notorious* (1952) with Marlene Dietrich; and Nicholas Ray's *Johnny Guitar* (1954) with Joan Crawford. Many of the reasons for this grouping are obvious. All these films aim to play havoc with western conventions, sometimes taking on provocative themes and being outrageous in tone. As part of their assaults toward this very male-dominated genre, all also focus on dominant women who ride herd over weak or troubled men. None of these women is an out-and-out, evil-to-the-core noir femme fatale, but all of them have their dark (sometimes very dark) sides. In *The Furies*, for example, the Stanwyck character has an unresolved Elektra complex and, in a fit of jealousy after hearing of her father's plans to remarry, attacks the bride-to-be with a scissors, leaving her forever maimed.

While all of these films have their fascinating quirky qualities, *Forty Guns* is probably the most intriguing to explore because it has such an uninhibited, I-don't-give-a-damn attitude about itself. Unlike these other "diva westerns," it's not trying to be an art house darling. And, unlike the others, it also works on a realistic level when it needs to in order to convey, as one contributor to the film website *IndieWire* put it, "an emotional depth that belies the set-up."[11] As a result, it is more successful as a satisfying entertainment, which—while it has some serious things to say—doesn't take itself too seriously and (at least in some respects) stays fairly rooted.

One of the challenges of delving into *Forty Guns* is its abundance of themes. In less than 80 minutes of running time, the film comments on quite a bit including the relationship between guns, violence, and sex; the challenges of dealing with wayward family members; the arrogance and abuse of power; and the inevitable evolution toward a more civilized world where a gunfighter such as Griff is increasingly considered a "freak."

Unlike *I Shot Jesse James*, it's virtually impossible to sum this film up in a sentence or two.

Of all the themes *Forty Guns* touches upon, perhaps the most interestingly handled is the guns-violence-sex relationship—one that immediately conjures up memories of Joseph H. Lewis' noir classic, *Gun Crazy* (1950), a film that ventures into much of the same psychological territory. In fact, *Forty Guns* repeatedly makes the point in such an overt and (for the time) outlandish and risqué way that the results are both startling and quite amusing. In the scene when we see the first sparks of attraction between Griff and Jessica, for example, she reminds him what a "popular killer" he is and then asks to "feel" his gun. He's hesitant to give it to her, he says, because "it might go off in your face." She's willing to take the risk, however, so he lets her hold it (which she does, very tenderly). In another scene, just after Wes and Louvenie have embraced, Wes says: "I've never kissed a gunsmith before." At this, Louvenie asks: "Any recoil?" These are clearly not the kinds of comments ingénues typically made in westerns, even in the increasingly irreverent 1950s releases.

While some scenes are humorous, however, the theme of violence and its relationship to manhood and self worth is also treated seriously. Brockie, for example, is a vicious, sadistic bully who feels that using his gun to do everything from terrorizing the town to wounding an old man, to killing one of the Bonnells is a legitimate way both to assert his manhood and to earn self-respect. When it comes to guns and violence, Brockie may be the story's biggest romantic and someone who reflects American attitudes more closely than many Americans would like to admit.

A second theme that harkens back to numerous noirs such as the Stanwyck vehicle *The Strange Love of Martha Ivers* is the arrogance and abuse of power. Again, Fuller handles the subject matter in his own distinctive, highly eccentric fashion. One scene that vividly shows this, of course, is the opening, when Jessica and her 40 gunmen ride roughshod over the Bonnells, leaving them caked in dust. Another scene is when Jessica orchestrates Brockie's release from jail as a lackey judge recites all the proper legal language to formally set him free. Still another is when Griff and Wes visit Jessica's house with a warrant. We see Griff enter her dining room. Then, we see her in a close shot as she asks Griff to pass the warrant to her. After this, we watch Griff and then no less than 16 well-dressed men sitting along a long row at the dinner table pass the warrant her way. It's a totally over-the-top and very original way of showing how everyone who's anyone in the greater vicinity is beholden to Jessica and does her bidding.

Still another noir-ish element in *Forty Guns* is the presence of the incomparable Barbara Stanwyck, certainly one of the reigning queens of noir and arguably the finest Hollywood film actress between 1930 and 1960. Key to the film's effectiveness is making an almost incredible, larger-than-life character such as Jessica—"the high-riding woman ... with a whip," as she is called—not only credible but also compelling and sympathetic, and no one acting in that era was better suited to this task than Stanwyck. Specifically, she brings a fascinating combination of authority and no-holds-barred sexuality that audiences hardly ever saw from actresses in westerns at the time. In fact, with Jessica's black leathers, her whip, and her willingness to use her whip on one of her male lackeys, Stanwyck also pulls off the suggestion that Jessica has a dominatrix side, a female trait audiences *never* saw in 1950s westerns. In addition, she gives Jessica—in her scenes with Griff—real emotional depth and vulnerability. We hear about her hardships and struggles to overcome them, and we understand how Griff can sincerely dislike things about her and, at the same time, fall in love with her. As Fuller—a fan of Stanwyck's uncanny ability to convey emotional truth even in outlandish situations—once noted: "To work with Stanwyck is to work with the happy pertinence of professionalism and emotion. She's superb as a queen, slut, matriarch, con girl, or on a horse—a viable criterion of dramatic impact because she naturally (bless her) eschews aspects of forced emotion."[12]

Forty Guns is Fuller at his eccentric best—sometimes odd, off-putting, and illogical, but also loaded with exciting, highly original visual statements; juicy, ironic dialogue; and startling, unpredictable camera work and cutting that all unite to serve its noir themes with great panache. It is Fuller's final western, and it remains one of a kind—a film that can never be duplicated, only imitated.

"Fuller aimed to make gut-punch movies, the kind you don't forget when you walk out of the theater..." Dombrowski writes. "His instinct was to challenge the classical, generic, and cultural norms by which Hollywood put stories on the screen, to upend audience expectations, and to shock and unsettle the viewer.... He wanted his audiences to go, 'Whoa!'"[13]

While Fuller understood and to some extent appreciated classical film conventions, his main focus and passion was—as Dombrowski suggests—in saying what he wanted to say in his inimitable, sometimes disconcerting, always provocative way. And his westerns certainly reflect this intent. For their time, they were radically different, shaking and stirring up a staid and steadfast genre with their insistence on bold originality, no-holds-barred irreverence, and conveying important truths as Fuller saw them. For our time, they remain both enormously important influences on everyone who's made a revisionist western from Peckinpah to Tarantino and—in their own right—fresh, lively, and thoroughly satisfying film experiences.

6

Delving Deeper into the Dark Side

Gregory Peck's Noir-ish Heroes in Henry King's *The Gunfighter* and *The Bravados*

> "It's a fine life, ain't it? Just tryin' to stay alive. Not really livin'. Not enjoyin' anything. Not getting' anywhere. Just tryin' to keep from gettin' killed."
> —*The Gunfighter*

Director-star partnerships that continue from project to project over many years have always been a staple of the film business, and—from Griffith and Gish to Scorsese and DiCaprio—examples abound. The reasons for these pairings vary of course, but usually the tie that binds is some kind of mutual benefit. Maybe the star becomes the director's muse, the person who can best express things the director wants to say. Maybe the director inspires the actor's confidence, giving the star the special opportunities to shine that all actors crave. Or maybe it's pragmatism that prevails, the star leveraging the director's prestigious name or the director capitalizing the star's popularity with audiences. Whatever the case, these pairings have been—and continue to be—enormously successful.

These pairings (almost always with male actors) have also been especially fruitful in the male-dominated western genre. In the late 1940s and 1950s alone, just a few of many well-known examples include John Ford and John Wayne, Howard Hawks and John Wayne, Anthony Mann and James Stewart, Budd Boetticher and Randolph Scott, and Delmer Daves and Glenn Ford. Often these partnerships extend beyond the genre, too. Both

Ford and Hawks directed Wayne in non-westerns. And Mann did the same with Stewart.

While much has been written about most of these partnerships, little attention has been paid to another major director-star pairing of the period: the partnership between veteran 20th Century–Fox staff director Henry King (1886–1982) and one of the era's great stars, Gregory Peck. Between 1949 and 1959, the two made six films together. They range in quality from flat-out masterpieces such as 1949's World War II psychological drama *Twelve O'Clock High* to handsomely produced but plodding exercises such as 1952's *The Snows of Kilimanjaro*, an adaptation of the Hemingway short story. And, while neither King nor Peck is well known for his work in westerns, two of the most interesting films among the six they collaborated on are in this genre, 1950's *The Gunfighter* and 1958's *The Bravados*.

What's fascinating about both is that, in terms of their subject matter, they are such innovative and noir-ish films. *The Gunfighter*, for example, has often been called the "first adult western" and the "first psychological western."[1] These claims may be debatable, but it is still a highly influential film, one that led the way to the darker, more complex and nuanced westerns of the 1950s and beyond. *The Bravados*, too, breaks new ground, venturing even farther into the disturbing side of the human psyche. "It's not a pretty story," says the film's trailer, which Peck personally narrates. "It's powerful and relentless and completely different from anything you've seen ... an unusual story told in a different way with characters such as you have never met before...."[2] While movie trailers are notorious for their hyperbole, this one, incredibly enough, mostly lives up to its claims. *The Bravados* has its flaws, but it is also powerful, relentless, and different.

Another interesting facet of the King-Peck partnership is Peck's willingness to be cast against type in the six films they made together. Unfortunately for the actor's legacy, the Peck persona most people remember today is based on his noble, decent characters in films such as 1947's *Gentleman's Agreement* and 1962's *To Kill a Mockingbird*. But the actor had a far greater range than that, and King was one director he felt he could trust when tackling roles that were quite different. Their efforts didn't always succeed, but when they did in films such as *Twelve O'Clock High*, *The Gunfighter*, and *The Bravados*, Peck can be a revelation to watch. His performances in both *Twelve O'Clock High* and *The Gunfighter* are among the best in his long career. In *The Bravados*, too—especially near the film's end when his character finally comes to terms with the consequences of his actions—he is riveting.

"He had steel in him": The Under-Appreciated Henry King

No one seems to talk much about Henry King these days. In fact, with the possible exception of Allan Dwan, whom we will discuss in an upcoming chapter, King is probably the most obscure director featured in this book. Yet, in his heyday—which was a long one, lasting from the early 1920s to the late 1950s—he was one of Hollywood's most bankable and critically acclaimed filmmakers. In the silent era, Lillian Gish declared King one of her favorite directors, and King helped to make stars out of both Ronald Colman and Gary Cooper, even suggesting to Colman that the grow the thin mustache the soon became the actor's trademark. While the coming of sound in the late 1920s meant the end of many silent film careers, the transition for King was, as film historian I.S. Mowis notes, "merely a formality."[3] In 1930, he signed a contract with Fox Studios (which became 20th Century–Fox in 1935) and stayed for more than 30 years. There he directed more than 40 films. At least 15 of them were nominated for Academy Awards in various categories, and, of these, seven were nominated for Best Picture Oscars. King himself was Oscar-nominated twice for Best Director, and, in 1944, he received the very first Golden Globe Award for directing for his work on 1943's *The Song of Bernadette*.

Born in Christiansburg, Virginia, in 1886, King dropped out of school at 15 just after the turn of the 20th century to work for the Norfolk & Western Railroad. Eventually, he found more enjoyable work as an apprentice actor in a theatrical touring company, and, in 1913, this led to Philadelphia's Lubin film studio, where he made enough of an impression to be hired to play villains in one-reel cowboy films. By 1915, he was directing in Hollywood. In 1921, he made *Tol'able David*, a powerful melodrama set in rural America. At the time, the Soviet director and film theorist V. I. Pudovkin called King's use of cutting to build a scene as effective as Griffith's.[4] More than 80 years later, film scholars Gerald Mast and Bruce F. Kawin also praised King's ability in this film to show "how to bring a story alive with significant and memorable detail by manipulating the visual [material]."[5]

Soon after this, King turned out a string of silent film hits such as 1923's *The White Sister* and 1924's *Romola* with Gish and Colman and then 1925's *Stella Dallas* and 1926's *The Winning of Barbara Worth* both with Colman.

After moving to Fox in 1930, King continued to make hits with such films as 1933's *State Fair* and 1937's *In Old Chicago* all the way through the 1950s with such films as the wildly popular Jennifer Jones-William Holden tearjerker, 1955's *Love Is a Many-Splendored Thing*.

He had his failures, of course. Perhaps the most resounding was *Wilson*, his 1944 Technicolor biopic of America's 28th president. While showered with recognition at the time (*Wilson* was nominated for 10 Academy Awards, winning five), it was not embraced by filmgoers and went down as a major dud. Seeing it today, it is understandable to see why. The film, while handsomely mounted and technically well crafted, is sentimental and idealized—more of a propaganda piece than a flesh-and-blood story.

Still, King's successes far outnumber his failures. He bounced back from *Wilson*, made his great films with Peck, made other successful films such as *Love Is a Many-Splendored Thing* and the 1956 film version of Rodgers and Hammerstein's *Carousel* and then retired in 1962 at the venerable age of 76.

One of the highlights of his later career was clearly his working relationship with Peck, which was filled with mutual respect. Peck, who often had trouble working with directors, looked to King much like a young person looks to a revered mentor or role model. "I think we were cut from the same cloth, not merely as fellow actors, but more as Middle Americans," Peck said in later life. "I think that I learned by example, not so much by what he told me but by his being the kind of man he was and of the personal code he had. I also think of him as very American in character, old fashioned in his ideals and extremely conscientious, kind, and considerate with everybody on the set, but demanding and tough when things did not go right. He had steel in him. Those times were among the best of my working life."[6]

So why is King virtually forgotten today? Certainly one explanation is his old-fashioned take on things, which resulted in many idealized and overly sentimental films. And certainly another—which was not necessarily his fault—is the ascendance of the auteurists and the belief that, to be a worthwhile work of art, a film must be the product of a single author's vision. By contrast, King was—for an era when the studios reigned supreme—the ultimate company man. While other directors often feuded with 20th Century–Fox's brilliant, supremely opinionated production chief Darryl F. Zanuck, King expressed respect for Zanuck's understanding of the filmmaking process and frequently sought him out for advice. As a studio employee, King also took his assignments as they came, moving quite naturally from unabashed tearjerkers to serious dramas, to adventure tales, to nostalgic Americana stories, to musicals, and to westerns. Believing always in the primacy of the story, he respected the original works of fiction that became the basis for most of his films, carefully adapting them to the screen rather than drastically changing them to accommodate his own expressive needs. And, unlike the consummate auteurs such as Orson Welles or Alfred Hitchcock, King did not have a specific visual signature that reflected his personality or his worldview. As Mowis notes: "Much of his [King's] work was characterized by an uncomplicated approach and a vivid visual style rather than cinematic tricks or technical individuality. For the most part, it was his meticulous attention to detail and his reliance on superior plots and good acting that got the job done."[7] Rather than a visionary/auteur/individualist, King was an interpreter/craftsman/collaborator whose films occasionally (*Twelve O'Clock High*, *The Gunfighter*, etc.) rise to significant artistic heights. No, maybe he wasn't Alfred Hitchcock, but that never was his intention, and it would be nice if the auteurists and others today would judge him more on his own terms rather than theirs.

Henry King capped a long and very successful directing career with several notable 1950s films, including *The Gunfighter* and *The Bravados*, both with Gregory Peck.

While Henry King is probably best known today as an adapter of works of fiction to film, his talent for adaptation also extended to his changing work environment. As the times changed, so did he. He would not, after all, have lasted in a place as fickle as Hollywood for nearly 50 years if he wasn't at least somewhat nimble. And perhaps one of the best examples of his ability to adapt professionally was his adjustment to the post–World War II sensibility. The audience required a different kind of story, and he was ready, willing, and able to provide it.

His first opportunity came with *Twelve O'Clock High*, one of Hollywood's first post–World War II films to explore the emotional toll of the war. Its main character, Brigadier General Frank Savage (Peck), takes over an underperforming "hard-luck" U.S. Army air bombing group early in the war, relentlessly drives the men under him, and eventually gets the results he wants. In the process, though, many lives are lost and—along with others—Savage pays an enormous emotional price. In the end, even he can't take the strain and suffers (what we assume to be) a breakdown. Although the story is told in flashback from another officer's point of view, we never find out what ultimately becomes of Savage, and the ambiguity is fascinating. Does he recover and go back to work? Or is his psyche permanently scarred? It's for us to decide—or wonder about.

Still very powerful today, the film must have had enormous impact on audiences used to seeing the romanticized, jingoistic World War II films popular at the time. With the story stripped of the sentimentality found in many earlier King films, there is a hard, brutal edge to the proceedings here. Characters speak in plain, factual, sometimes almost clinical terms—underplaying their fear, anger, sadness, and other emotions and, by doing so, making them seem more real. The cinematography by Fox veteran Leon Shamroy, reflects all of this quite vividly, too. The film is very noir-ish in its placement of cameras, use of light and shadow, and other techniques to reflect the dark emotional tone.

Released in Los Angeles in December 1949, *Twelve O'Clock High* was widely praised and went on to receive four Academy Award nominations, including a nod for Best Picture. Sadly, King, who had been twice nominated for lesser films, was not nominated for this, arguably his best.

By that year's awards season, however, King had moved on, turning his attentions to another dark, noir-ish story that explored the psychological effects of hard times, a western called *The Gunfighter*.

"He looks mighty average to be such a big man": The Gunfighter

Often called the "first adult western," *The Gunfighter* actually follows in a long line of stylish, complex, grown-up westerns that began with 1939's *Stagecoach*, took on darker subject matter in films such as 1943's *The Ox-Bow Incident*, and became more prominent in the mid- and late 1940s in films such as *My Darling Clementine*, *Pursued*, *Ramrod*, *Fort Apache*, and *Colorado Territory*. Calling it an early psychological western is probably more accurate. While all of these films explore the inner lives of key characters to some extent, *The Gunfighter* looks at its hero, Jimmy Ringo—a doomed man who, try as he might, can never escape his past—in significantly greater depth. And, especially for the time, the shift seemed seismic. As Bosley Crowther of the *New York Times* noted in his 1950 review: "The addicts of western fiction may find themselves rubbing their eyes and sitting up fast to take notice before five minutes have gone by in 20th Century–Fox's *The Gunfighter*,... For suddenly, they will discover that they are not keeping company with the usual sort of hero of the commonplace western at all. Suddenly, indeed, they will discover that they are in the exciting presence of one of the most fascinating western heroes as ever looked down a six-shooter's barrel."[8]

The film's greater emphasis on character rather than action also sets a important trend, paving the way for numerous westerns made during the 1950s and afterwards that delve deeper into the inner workings of their heroes.

Finally, the film's noir-ish, deterministic take on its hero is very much in evidence. While Ringo wants to change and make a clean start, the world will simply not let him. In this respect, he is more like Robert Mitchum's Jeff Bailey in *Out of the Past*, Richard Widmark's Harry Fabian in 1950s *Night and the City*, and numerous other classic noir heroes than most other western figures. From the first scenes of the film, we sense that he is a doomed man.

The Gunfighter begins with a succession of wonderful shots by the great cinematographer Arthur Miller of Ringo (Peck) riding alone across a dramatic western landscape. He is not traveling during the bright daylight but across a shadowy, almost dream-like landscape at night, and the dark tone of the film is quickly established.

He arrives at a nameless town, asks for a drink, and is immediately challenged by a young "squirt" itching to make a name for himself by bumping off a gunfighter as prominent as Ringo. Ringo, of course, shoots the upstart. The shootout is clean (all observers agreeing it was self-defense), but Ringo immediately learns that the young man he has just killed has three brothers who won't care which person drew first.

Ringo leaves, and the three avenging brothers follow in hot pursuit. At a watering hole in the desert, he catches them by surprise, takes their horses away, and tells them to "git." But they know he is headed to the nearby town of Cayenne, and they are determined to follow.

When Ringo arrives in Cayenne, we soon find out why he has come. This is where his estranged wife Peggy (Helen Westcott) and the son he has never known, also named Jimmy (B. G. Norman), have created a new life for themselves. Ringo also reunites with Mark Strett (Millard Mitchell), a friend from the past who has settled down and become Cayenne's town marshal. Mark hears about Jimmy's pursuers and is worried that some hothead in town might want to go after Jimmy as well. He wants Jimmy to leave ASAP. Jimmy agrees to but first he convinces Mark to visit Peggy and ask her to meet with him. Mark agrees, telling Peggy on his visit that Jimmy's "not as cocky as he used to be." But, while she's conflicted about what to do, Peggy ultimately decides that she doesn't want to see him.

Someone who does, however, is Hunt Bromley (Skip Homeier), a local tough who is fascinated by what a name he can make for himself by gunning down the great Jimmy Ringo. Hunt's in the barbershop when he hears that Ringo is in town.

"He looks mighty average to be such a big man," says one man.

"About as big as they come, I guess," says another.

Hunt asks smugly: "How many hands has he got?"

"Well, I never counted them, to tell you the truth," says another.

"He's got two hands, like anybody else," Hunt says. "And some of these days somebody's gonna to make a big name for himself by provin' that's all he's got.... Well, it's gotta come sooner or later, ain't it? Don't expect him to go on forever, do ya?"

Basically confined to the town saloon and its vicinity for the rest of the story, Jimmy has a series of encounters with various townspeople—Bromley, who wants to size Ringo up; an old friend named Molly, who offers to help persuade Peggy to see him; an old man, who mistakenly thinks that Ringo has killed his son; a group of morally outraged local women, who want Ringo out of town; and finally—with Molly's help—Peggy and little Jimmy.

As these events occur, we also know that the three avenging brothers have gotten horses and guns and are riding hard toward Cayenne. And, from time to time, we see and hear a clock that reinforces that time is running out before several story lines come to a head.

Finally, after meeting with Peggy and Jimmy, Ringo agrees to leave. But the three brothers have arrived in town, and Bromley also wants his crack at him.

As Ringo rides out, Bromley guns him down. Although Bromley drew first, surprising Ringo, and is quickly arrested, Ringo—as he lay dying—says that he drew first and that Bromley should go free. Bromley arrogantly says he doesn't want Ringo to do him any favors. But Ringo—looking him straight in the eye—counters: "If I was doin' you a favor, I'd let 'em hang ya right now and git it over with. But I don't want ya to git off that light. I want you to go on being a big, tough gunny. I want ya ... ta know what it's like to live like a big, tough gunny. So, don't thank me yet, pardner. You'll see what I mean. Just wait."

6. Delving Deeper into the Dark Side

With those words, Ringo dies. And, with that, an enraged Mark takes Bromley into a nearby barn, roughs him up, and tells him: "Ringo's fixed you good. You're goin' to get it exactly like you give it to him. Because there's a thousand cheap, dirty, crooked little squirts like you waiting right now for the chance to kill the man that killed Jimmy Ringo. But it ain't goin' to be here, sonny, not in my territory. So get goin' now. Get killed somewhere else."

Afterwards, the town gathers for Ringo's funeral. Peggy and little Jimmy arrive, tell others they are Ringo's wife and son, and take their seats in the church.

―――

Instead of the dramatic gunfights, battles with Native Americas, and virtuous, God-fearing homesteaders—all surrounded by expansive scenery—that most fans of westerns were accustomed to in 1950, *The Gunfighter* offers a starkly

In King's gripping 1950 film *The Gunfighter*, a wise but weary gunman named Jimmy Ringo (Gregory Peck) faces down yet another young "squirt" looking to make a name for himself, Hunt Bromley (Skip Homeier), as Mac the bartender (Karl Malden) looks on. The film, often called the first "psychological" western, was key to ushering in a new era of more complex characters and moral ambiguity in the genre.

different view of the time and the place. As film writer Mike Lorefice writes, "[T]he film depicts western life as a vicious cycle of brash wild young punks being hunters until they've knocked off one of the top dogs, at which point they graduate to being the hunted. The thing is, they don't know what the real west is like until they've tried going out in it. The difference between the hunter and hunted is seen in how they act. The hunters are braggers and showoffs, annoyances that are just out for glory and attention, while the hunted act like they've done it before and don't draw attention to themselves with any special emotion or expression. The hunters want what the hunted have, while the hunted want what they left behind."[9] If we accept this appraisal of things, it paints a grim picture.

There are clearly many noir-like elements in *The Gunfighter*. Certainly, one of the most obvious is Ringo's inability to escape his past. He is its prisoner. And one way the film emphasizes this is by keeping him confined in Cayenne's saloon for much of the time. It's a highly restrictive, if not suffocating, environment, one that frustrates and occasionally maddens Ringo. Another is the hero's doomed aspiration. Ringo desperately wants to change. He wants to make things right again with Peggy and little Jimmy so he can now have a normal life with them. While he is a realist in many ways about his situation, he still holds this pipe dream near and dear. Both Mark and Peggy are sympathetic to this desire, but they are also clear-thinking realists who know that it's probably already too late for the happy ending. In addition, there's something at stake for them. They've both worked hard to distance themselves from their lives with Ringo and to build respectable lives for themselves and, in Peggy's case, for little Jimmy as well. They don't want to throw all this work away, either. As Lorefice notes: "[This] illustrates the point that you can adjust all you want, but that can do you no good if others are totally unwilling to adjust to your adjustment."[10]

Perhaps the most fundamentally noir part of this film, however, is its prevailing view of human beings. While there are good people in the film, people are, more often than not, portrayed negatively. Just among the characters we meet are three vengeful brothers who want to kill Ringo, whether or not he was merely acting in self defense; two groveling bartenders; two arrogant young "squirts" who aspire to be gunfighters; a group of school children who are bursting with curiosity to see gunplay and blood; an old man who wants to kill Ringo even though he's not even sure that Ringo had a hand in killing his son; and a gaggle of "respectable" women who demonize Ringo without even knowing that the thoughtful, witty stranger listening to them is indeed Ringo. Generally speaking, the story does not speak well for the human race. In fact, it appears to be the antithesis of the much more neighborly world portrayed in another great western released in 1950, Ford's very life-affirming *Wagon Master*.

As well as being a riveting noir, *The Gunfighter* is also well done on almost every level. Among the actors, Peck is superb as Ringo, playing against type and capturing the character's vulnerabilities as well as intimidating qualities quite well. The very under-rated Millard Mitchell is also very good as Mark, Ringo's old friend who now wants him out of town. The tight script, mostly the work of writer William Bowers (with an assist from director André de Toth on the story) crackles with humor, irony, and understated heartbreak. Critics rarely talk about the film's dark humor, but it is everywhere. One especially funny line comes from a barbershop loafer who says he doesn't want to see Ringo because it might be dangerous and that he has to consider his mother, "who's my sole support." The script also gives real personalities not just to a handful of characters but to many of the townspeople of Cayenne from Karl Malden's Mac the bartender to Jean Parker's Molly the saloon "singer" to Anthony Ross's Deputy Charlie Norris. As viewers, we feel more like visitors to an actual community than we do in many films. Of course, there's Arthur Miller's poetic black-and-white cinematography to add to the sense of foreboding. And King orchestrates it all with great aplomb. The entire experience is gripping from beginning to end.

The Gunfighter isn't perfect, of course. It's unfortunate, for example, that the film doesn't end with Ringo's death and Mark's warning to Bromley ending with "Get killed somewhere else." Instead, there's a tacked-on funeral service (that's totally out of synch with the overall thrust of the story) and then a shot of a silhouetted Ringo riding through the desert at night, both scenes perhaps intended to give the film some uplift at the end. These are unnecessary and distracting. The film is designed to be a classic noir downer and should end on a down note. But, in the great scheme of the film, this is a nit—a minor glitch in an otherwise superior experience.

"The face of a hunter": The Bravados

"I've ridden a hundred miles to see this hanging," says a mysterious stranger played by Gregory Peck as he approaches a normally peaceful U.S.-Mexico border town named Rio Arriba in the first moments of King's 1958 western, *The Bravados*. And already, we're bursting with curiosity. Who is this man? Why has he ridden all this way? What's going to happen here?

The second and last of the westerns Henry King and Gregory Peck made together, *The Bravados* is a fascinating study of vengeance and remorse. Redemption is suggested, but, even as the story ends, peace of mind remains elusive.

While this film has some faults, it's also one of the most underappreciated near-great western noirs of the 1950s. *The Gunfighter* has become a classic, but *The Bravados* remains little known and largely ignored. Writing for *IMDb*, I. S. Mowis has called the film "uncompromisingly tough," "offbeat," and "under-rated."[11] And, writing for *DVD Talk*, Stuart Galbraith IV has also called it "excellent" and "a film ripe for rediscovery."[12] But other than these and other occasional comments here and there on the blogosphere, little is said about this fascinating film.

Part of the reason for this might be the film's grim tone, or part might be for its religious component, something that on the surface may seem dated to today's audiences. But, if we look at his film closely and evaluate its assets, it is a powerful experience, a film that takes western noir into even darker, more disturbing territory than *The Gunfighter* does.

—⁂—

The story opens, of course, with that mysterious stranger, a rancher named Jim Douglas (Peck), coming to Rio Arriba for the hanging of four men who were involved in a fatal bank robbery. He hasn't met the condemned men, but, as he tells the sheriff (Herb Rudley), he feels he knows them. In addition to meeting the four men and looking them over, he also meets an old romantic interest, Josefa (Joan Collins), but, to her disappointment, he now seems distracted and aloof.

That night, as almost everyone in town is in church, an accomplice of the four men, posing as the hangman, stabs the sheriff and helps the four escape. On their way out of town, the men kidnap Emma (Kathleen Gallant), the daughter of a local merchant.

We hear Douglas' story. He believes that these four men also stole money from him and then raped and murdered his beloved wife. For the past six months, while his housekeeper has taken care of his three-year-old daughter, he has pursued them.

Douglas now joins the posse the townspeople have formed to find and recapture the four men, and, because he is clearly one of the most competent among them, he quickly takes on a leadership role.

As the hunt proceeds, Douglas manages to have personal confrontations with two of the four men. He shows the first (Lee Van Cleef) a photograph of his wife, but the man doesn't recognize it. His reaction seems honest, but— even though the man is on his knees pleading for his life—Douglas kills him.

The action shifts to the home of a neighbor of Douglas, a solitary miner named Butler (Gene Evans). The two remaining men, Zachary (Stephen Boyd) and Lujan (Henry Silva), and their hostage, Emma, all stop for food. Butler, sensing that this means trouble, grabs a bag of money and tries to escape. But Zachary sees him, shoots him, tells Lujan to see what's in the bag, and then—finally seeing his chance to do what he's wanted to do since escaping the gallows—proceeds to rape Emma. Meanwhile, Lujan takes the bag and hides it on his person. Immediately, he sees a couple of riders in the distance. He assumes they are part of the posse, but they turn out to be Josefa and an escort on their way to the Douglas ranch, where Josefa plans to stay and care for Douglas's young daughter. Fearing the posse, Zachary and Luhan jump on their horses and gallop away. A moment later, Josefa and the escort see Douglas and then the posse. All converge on the scene, where they find Butler's body and the raped Emma. Douglas is enraged both by what's happened to Emma and at the death of his neighbor, a man who "never harmed anybody in his life."

After dropping off Josefa at his ranch, Douglas rejoins the posse at the international border. By law, the posse can't enter Mexico. But this doesn't deter Douglas, who crosses the border, kills Zachary, and then tracks Luhan to his modest adobe home, where he comes upon Luhan's wife and young son. The wife sees that Douglas wants to shoot her husband, and, when he isn't looking, knocks him unconscious with a vase.

As Douglas awakes from his blow, he sees Luhan looking over him with a gun on his lap. He wonders why Luhan hasn't killed him. But Luhan responds: "I have no reason to kill you. Why do you hunt me?"

Again, Douglas shows the photograph of his wife, and again one of the men he has been pursuing honestly says that he has never seen her. Douglas also sees the bag of money, recognizes it as the money stolen from his home when his wife was killed, and accuses Lujan of taking it. Lujan corrects him, saying he took it instead from Butler's dead body.

"Where did Butler get that money?" Douglas asks.

Then it all becomes clear. It was Butler—not the four men—who had robbed Douglas and then raped and killed his wife. Later that day, he had told Douglas about the four men, who had by chance passed through the area earlier. This revelation stuns Douglas—in his rage, he had killed three men for a crime they had not committed.

Douglas returns to Rio Arriba and goes into the church in the hope of finding some forgiveness for his sins, some kind of personal peace. He tells a sympathetic priest (Andrew Duggan) what he's done and hears some comforting words from him, but he still doesn't feel better. "It doesn't help," Douglas tells the priest. "I was wrong ... wrong ... wrong."

Flanked by the town sheriff and the "hangman" (actors Herb Rudley and Joe DeRita) are the four title characters of Henry King's last western, 1958's *The Bravados* (actors Stephen Boyd, Albert Salmi, Lee Van Cleef, and Henry Silva). After these men escape from jail, an obsessed rancher (Gregory Peck), who believes that they have raped and murdered his wife, relentlessly pursues them.

The townspeople, seeing that Douglas has returned, flock to the churchyard to hail him as a hero for killing three of the four men responsible for the fatal bank robbery and the kidnapping and rape of Emma. Josefa and his daughter are also there and join him inside the church. A few moments later, as the three leave the church, everyone cheers him as a hero. "The emergency arose," the sheriff tells the appreciative crowd, "and the man appeared."

But Douglas does not feel anything like a hero. He walks away with Josefa and his daughter, a haunted, guilt-ridden man.

—⁂—

Like *The Gunfighter*, *The Bravados* certainly possesses a pronounced noir sensibility and style. Both films are about trapped men: Ringo who can't escape his past and Douglas who, for almost the entire film, is a prisoner of his own hatred and thirst for vengeance. Both films also explore the dark side of the human psyche in uncompromising ways and—reminiscent of the plays of the ancient Greeks—are unflinching in how they see human tragedies through. Like Oedipus, for example, both Ringo and Douglas have learned to see too late and must now face the consequences of their earlier rashness. For Ringo, of course, this means a bullet from Hunt Bromley. For Douglas, this means living with actions he considers unpardonable sins. And, although *The Bravados* is shot in color, many of its night scenes have an eerie, dreamlike, distinctly noir-ish look and feel to them. Most of these scenes are shot with intense blue filters showing an unreal sapphire-blue sky with either darkly lit or silhouetted settings and human figures. The brainstorm of frequent King collaborator cinematographer Leon Shamroy, the effect is almost monochromatic, suggesting the unreal nature of classic black-and-white noir cinematography while still remaining consistent with the film's color scheme. Fascinating, too, in *The Bravados* is the occasional use of background sounds to underscore grim events. One that's particularly interesting during the early jail scenes is the persistent off-camera noise of workmen hammering and sawing as they build the gallows for the hanging. In its own way this is as effective as the ticking of the clock in *The Gunfighter* is to reinforce the idea that—indeed for certain characters—time is running out.

One major difference between the two films, however, is the degree of ambiguity. While both are morality tales, *The Bravados* is much less cut and dried than *The Gunfighter*. Throughout *The Gunfighter*, we know pretty much where everyone is on the moral spectrum. Mark and Peggy are the "good" characters, who, while sympathetic to Ringo, realize the futility of his position and the harm his continued presence in town could bring. Bromley, of course, is the "bad" character, who wants to make a name for himself by killing Ringo and will eventually get his comeuppance. And Ringo, who was once "bad," has now become wiser and better—basically a good man who cannot shed his dark past. It's all fairly clear. But in *The Bravados*, the morality is murkier ... and messier. Just consider the actions of Douglas, whom most see as a "good" man, after his wife's death.

Is it acceptable, for example, for him to become a vigilante? No, but it's also suggested that local law enforcement will probably not be successful in catching his wife's killer or killers. And it's clear that, as a natural "hunter," he's by far the most competent person for the job.

Is it acceptable for him to leave his three-year-old daughter just after she has lost her mother? No, but, if he isn't actively trying to catch the killer or killers, they will probably get away.

Is it acceptable when, acting as part of a posse, he kills two of the four men he is pursuing, even when they are defenseless? No, he should capture them alive and make sure they are returned to Rio Arriba. But they have already been sentenced to hang and will soon die anyway. Besides, both have already admitted to doing lots of bad things in the past.

Is it acceptable for him to leave the posse at the international border and pursue the remaining two men, Zachary and Luhan, into Mexico? No, but Zachary is easily the most despicable of the group; he is safe from U.S. law enforcement in Mexico, and, unless Douglas stops him, he will continue to act despicably.

Is it acceptable for him to feel horrible inside *only after* he discovers that these men did not kill his wife? No, but that's what it takes to get him to realize what he's done.

And would he have eventually felt as bad about his own actions if the men had actually killed his wife? Probably not, but we don't know and can only guess.

All of these questions also beg us to consider the state of Douglas's mind. He begins his hunt on hearsay; he never has any proof to tie the four men to his wife's murder. And what's especially intriguing—even after Douglas kills the first man and it becomes more apparent to him and others that—although they are bank robbers, killers, and kidnappers—these men may *not* be the ones who killed and raped his wife, he continues to hunt and kill them. This is a man locked into a course of action he cannot extricate himself from, a man truly trapped by his blind rage.

The morality of the community is murky and messy, too. Although Rio Arriba has given the four men their day in court and gone to the expense of a proper hanging, the anger over the bank robbery and killing of a bank employee remains intense. For example, near the beginning of the film, when one of the townspeople mistakes Douglas for the hangman, he says: "Hang 'em slow." Later, the escape of the four men and their kidnapping of Emma only enrages the townspeople more. Their interests are different from Douglas's, of course: they want these men dead for the wrongs they've committed in their town. But, even though they probably know that Douglas's killings of the first two men are not acts of self-defense but rather murder, they really don't care. From their point of view, Douglas has dispensed justice, and his motives and methods are irrelevant. Finally, when they learn that Douglas has killed three out of the four men, he is even cheered as a hero. In the end, vigilantism is just fine with them.

In *The Bravados*, no one really comes out in a good moral light. At the miner's cabin, even sweet Josefa begs Douglas to kill the remaining two men. And back in Rio Arriba, even the kindly local priest more or less gives Douglas a pass when he hears what Douglas has done. Everyone wants to close the book and move on. But, to his credit, Douglas is the only one who feels any moral misgivings.

As the film ends, the morality remains murky and messy: three men are killed for a crime they did not commit, a vigilante murderer is hailed as a hero, and the only one who seems even remotely concerned about it is him.

Since *The Bravados* isn't as neat or as tidy as *The Gunfighter*, it may come closer to being a more accurate reflection of how people acted in the west and to some extent have always acted in morally complicated situations. So much of life is about murky, messy moral issues that people do not want to consider too deeply and would prefer to forget about, and the film's uncompromising exploration of this unpleasant reality is certainly one reason why *The Bravados* remains such a powerful experience more than half a century after its release.

In addition to its powerful story, *The Bravados* has several other major assets. Peck's performance, especially in the scenes when he comes to grips with his actions, is quite moving. As the four pursued men, Stephen Boyd, Henry Silva, Lee Van Cleef, and Albert Salmi, are also very good at portraying distinct characters each with different moral shadings. Boyd, in particular, goes all out in his turn as the reprehensible Zachary, and Silva is masterly as the wise and calmly authoritative Luhan. The film—thanks to Leon Shamroy—is an exciting visual experience during both vivid day and eerie night scenes. And King's handling of shots and scenes is occasionally inspired. Before the four men escape, for example, King includes both the gallows and the town church in many shots and from many perspectives, artfully suggesting intriguing parallels between the two structures and their meanings to the people in the story. Some contemporary film writers have criticized the prominence of religion in the film. But it's important to note that religion or faith does not save Douglas. He is a man looking for peace. He hopes to find some peace through religion. But all he really gets are some priestly platitudes, which, as he admits, don't really help him.

Perhaps the most noticeable of the film's shortcomings is the Josefa role and Joan Collins's clumsy portrayal of this character. The role isn't well written or even necessary to the story, and Collins, at the beginning of her long career, is anything but accomplished in it. But it's reasonable to assume that—especially for a story as grim as this—the studio insisted on a romantic interest and a beautiful actress to play her.

―――∽∞∽―――

In its 1982 obituary for Henry King, the *New York Times* led with the headline: "Henry King, Movie Director Known for Book Adaptations."[13] That's certainly true: King made major films of famous novels such as *A Bell for Adano*, *The Sun Also Rises*, and *Tender Is the Night*. But, as many obituaries do, it failed to adequately sum up the person and the person's achievements. King was, after all, a top Hollywood director for more than 40 years, his films were nominated for scores of Academy Awards, and several of his films—including *The Gunfighter* and *The Bravados*—deserve classic or near-classic status today. While not an auteur, he was nevertheless a leading film industry player who inspired the confidence of hard-driving moguls from Sam Goldwyn to Darryl Zanuck, great actors from Lillian Gish to Gregory Peck, master cinematographers from Arthur Miller to Leon Shamroy, the legendary 20th Century–Fox film editor Barbara McLean, and major American writers from John Hersey to Ernest Hemingway. He was, by no means, a minor figure.

King directed relatively few westerns during his long career, but, when he did, the films usually mattered. His last two westerns, *The Gunfighter* and *The Bravados*, are both highly innovative, distinctive, and excellently orchestrated examples of the dark, psychologically rich western that captivated audiences in the 1950s and continues to fascinate us today. These two films, especially *The Bravados*, deserve more attention than they get.

And the same, of course, can be said of their director.

7

Deliverance on a Down Note
The Tortured, Grimly Determined Heroes of Anthony Mann's *Devil's Doorway, The Naked Spur* and *Man of the West*

"There's nothing an Indian needs like a speech from a lawyer telling him to give up."—*Devil's Doorway*

In a television interview shortly before his premature death at age 60, director Anthony Mann (1906–1967) made a curious comment about the heroes in his films—or "anti-heroes," as he preferred to call them. "It was always a man who had gone through so much that, when the time came and he finally got there, he was exhausted," Mann said. "He was not exalted, but exhausted. Therefore, it gave [each film] a great reality, because very few people are exalted.... I don't think I've ended any of my films with any kind of exaltation, really more tired. He's done the job, and thank heaven it is done."[1]

After seeing Mann's films, especially the 11 westerns[2] he made between 1950 and 1960, it's easy to understand why his heroes, or anti-heroes, are so tuckered out. Typically, they must face brutal antagonists in intense conflicts that often lead to grueling physical combat. In addition, they must come to grips with some demon within—some deep-seated rage or other nasty part of themselves—that these conflicts have unleashed. Finally, they must also cope with ongoing emotional pain from a dark, traumatic experience from their pasts, something that's held these heroes back personally and must be exorcised. In the end, they are delivered from both evil adversaries and inner turmoil, but to get to that place they have had to go through hellish ordeals. If they've survived, they may be better for the experience, but, as Mann himself noted, "very few people are exalted." In the gritty, often violent world of a Mann film, survival in itself is quite an accomplishment.

Dismissed by many film critics during his time as a mere "action" director, Mann has gradually won a strong cadre of partisans for both a string of superbly crafted noir crime dramas in the late 1940s and his 1950s westerns, most of which are at least somewhat noir-ish in their sensibility and styling. We might even go as far as to say that, in terms of the number of high-quality noir-ish westerns he made, he was first among his peers—no other director's work captures the dark spirit of the post-war western as well as his films do as often as they do.

When evaluating Mann's westerns much of the adulation has gone to the series of five of them he made with the actor James Stewart between 1950 and 1955: *Winchester '73* (1950), *Bend of the River* (1952), *The Naked Spur* (1953), *The Far Country* (1955), and *The Man from Laramie* (1955). Along with Henry King's *The Gunfighter* (also 1950), *Winchester '73* is usually regarded as one of the first so-called "psychological" westerns, films that probed deeply into the inner workings of their highly competent but also haunted, flawed, and conflicted heroes. Yet, while King and other directors dabbled with the psychological western, Mann immersed himself in it, working closely with Stewart (who at the time was very interested in taking on darker, more complex roles) in four more westerns to create a major body of remarkably consistent work. In all five films, for example, Stewart plays slightly varied but always quite similar versions of the competent, haunted Mann western hero. (He even makes a point of wearing the same scruffy cowboy hat in every one of the films.) Several character actors also appear and then re-appear in similar kinds of roles throughout the series. Arthur Kennedy, for example, is Stewart's evil alter ego in both *Bend of the River* and *The Man from Laramie*. And Millard Mitchell is Stewart's crusty sidekick in both *Winchester '73* and *The Naked Spur*. Finally, three of the films are the work of acclaimed screenwriter Borden Chase, who often exerted a considerable influence on his scripts. Together, the five films have a powerful cumulative effect, each complementing and enriching the others the way the films do in Ford's "Cavalry Trilogy" or Budd Boetticher's Ranown cycle (see Chapter 10).

While the adulation these films have received is absolutely warranted, it has (unfortunately) overshadowed the achievement evident in the six other westerns Mann made immediately before and after his partnership with Stewart. Unlike the Stewart films, these are more of a mixed bag. All feature different lead actors who together play a much broader range of characters with widely varying concerns. All involve the work of different scriptwriters, each with distinctive styles. And qualitatively, they range from the superb *Man of the West* (1958) to the lackluster *Cimarron* (1960). But they all have one element in common that sets them apart from the vast majority of westerns during the period. That is, of course, the driven, gifted Anthony Mann.

The first two of this group, *Devil's Doorway* and *The Furies*, were both released in 1950 and are both transition films, representing Mann's shifting interest away from noir crime dramas and toward westerns. Among Mann's westerns, these two—in terms of both content and visual styling—are probably the most noir-like. *Devil's Doorway*, especially, is unrelentingly bleak in its take on human nature and unsparingly honest in the way its story plays out. The down note here is emphatic—and very disconcerting. Both films also use seasoned noir cinematographers, John Alton and Victor Milner, respectively, to underscore the dark themes with striking dark images, extreme camera angles to provoke viewer anxiety, and other standard noir techniques. And both include unusually (for the time) intense and sometimes twisted noir violence.

Among Mann's post–Stewart westerns, his most effective and powerful is also his most noir-like: 1958's *Man of the West*. In many respects, its story is similar to the noir masterpiece *Out of the Past* by Jacques Tourneur. A man with a brutal outlaw past has mended his ways and settled into respectability, but, quite by chance (or fate), he is pulled back into the violent noir underworld he thought he had escaped from for good. Once there, he's forced to revert to his old ways to survive and is sickened by the whole experience.

With so many fine westerns—all with a moderate to heavy share of noir content in them—to choose from, it's difficult to focus on just a few to examine in greater detail in this chapter on Mann's contribution to the noir western. So, at the risk of being totally arbitrary, we'll look at *Devil's Doorway* as an example of Mann's brief but fruitful noir-to-western transition period; *The Naked Spur*, perhaps Mann's finest collaboration with Stewart; and the still very under-appreciated *Man of the West*.

For those who would like to dig deeper into Mann's work, two excellent resources are Jim Kitses' *Horizons West: Directing the Western from John Ford to Clint Eastwood* (2004), which includes a lengthy chapter on Mann, and Jeanine Basinger's book-length study *Anthony Mann* (2007). While Kitses focuses mostly on Mann's westerns, Basinger examines all the 40-plus films Mann made during his 25-year directing career, putting his westerns in the larger context with his early B-films, noirs, later epics, and other efforts.

Remembering the Forgotten Mann

For a Hollywood figure who accomplished as much as Anthony Mann did, it's amazing how little is known about his life, especially before he became a film director. In fact, some of the key facts remain in question. He was born in Southern California in 1907, but was his birthplace San Diego or Port Loma? He changed his surname from Bundsmann to Mann, but was his original first name Emil or Anton?

It is known, however, that, after his family moved to New York City when he was 10, his parents, Emil and Bertha Bundsmann, encouraged their son to pursue his passion for stage acting. In his teens, he left formal schooling for the theater and never looked back. Beginning with walk-on roles, he soon was playing major parts in various stock company productions. And, eager to learn about all aspects of theater, he also worked as a stage manager, production

Anthony Mann (center, directing Julie London and Gary Cooper in 1958's *Man of the West*) excelled in 1940s crime noir and then topped himself with a series of exceptionally fine (and often very dark) westerns in the 1950s.

manager, set designer, and director. After directing a series of plays in the mid- and late 1930s, he caught the attention of David O. Selznick, who lured him to Hollywood to be a talent scout. This led to assignments directing screen tests for actors Selznick was considering for roles in such films as 1939's *Intermezzo* and *Gone with the Wind* and 1940's *Rebecca*. From there, Mann went to Paramount as an assistant director, working for three years in this capacity for several established directors, including Preston Sturges.

In 1942, Mann was handed his first film-directing assignment, a low-budget comedy called *Dr. Broadway*, and for the next five years he learned his craft by directing nine more low-budget features for several studios. Based on poor scripts, dependent upon meager budgets, and often made with marginally talented actors, these films taught Mann how to make the most of threadbare resources. Another facet of Mann's work—his commitment to the visual (rather than the verbal) as the primary medium of expression in film—was also in full evidence in these films. Unlike many other stage directors who had moved to film after the birth of the "talkies" and remained dependent on words to tell stories, Mann immediately understood that, in films, the visual trumped the verbal almost every time. While the films he made during this period were far from great, they usually adhered to this commitment.

Mann's breakthrough year was 1947, when his fine noir films *T-Men*, *Railroaded!*, and *Desperate* were all released. Following on these between 1948 and 1950 were more superb noirs, such as *Raw Deal*, *Border Incident*, and *Side Street*, which together cemented Mann's reputation as one of the best noir directors around. One great asset during this time was Mann's partnership with the gifted cinematographer John Alton, whose poetic, often dream-like work in black and white gave films such as *T-Men*, *Raw Deal*, and *Border Incident* exceptional depth and power. But this was also the period when it all came together in Mann's head, too. "By the end of his noir period, Mann had achieved remarkable technical mastery," Basinger writes. "His basic unit of expression became composition. Mann forced a viewer to contemplate characters in the space of the frame, and to take from their position and background an understanding of their situation in the narrative. Because the compositions were done with such extreme care, the understanding was not just about the surface level of the story, but also about the internal, psychological state of the character."[3]

In 1950, Mann had a very impressive year. In addition to the fine noir *Side Street*, three additional Mann films were released: his first three westerns. They were, of course, his two very noir-like efforts, *Devil's Doorway* and *The Furies*, and another breakthrough, *Winchester '73*.

Originally, the legendary Fritz Lang was set to direct *Winchester '73*, but at the last minute he dropped out of the project. Partly at the urging of James Stewart, who was set to star and who had been impressed with *Devil's Doorway*, Mann was brought in. Dissatisfied with the script, Mann turned to Borden Chase to do a rewrite. Then, at long last, the project was a "go."

Winchester '73 was a breakthrough in a number of ways. First, it represented a new period in Mann's artistic development. While keeping the psychological complexity; raw, visceral power; and grim worldview of his noir films, he now added a simpler, more direct visual style—a combination that would serve him well for many more westerns. Second, it represented a new period in Stewart's artistic development. Now in his 40s and too old to be playing the "aw shucks" kinds of roles that had served him well in the 1930s, he was looking for different, darker, more psychologically nuanced characters to play. Now, with Mann and Chase, he had found partners to help develop these characters. Finally, *Winchester '73*—along with films such as King's *The Gunfighter*—represented the birth of a new era for the western. There had certainly been dark characters in westerns before, but now neuroses and nasty behavior, even when exhibited by the central characters, were in.

While *Devil's Doorway* and *The Furies* failed at the box office despite popular stars (Robert Taylor and Barbara Stanwyck, respectively), *Winchester '73* was an enormous hit. Mann and Stewart had found a winning formula, one they would revisit four more times.

In addition to their western collaborations, Mann and Stewart also made three non-westerns together: 1953's *Thunder Bay*, 1954's *The Glenn Miller Story*, and 1955's *Strategic Air Command*. All were commercial successes, but all have also dated over time.

Mann and Stewart were all set to do a sixth western together called *Night Passage* when the two had artistic differences and Mann dropped out of the production. The film, released in 1957 and directed by James Neilson, is reminiscent of the Mann-Stewart westerns but not nearly up to the quality. For both Mann and Stewart, this split was not a pleasant one, and, even in interviews later in his life, Stewart (who outlived Mann by 30 years) refused to discuss their work together.

In the late 1950s, Mann continued to make both westerns and non-westerns. In addition to *Man of the West*, two respected westerns include 1955's *The Last Frontier* with Victor Mature and 1957's *The Tin Star* with Henry Fonda and Anthony Perkins. Two widely praised non-westerns include the 1957 war film, aptly titled *Men in War*, and 1958's *God's Little Acre*, an adaptation of the Erskine Caldwell novel, both featuring Robert Ryan.

Mann's last western, 1960's *Cimarron*, is really an epic set partly in the west. It became a victim of studio tampering, and the result is a film far below Mann's standards.

During the 1960s, Mann continued to make epics, all the rage at the time. His 1961 film, *El Cid*, about the 11th century Spanish hero Don Rodrigo Diaz de Vivar—called "El Cid"—with Charlton Heston and Sophia Loren, was a huge success both commercially and critically. But his three later films were commercial failures, and one of them, 1964's lavish *The Fall of the Roman Empire*, even bankrupted its producer, Samuel Bronston.

While working on the spy thriller *A Dandy in Aspic* in 1967, Mann suffered a fatal heart attack. The film's star Laurence Harvey directed the remaining scenes.

Curiously, the year after Mann's death, the influential film critic Andrew Sarris published *The American Cinema: Directors and Directions 1929–1968*, a book that radically changed perceptions and perspectives about directors during Hollywood's classic period. Among many whose work had previously been overlooked or discounted, including Nicholas Ray, Douglas Sirk, and Sam Fuller, Sarris designated Mann as a true "auteur" whose films expressed a strong personal vision and had enduring artistic merit. For most of the other directors Sarris had selected, this was a time of joy and vindication. At long last, they and their films could receive the attention and praise they had long deserved. And some, such as Fuller, remained the darlings of the film festival circuit for another 30 years.[4] Mann, however, would never hear the tributes from admirers at film festivals or receive a Lifetime Achievement Academy Award. He had already passed from the scene, respected by his colleagues but virtually unknown to most filmgoers.[5]

Nevertheless, his work—as they say—lives on. And among his films, his westerns have a special place not just in Mann's body of work but also in the development of the western itself as serious art form. As Basinger observes:

> Mann's westerns present a story about a hero who is undergoing a psychological change. The landscape, or background, is aligned with him and used to illustrate his internal change through the device of the journey. The internal change, demonstrated visually by background (and position in frame) and revealed by plot, causes the hero to demonstrate his emotional stress through action. The action, usually culminating in violence, creates an emotional effect on the audience, which is like what the hero is undergoing in the narrative. The story, the internal and external life of the hero, and the effect on the audience are all unified.
>
> This remarkable achievement of Mann's is among the greatest in all of film. Because its nature is primarily emotional for the audience and technical in terms of presentation, it has been totally overlooked by critics and scholars attuned only to intellectual, political, or sociological achievements on film.[6]

"Don't cry, Orrie. A hundred years from now it might have worked": Devil's Doorway

Although Mann's westerns starring James Stewart have overshadowed the two non–Stewart westerns Mann made during his noir-to-western transition period in 1950, the two—*Devil's Doorway* and *The Furies*—remain very impressive accomplishments. Of the pair, *Devil's Doorway* has a couple of assets that give it an edge over *The Furies*. First, the story is told with the absolute clarity that Mann delivered in his best noirs and would deliver in his best westerns. We know what this film is about, and every word and visual exists to illustrate and enhance meaning. *The Furies*, while riveting at times, can stretch credibility at other times, such as when the heroine's Mexican lover faces execution in a casual, almost blasé manner. We have to wonder what's going on here—and why he's motivated to act in such a carefree way. Second, *Devil's Doorway* is a more harmonious blend of the noir and western styles. Both in terms of content and style, we feel that the integration here is a natural one. *The Furies*, in contrast, often seems contrived, as though the two different film styles are being jammed together for the sake of effect rather than to create a natural storytelling scheme.

Devil's Doorway begins with shots of a lone rider, ant-like even on the big screen, galloping across wide landscapes bordered by gigantic rocks—perhaps a suggestion of the enormity (and perhaps futility) of the challenge that will eventually await him. As he rides into Medicine Bow, Wyoming, we see that he is a dark-skinned man in a U.S. Cavalry sergeant major's uniform. He is Lance Poole, or Broken Lance (Robert Taylor), a Shoshone who has adopted many of the white man's ways, fought bravely in the Civil War, and even received the coveted Medal of Honor.

Lance is eager to reunite with his family and resume cattle ranching in his beloved Sweet Meadow just beyond a natural gateway near Medicine Bow called the Devil's Doorway. But the times have changed. More whites—especially sheepherders from the Midwest—are moving into the territory, making good land such as Sweet Meadow all the more valuable. In addition, the federal government has passed a new homesteading law, which not only forbids Native Americans from owning land, but also declares them "wards of the government."

7. Deliverance on a Down Note

Lance consults a lawyer, an "A. Masters," who, to his surprise, is a woman named Orrie (Paula Raymond). He is uncomfortable with this, just as she is with him. But just as she puts aside her racism, he puts aside his sexism: they agree to work together, she navigating legal channels to help him retain ownership of his land.

But the government, a growing number of people of Medicine Bow, and the increasing numbers of incoming sheep herders will have none of this. Orrie tries to convince Lance to accept the futility of his position. He fires back bitterly: "I envy you, M'am, you being a lawyer. You got a faith, something to go by—like a religion. With you, it's the law.... I've always wanted something like that—something to tell me what's right or what's wrong ... because then you don't have to bother about your conscience. It's written out for you to follow. No matter what it does to people, it's the law. Changing the law isn't something you have to worry about."

Orrie is moved by this and initiates a petition to change the law. But again her efforts fail.

The sheepherders need Lance's land, so does Lance, and—despite Orrie's attempts to find a compromise—a fight is inevitable.

The series of battles, which takes up most of the last 25 minutes of the film, is a grim affair. The sheepherders, with both their wagons and men on horseback begin to move up the Devil's Doorway. After pleading with them to stop, Lance and his hands dynamite the wagons and the sheep. Many people are left dead.

As Lance and his hands retreat to Sweet Meadow and build defenses around their ranch house, the townspeople form a posse and ride to the ranch. Fearing even more of a bloodbath, Orrie contacts the local cavalry contingent, asking for aid. The cavalry agrees to come.

But at the ranch, a new battle is beginning. Now, the townspeople start throwing dynamite at the ranch house. Lance and his hands inflict losses on them, but they suffer losses, too.

The cavalry arrives, but its orders are to use force to take Lance and the rest of the Shoshones who've come to live at his ranch to the reservation, for them a fate that might very well be worse than death.

Orrie, who's also arrived on the scene, tries to talk with Lance one last time, but he will have none of it. "There's nothing an Indian needs like a speech from a lawyer telling him to give up," he says with great sarcasm and anger.

Finally, as she agrees to leave, they almost kiss but keep themselves from doing so. She begins to cry as she walks away. "Don't cry, Orrie," Lance says,

Robert Taylor is surprisingly effective as Lance Poole, a Shoshone who adopts many of the white man's ways and then is disillusioned when whites betray him and his tribesman in Mann's *Devil's Doorway* (1950). The film's cinematography by noir veteran John Alton is especially compelling.

this time with genuine compassion mixed with sadness. "A hundred years from now it might have worked."

Lance goes out to fight one last time, seemingly wanting to be hit; is wounded; and asks if the women and children can be spared and sent to the reservation. The cavalry lieutenant in charge agrees.

Finally, Lance retreats to the house, gathers the women and children huddling in the wreckage, and follows them out in a procession leading to the lieutenant and Orrie. We don't see Lance clearly at first, but after a moment we realize that he is wearing his sergeant major's uniform from the Civil War with his Medal of Honor still pinned on it.

He walks up to the lieutenant and, in one last bitter, ironic gesture, salutes.

"Where are the others?" the lieutenant asks, meaning the other men.

Emphasizing his first word, Lance says: "We're all gone." Immediately, he falls to the ground dead.

There is no doubt that, except perhaps for lacking a femme fatale and a flashback or two, *Devil's Doorway* is an impressive, near-perfect textbook noir. First, few other westerns are as unrelentingly bleak. After all his struggles, for example, the proud, stubborn, resourceful Lance finds deliverance only in death. For him, there really is no other viable solution—no other way through the conflict he faces. And, except for Orrie and her mother (Spring Byington), none of the other characters really learns anything from this tragedy. In fact, except for Orrie and her mother, all the featured characters from the manipulative and racist Verne Coolan (Louis Calhern) to the amiable but weak Zeke Carmody (Edgar Buchanan) to the earnest young sheepherder Rod MacDougall (Marshall Thompson) to the loyal Red Rock (James Mitchell) are all killed in the fighting. Second, the film's visual design and staging reinforce the dark worldview from start to finish. Many of the scenes, for example, are set at night; many of the interiors show dark, cramped spaces to suggest the darkening realities settling over the proceedings; fights (particularly the bar brawl between Lance and Coolan's henchman) are particularly gritty and nasty to look at; at one point dark clouds and thunder accompany ominous news for Lance; and dark shadows often fall across the faces of characters to underscore everything from Coolan's dark, racist thinking to Lance's hardening attitudes and growing alienation. In almost every respect, this is one downbeat experience.

But *Devil's Doorway* is much more than an excellent example of western noir, and one of its great assets is its very honest, unusually modern handling of the story's various social themes. Even though it was made in 1950, it possesses the values and the sensibility of a film made in the 1970s or afterwards, a film such as 1970's *Little Big Man* or 1990's *Dances with Wolves*. No doubt, Mann—who also featured a strong female lawyer in his noir, *Raw Deal*—was influential in the script development, but a great deal of the credit here must go to scriptwriter Guy Trosper for his uncompromising original screenplay. Trosper brought a strong political point of view and a real sense of social outrage to this script, elements we rarely see in other Mann films.

What is exceptional (and perhaps even enlightened) about the film for its time is its honest portrayals of both Native Americans and the way white Americans typically treated them. For decades, of course, nearly all westerns portrayed most Native Americans simply as savages and killers. While some late 1940s films, such as Ford's *Fort Apache* (1948), offered a more progressive view, showing the racism, imperialistic values, and corruption of some whites as well as the legitimate complaints of the Native American leaders, the Native Americans were—in 1950—still mostly just the bad guys.

For many, a major game changer in depictions of Native Americans was the release of Delmer Daves' *Broken Arrow* in July 1950. Receiving great acclaim for its unusually sympathetic treatment of its Native Americans, the film was hailed as a major step forward in "righting" the story of the settling of the west.

Although there is much about *Broken Arrow* to respect (see Chapter 9), it does, however, present a relatively simplistic, somewhat naïve treatment of this conflict. Most whites and most Native Americans—the film spells out for us—are good, reasonable people, and, if we only listened more to each other—and learned more about each other's ways—then we can eventually achieve peace through understanding. Although bad things happen in *Broken Arrow*, the overall tone is uplifting, softened, comforting. And, probably to accommodate the mostly white movie-going audiences in 1950, it pretty much absolves "good" white people from any responsibility for the atrocities the "bad" white people inflicted upon the Native Americans.

In stark contrast, *Devil's Doorway*, which opened in theaters that September, just two months after *Broken Arrow*, offers no such comfort or consolation. Here, the perpetrators of injustice aren't merely a few crooked, conniving white men but everyone, including Orrie, the film's most sympathetic white character, and the U.S. Congress, which passed the racist homesteading law. If we consider ourselves loyal Americans, this film is clearly saying, we must all share in the blame. Of the two films, *Devil's Doorway* is by far the angrier, more scathing in its criticism, and more honest.

Writer Glenn Erickson also points out still another element of the film, which might have seemed quite radical for the time. "The inevitability of violent struggle is *Devil's Doorway's* most subversive aspect," he notes. "Most dramas about the fate of Native Americans are pessimistic tragedies, the difference here being that Lance Poole fights back. His rebellion is joined by a small band of dispossessed Shoshone holdouts. Anthony Mann dwells on violent scenes of Lance and his warriors shooting and stabbing members of Cooley's posse. Lance is even shown strangling one enemy in a bloodthirsty rage."[7] Not only are the Native Americans violent, but their violence also has legitimacy, since the whites offer them no reasonable way out.

Still another way in which *Devil's Doorway* seems unusually modern for a 1950 film is its depiction of the main female character, Orrie, and her relationship with Lance.

Orrie isn't just a potential frontier wife or a saloon "singer." She is an educated, competent person working in a serious profession who wants to be treated as an equal to men—for all intents and purposes, a feminist.

As a female, her character also brings nuance and resonance to the story in a couple of very intriguing ways. First, it shows how all kinds of people—even the oppressed—are capable of some form of prejudice. When she and Lance first meet, for example, their first inclination is not to work together because she's uncomfortable with his being a Native American and he's put off because she's a woman. They both must overcome these initial prejudices, suggesting that even they—good people who are victims of racism and sexism—are also capable of discrimination. Second, it opens the door to the possibility of romance. In addition to both being outsiders, Orrie and Lance have much in common: intelligence, integrity, a sense of fair play, great mutual respect, and perhaps even deep mutual attraction and affection. In another kind of world they might have become lovers, but in this world that is simply not possible, and the film treats this in a painfully honest way. At one point, Lance wants to help Orrie step off her buckboard but stops because he knows how inappropriate it would be for an Indian to hold a white woman's hand. At another point, the two almost kiss, but they don't because their worlds forbid them to. Then, as Orrie leaves Lance shortly after this, he tells her, "A hundred years from now it might have worked." This is a wonderfully ambiguous line, suggesting not only peaceful coexistence between whites and Native Americans but also a romance between the two of them.

Finally, although Robert Taylor and Paula Raymond were far from being Hollywood's finest actors at the time, both bring great conviction to their portrayals of Lance and Orrie. Certainly, Trosper's original, intelligently drawn, and very sympathetic characters helped to inspire their work on *Devil's Doorway*. But here they are both also summoning something special within themselves that we rarely see in their other work. In Taylor's case, this could very well be the best performance of his career.

"He's not a man; he's a sack of money. That's why we're all here...": The Naked Spur

"*The Naked Spur* is a masterful achievement," writes Jeanine Basinger. "It is one of the most mature and intelligent films ever made, yet at the same time it has the vitality of the most straightforward storytelling westerns."[8]

This is high praise indeed, and it is shared by just about everyone who loves westerns, dark or otherwise. The five westerns Mann made with James Stewart are the best known and most widely acclaimed part of the director's work. And, of these collaborations, *The Naked Spur*—the third in the series—might just be the best. From first shot to last, this beautifully balanced, beautifully modulated game of cat and mouse just rips—delivering action, developing characters, sharpening conflicts between those characters, and building tensions every step of the way.

The film begins as Howie Kemp (Stewart) chances upon a grizzled prospector named Jesse Tate (Millard Mitchell). Kemp is tough and extremely cautious. Implying that he is a law officer, he tells Tate he is looking for Ben Vandergroat (Robert Ryan), a murderer on the run, and that he has lost Vandergroat's trail. Tate mentions that he had recently seen a cold campfire nearby and that maybe it had been Vandergroat's. Intrigued, Kemp offers to pay Tate to help him look for Vandergroat.

As the two are riding around a rock cliff, an avalanche of boulders tumbles down on Kemp. Miraculously, he and Tate get out of the way just in time. But the timing of this avalanche has made Kemp suspicious. Checking out the cliff from behind, he sees a black hat and takes a few shots at it. Roy Anderson (Ralph Meeker), a cavalry lieutenant recently (and dishonorably) discharged from the military for raping a Blackfoot woman, rides up. He's heard the shots and wants to see what the commotion is about. Tate tells him, and, though Kemp would prefer that he leave, Anderson hangs around, offering to help.

Eventually, with Anderson's assistance, they capture Vandergroat.

7. Deliverance on a Down Note 129

When they do, they find that he is traveling with a young woman, Lina Patch (Janet Leigh), the daughter of one of Vandergroat's outlaw friends. She knows Vandergroat is wanted for murder, but she is convinced that he is innocent.

Vandergroat, who knows Kemp from the past, reveals that Kemp isn't a law officer but instead a bounty hunter intent to bring him in back to Kansas dead or alive for the $5,000 reward. Angry with Kemp for deceiving them, both Tate and Anderson insist that he split the reward with them. Realizing that he has no other choice, Kemp agrees.

Now, as the five head back to Kansas, Vandergroat plays mind games with his three captors, using greed to divide them and suggesting that Lina use her beauty to create tension between Kemp and Anderson.

The group has a run-in with several Blackfeet who've been pursuing Anderson to avenge what he's done to the Blackfoot woman. In the skirmish, Kemp saves Lina from harm but is wounded in the leg. The leg wound causes Kemp to pass out on the trail, and that night he wakes from a traumatic nightmare, thinking that Lina is his former fiancée, Mary. Vandergroat shares the dark backstory with the others, explaining that Kemp had entrusted his ranch to Mary when he went off to fight in the Civil war and that she had sold it and run off with another man. Lina feels great sympathy for Kemp and becomes increasingly conflicted between her growing affection for him and her loyalty to Vandergroat.

Later, when the group huddles in a cave during a storm, Vandergroat convinces Lina to distract Kemp, so that he can try to escape. As she and Kemp talk, they have a tender moment, she sharing her dream of getting a fresh start in California, he telling her of his plan to buy back his ranch, and the two of them kissing. But, as Vandergroat tries to escape, Kemp catches him and realizes that Lina—at least in part—has also been deceiving him.

At the group's camp the next day, Vandergroat focuses on manipulating Tate, telling him about a nearby gold mine he knows about and suggesting that he will take Tate there if Tate will set him free. That night, the two sneak away, taking Lina along. The next day, Vandergroat creates a diversion, grabs Tate's rifle from him, and kills him. He then fires two more shots to draw Kemp and Anderson in so he can kill them, too. Appalled by all this, Lina finally sees what kind of man Vandergroat actually is.

Just as at the beginning of the film, Vandergroat chooses to fight from atop a rock cliff. This time, however, he has guns and ammunition. An action-filled chain of events ensues, in which Kemp uses his spur like a mountaineer's piton to climb the cliff, Anderson shoots a distracted Vandergroat, Vandergroat falls into the treacherous river below, Anderson goes in to retrieve his body for the reward money and is killed by a fast flowing tree stump, Kemp finally retrieves Vandergroat's body, and in a rage he declares his intention to bring the body back and claim the reward money.

Lina, however, begs him to reject the blood money and offers to go with him—any place he wants—to start a new life. Realizing that his anger is hurting them both, Kemp stops, begins to dig a grave for Vandergroat (thus giving up any chance to claim the reward money), and agrees to go with Lina to California. At long last, he seems to be at peace.

In terms of its visual design, *The Naked Spur* is not at all noir-ish. At this point in Mann's career, the frequent nighttime settings, use of blackness and shadows to suggest dark intentions, and other traditional noir trappings prevalent in *Devil's Doorway* (as well as *The Furies* and the director's crime noirs) play a much less prominent role in Mann's work. Both the transition to westerns and the transition to color photography (*The Naked Spur* was Mann's second Technicolor effort) changed all of that. In fact, most of *The Naked Spur* was filmed in Colorado's breathtaking San Juan Mountains, and most of the scenes occur during bright sunny days.

In terms of its sensibility, however, *The Naked Spur* is very noir-like. Its story revolves around five people who at one time or another all betray others who have put their trust in them, many of these betrayals involving good old-fashioned greed—people selling each other out for money. Its protagonist is a classic noir anti-hero who is an outsider, has endured a past trauma that continues to torture him, identifies in certain ways with the villain, and is not above doing some double-dealing. Finally, while its settings and visual design are not noir-ish in the strictest sense, they suggest—through an emphasis on settings from harsh rock cliffs to treacherous rivers—the noir viewpoint that the world is usually a cruel, punishing place.

The theme of betrayal, the heart and soul of so many crime noirs, is central to *The Naked Spur*. At one point or another in the story, each of the film's five characters—even the good ones—betrays at least one other person. Kemp, for example, lets both Pike and Anderson believe that he is a law officer when he is actually a bounty hunter after a $5,000 reward. Concerned that anyone else might get ideas of capturing Vandergroat, he has even cut off the bottom portion of the "Wanted" poster that offers the reward. Pike, normally an

7. Deliverance on a Down Note

Perhaps the best of the highly praised Mann–James Stewart collaborations, 1953's *The Naked Spur* tells the story of a bounty hunter (Stewart) determined to bring in a killer (Robert Ryan) for the reward money. Pictured here are Millard Mitchell, Ryan, Janet Leigh, Ralph Meeker, and Stewart.

upright fellow, agrees to let Vandergroat go free in return for Vandergroat's leading him to a gold mine. Because she still believes in Vandergroat's innocence, even kind, good Lina agrees to sweet-talk Kemp to distract him and allow Vandergroat to escape. All of us, the film seems to be saying, get our hands dirty at some point. For any number of reasons, all of us are capable of selling others out. That master of noir betrayal stories, André de Toth, would probably have loved this aspect of *The Naked Spur*.

One of Mann's most tormented and neurotic protagonists, Howie Kemp has nearly all the ingredients of the classic noir anti-hero. He was building a life when the war intervened, enabling his fiancée to betray him by selling his land and running away with another man. This experience, as we see in the film, still gives him nightmares and has hardened him in numerous ways. He is, for example, intensely suspicious of everyone. We see this from the film's first scene, when he interrogates the amiable Pike. He has a complex relationship with the villain, Vandergroat, someone he's known in the past who also has a special connection with Lina. In addition, Kemp is cynical about money and how he can make it. He wants to buy his ranch back, a noble goal, but to do so he adopts the "unclean" profession of bounty hunter. As Anderson, referring to Vandergroat, reminds Kemp late in the story: "He's not a man; he's a sack of money. That's why we're all here, especially you."

Like many (but certainly not all) noir anti-heroes, Howie Kemp is eventually able, in the film's final scenes, to put his demons to rest, commit to a relationship with Lina, and move on to that "fresh start" in California. It is a cathartic moment that—considering all Kemp has gone through—is quite moving and even reminiscent of such fine noirs as Abraham Polonsky's 1948 masterpiece, *Force of Evil*, in which we truly believe that the main character has come through a major, life-changing journey.

Visually, of course, *The Naked Spur* is not noir-ish in the traditional sense, but, even in a beautiful, expansive visual environment, Mann—as he does in his other westerns as well—uses landscape to underscore the noir precept that the world often is a harsh, hostile, bruising, and even deadly place. Throughout the film, scenes are staged to show the separation that exists between characters (often with trees dividing them), the perilous nature of the mission (with steep cliffs beside the characters), the difficulty of success (with high distant mountains), and other realities inherent in the story. When the film reaches its climatic moments, the terrain becomes even more daunting and threatening, focusing, as Jim Kitses notes, "on the unnatural struggle of extreme men, trapped in the ugly, unyielding rocks of a horrific landscape."[9] In *The Naked Spur*, this terrain is the rock cliff beside the powerful, swiftly flowing river that serves as the site of the film's climatic fight. Here, the danger is everywhere, coming from the environment as well as the other characters. This point is made quite emphatically, for example, when—after Vandergroat has died—the exuberant Anderson goes into the river to retrieve his body and is unexpectedly killed by an onrushing tree stump. As any noir worth its salt is telling us: the world is a very unpredictable, often very perilous place.

One of the amazing facets of *The Naked Spur* is its very small cast, each character perfectly juxtaposed to the others in some way in the deadly cat-and-mouse game they all play. And, in addition to the fine direction and writing (by Sam Rolfe and Harold Jack), the five actors who portrayed these characters—Stewart, Leigh, Ryan, Meeker, and Mitchell—all did exceptionally good work. A good deal of the credit for the film's enduring fame belongs to them as well.

"I want to kill every last one of those Tobins. And that makes me just like they are": Man of the West

While not as well known as the westerns he made with Stewart, Mann's 1958 *Man of the West* has steadily grown in stature among film scholars and writers over the last few decades. Glenn Erickson, for example, has called it "a western ahead of its time."[10] Jim Kitses has proclaimed it "a personal achievement of the highest order."[11] Derek Malcolm has said that it is "the greatest of all" Mann's westerns.[12] And Jeanine Basinger has dubbed it the "culmination" of Mann's work in the western genre, his "crowning achievement," and "one of the greatest westerns ever made."[13]

In addition to being a superb western that does look forward to some of the brutally tough revisionist westerns of the 1970s, *Man of the West* is also a very noir-ish one. In some ways, in fact, its gallery of grotesque villains and occasionally sadistic violence takes us back to Mann's noir thrillers *Raw Deal* and *Border Crossing*, making it as much a horror story as a western.

—⁂—

The story begins as Link Jones (Gary Cooper) arrives in Crosscut, Texas. He's going to take a train from there to Fort Worth, where he plans to hire a schoolteacher with money entrusted to him by the people of his small community of Good Hope. Despite his upright intentions, however, he seems uneasy when people ask him questions about himself. So he sometimes makes up false answers.

On the train, he talks with an aging con man, Sam Beasley (Arthur O'Connell), and a saloon singer who's just left Crosscut, Billie Ellis (Julie London). When the train stops to load on wood and the men are asked to help out, a gang of three—Coaley (Jack Lord), Trout (Royal Dano), and Ponch (Robert J. Wilke)—with the assistance of an inside man named Alcutt try to rob the train. In the scuffle, Link tries to stop them and is knocked out. A guard orders the train to start again, thwarting the robbery, but the robbers still manage to steal the money Link has been carrying.

When Link awakes, the train has gone, and he, Beasley, and Billie have all been left behind. Miles from the nearest town, the only place Link can think of going is a broken down farmhouse nearby.

"How did you know about it?" Billie asks.

"I used to live here once," Link says.

"When you were a boy?"

In this scene from Mann's very dark *Man of the West* (1958) Coaley Tobin (Jack Lord) gets saloon singer Billie Ellis (Julie London) to strip for his pleasure by threatening to cut the throat of Billie's protector, Link Jones (Gary Cooper). The film mirrors the decent-into-hell plots found in many late 1940s and early 1950s crime noirs.

"I don't know what I was," he responds cryptically.

Seeming very cautious, Link tells Beasley and Billie to wait in the barn while he checks out the house. He enters the dark, cramped building and finds the robbers hiding inside. Within minutes, an older man joins the group. He is a man Link knows all too well—Dock Tobin (Lee J. Cobb), Link's uncle and the man who, in this very farmhouse years before, had raised Link to be a robber and a killer. He introduces Link to the trio who now work for him, including Coaley, who is, Link learns, also his cousin, and he complains about how hard his life has been since Link left him more than a decade ago.

Seeing that he, Beasley, and Billie are now in real danger, Link brings them in from the barn and lies to Tobin, telling him that he deliberately sought him out after the train left the three behind. While Dock wants to believe this story, Coaley is suspicious. The old man then shares a longtime dream to rob a bank in the town of Lassoo and announces that, with Link's return, the gang finally has the resources to make this possible. Coaley, meanwhile, finds Billie attractive and wants her to strip for the men. Link tells the group that she is his woman, hoping that Coaley will back down. Instead, the determined Coaley holds a knife to Link's throat and insists that she strip. Humiliated, she begins. Eventually, Dock stops the proceedings, sending Link and Billie out to the barn to sleep. When they are finally alone, Link tells Billie that he has a wife and two sons back in Good Hope. Moved by how Link has cared for her and attracted to him as well, she is disappointed to hear this.

The next day, Claude Tobin (John Dehner), another of Link's cousins, shows up. Suspicious of Link, he joins with Coaley in advocating that they simply kill Link, Beasley, and Billie. Still the leader, however, Dock overrules them, and the group begins a four-day journey to Lassoo, where they will rob the bank. Along the way, Link and Coaley get into a fistfight, Link beats him severely, and then—adding to Coaley's humiliation—strips him to avenge the humiliation he put Billie through. Coaley then tries to kill Link, but Beasley steps in the way, sacrificing himself. Annoyed with Coaley for disobeying him, Tobin shoots him. As he lay dying, Beasley tells Link that, if Link had been killed instead, then Beasley's own chances of survival would have been nil. At least this way, Link and Billie might still have a chance. Link is quite moved by Beasley's gesture.

Nearing Lassoo, Link volunteers to rob the bank. Dock stays at their camp with Billie, while Link and Trout, and then Claude and Ponch, ride into Lassoo. But Link finds that the bank no longer exists and that Lassoo is now a ghost town. A series of gunfights take place, Link killing Trout, Ponch, and finally Claude.

Returning to camp, Link discovers that Dock, who had given his word not to harm Billie, has beaten and raped her. He finds him; tells him that, like Lassoo, he is a ghost and finished; shoots him; and finds the bag of money he had been carrying for Good Hope on him.

Finally, as Link and Billie ride back to civilization, she says that, while she knows that Link will return to his wife, she also feels a love for him that she considers—and will always consider—very special.

While not as overtly noir as *Devil's Doorway*, *Man of the West* is still much darker in its sensibilities than *The Naked Spur* and most of the other Mann-Stewart westerns. Its hero, Link Jones, is not only a man who has been traumatized by a past experience and shares some affinity with the villain, he has actually been a villain, a man who has robbed and even killed people—a man, who, by the prevailing standards of frontier justice, should have been hanged years ago. As his name suggests, he is intimately and perhaps forever "linked" to major evil-doing, and he is deeply concerned that his own violent tendencies will re-emerge. In addition, his hero's journey is a darker one, a descent into a living hell populated by the grotesque people who mirror his own evil beginnings. Finally, the visual expression of this journey is much darker and noir-ish. Gone, of course, are the enormous mountains and beautiful wilderness expanses we see throughout *The Naked Spur* and other Mann-Stewart westerns. This world, while it begins in a bustling human community surrounded by verdant countryside, moves into a variety of bleaker and more hellish settings to suggest the hero's descent into a very dark, harsh world.

Many traditional noir heroes, such as Joe Sullivan in Mann's *Raw Deal*, have dark outlaw pasts, but relatively few have been murderers who've gotten away with it as Link Jones is. When Billie tells Link that he is not like the members of the Tobin gang, for example, he soberly responds: "I was. There wasn't any difference at all." Before the film's story begins, of course, Link has already gone through an enormous personal change. He has left the Tobin gang and completely transformed his life: marrying a good woman, having two children, becoming a respected member of the small (probably religious) community of Good Hope, and even confessing his past to his community. As he tells Billie, he is also deeply moved that the people of Good Hope have forgiven his past sins. Now, however, he fears what reconnecting with the Tobins might mean for him. On one hand, Link (who has renounced killing) understands that killing is probably the only way he and Billie can get out of the mess they are in. On the other hand, he also wants to kill the Tobins out of pure rage and hatred. "Do you know what I feel like?" he says to Billie. "I feel like killing—like a sickness come back. I want to kill every last one of those Tobins. And that makes me just like they are." Just being around them makes Link want to murder again, and, while he finds the inevitability of killing troubling, he finds his own volcanic feelings even more so. He fears that he may revert to his old ways—their ways; become like them again; and, in the process, lose all he has worked so hard for. This internal struggle is perhaps best illustrated through the film's two "stripping" scenes. After Coaley has humiliated Billie (and enraged Link) by forcing her to strip in the farmhouse, Link goads Coaley into a fight and, when he defeats Coaley, pulls his clothes off so he can feel as humiliated as Billie did. This second stripping scene shows that Link's own fears may be warranted. Merely being around the Tobins brings out the worst in him—something that's still (and may always be) there. Just as Billie and Coaley are stripped of their clothes, Link is being stripped of his hard-won humanity. The one bright spot is that, when Link has the chance to kill a defenseless Coaley, he can't bring himself to do it. He hasn't entirely reverted to his old ways. This good-evil duality that resides within us all—this struggle for one's own soul—a central theme in numerous noirs, is a central theme here, too. Can Link both defeat the Tobins and contain his own propensity for evil? Throughout much of *Man of the West*, this is a major concern for him.

Some scholars have seen strong similarities between Link's journey and a classic Greek hero's journey, such as Odysseus' trip to the underworld in *The Odyssey*.[14] This parallel is certainly appropriate, fitting with Mann's preoccupation with Greek and Biblical myths and themes in films such as *The Furies* (Electra) and *Winchester '73* (Cain and Abel) as well as with his fondness for journey stories. But another and perhaps even more striking parallel might be with a noir hero's reluctant journey from a place of respectability in the mainstream world back to a hellish noir underworld in order to settle unresolved issues/conflicts from his past. Let's look, for example, at some of the hero's journey parallels between *Man of the West* and perhaps the quintessential noir, Jacques Tourneur's *Out of the Past* (1947). Like Link Jones, Jeff Bailey (Robert Mitchum), the hero of *Out of the Past*, is a reformed outlaw who is leading a modest but upright life in a small town and who has even found love. Then, a twist of noir-ish fate, or bad luck, occurs. For Jeff Bailey, it's when an old hoodlum colleague stumbles into his life and then reports his whereabouts to the outlaw leader. For Link, it's the misfortune of finding Dock Tobin and his gang in the seemingly abandoned farmhouse. Once pulled back into his dark past, the hero must perform an undesirable task for the outlaw leader. Jeff must retrieve some incriminating income tax records. Link must rob the bank in Lassoo. But accomplishing the task is not enough. In both cases there must be a reckoning in which the heroes kill not just the outlaw leaders but also all the other bad guys. Finally, the "good" woman in each story must resign herself to life without the hero. In *Out of the Past*, Jeff dies and Ann (Virginia Huston) is left with another man she doesn't love. In *Man of the West*, Link goes back to his wife in Good Hope and Billie is left alone. Like *Out of the Past* and numerous other noirs, *Man of the West* is about the difficulty (and often futility) of trying to escape a disreputable past and the dark consequences that can occur when one is pulled back into that past. And, as in these noirs, this theme is expressed (at least in part) by the course of the hero's journey. In fact, *Man of the West* could have just as easily been titled *Out of the Past*.

As in other Mann films, the noir-ish use of landscape and other settings to suggest the interior lives of the characters is quite evident in *Man of the West*. Here, especially, the use of visuals reflects the states of mind the characters are experiencing. For example, in the first part of the film—before the descent into the noir underworld of the Tobins—visuals are generally calm and pleasant. The town of Crosscut is portrayed as both bustling and upbeat. The countryside surrounding it consists of green rolling hills. There are ominous moments, of course, from a sheriff's suspicions about Link at the train station to the train robbery, but in this part of the film the tone is generally relaxed and the visuals reinforce this. Suddenly, however, the story shifts dramatically, becoming much darker and more desperate. This occurs as soon as Link enters the farmhouse and encounters the train robbers and then Dock Tobin. In visual terms, the farmhouse interior scenes are probably the most traditionally noir part of the story: the setting dark, cramped, and sinister—the villains' movements and behaviors unpredictable and unnerving. Then, after leaving the farmhouse, the settings shift to arid desert; then to the stark, near-deserted ghost town of Lassoo; and then—for the final, brutal reckoning—to forbidding rock crags. These all suggest the harsh, bleak battle Link and the various gang members wage against each other. Finally, as Link and Billie travel back to civilization, the landscape is greener and less forbidding, reinforcing the point that calmness and civility have returned. Throughout the film, the effect is quite powerful—not only do these visuals reflect Link and Billie's psychological journeys but they also help give great resonance to them.

As well as being a western ahead of its time, presaging the dark, brutally tough westerns of the 1970s and afterwards, *Man of the West* owes much to the noir tradition that Mann himself helped create and extend to the western. As Basinger has rightfully called it the "culmination" of Mann's work in the western genre, we can also call it the culmination of his work in noir.

As with all great talents who die before their time, it's curious to speculate whether or not Anthony Mann had more great films in him, and, if so, where they would have taken both him and the art of filmmaking. When he died, there was talk that he wanted to do a western version of Shakespeare's *King Lear* with none other than John Wayne. That would have been—at the very least—quite interesting to see.

The reality, however, is that Mann didn't get the chance to make more films, westerns or otherwise, and that, in terms of his work, what we have is what we have. This duly noted—we have quite a bit. During his prime years—between 1947 and 1958—Mann made more than two dozen films, many of them (with the help of John Alton and others) shaping and sharpening the noir style and sensibility and many more (with the help of James Stewart, Bordon Chase, and others) reshaping and redefining the western genre for a new era. His ability to present psychologically nuanced characters and morally complex stories through stunning visual images might just—with the possible exception of John Ford—be unmatched by anyone who has ever directed westerns. He was a master, and his influence is very much with us today.

8

Nightmare in Broad Daylight
Evil Poses as the Law in Allan Dwan's *Silver Lode*

"We're the law, remember. If anybody starts anything, shoot to kill."—*Silver Lode*

Virtually unknown today, Allan Dwan (1885–1981) was a true film pioneer whose most successful and prestigious years as a director were over by the time he was in his mid–40s. He entered the motion-picture business in 1909, just a year after D.W. Griffith had made his first film. By 1911, he was directing one- and two-reel shorts at a furious pace, one every three or four days. Within a few more years, he was directing the great stars of the era—among them, Lillian Gish, Mary Pickford, Douglas Fairbanks, and Gloria Swanson—in major feature-length films that won over audiences and critics with their intelligence, wit, exuberance, and masterly craft. One great triumph during this time was his 1922 *Robin Hood* with Fairbanks, a film that noted playwright and critic Robert E. Sherwood called "the high-water mark of film production—the farthest step that the silent drama has ever taken along the high road to art."[1] Throughout the 1920s, he remained a directing "rock star," churning out hit after hit for Fairbanks, Swanson, and other great silent era stars.

After his last Fairbanks success, 1929's *The Iron Mask*, however, Dwan's fortunes changed considerably. The studios were tightening creative controls, and, to keep working within the evolving studio system, Dwan increasingly accepted the projects as they came—even if the scripts were inferior, the budgets low, and the production teams less than stellar.

While Dwan wasn't particularly fond of these new realities, he still loved the task of telling stories in his straightforward, energetic, unaffected way.

8. Nightmare in Broad Daylight

Shown here with Barbara Stanwyck while shooting 1955's *Cattle Queen of Montana*, Allan Dwan began in films in 1909, and, over a 50-year career, often produced remarkable results with limited budgets and scant resources.

And for the next 30 years he soldiered on, making more than 70 sound films. A few—including three Shirley Temple vehicles, 1938's *Suez* with Tyrone Power, and 1949's *Sands of Iwo Jima* with John Wayne—were "A-list" pictures with big stars and the big budgets that came with them. But nearly all the others were low-budget efforts often compromised by studio tampering. Although Dwan usually had to put up with difficult conditions, his ability as a pragmatic and inspired problem solver often prevailed, and a number of these films hold up quite well after many decades. In addition, Dwan—already a proven hand at many kinds of films—continued to adapt to emerging film fashions. When the public wanted gentle comedies during World War II or edgy westerns in the 1950s, for example, he was quick to accommodate. In fact, his very last film, *Most Dangerous Man Alive* (shot in 1958 and released in 1961 when Dwan was 76) is a sci-fi/adventure about a survivor of a cobalt bomb explosion who learns that his body is turning to steel—a subject that was quite trendy for the time.

Among Dwan's 1950s westerns, one that excellently demonstrates both his filmmaking ingenuity and his ability to adapt to current fashion is the very noirish *Silver Lode* (1954). Long dismissed as a low-budget "rip-off" of a better known and more widely admired western of the period, Fred Zinnemann's *High Noon* (1952), *Silver Lode* has, in recent years, cultivated a small but steadily growing group of partisans. Writing for *The New Yorker* in 2012, Richard Brody proclaimed that, in its "understated lucidity," it is "one of the greatest" westerns ever.[2] In 2013, the blog site *Cinema Talk* called it an excellent example "of what made Allan Dwan so vital."[3] In 2010, the blog site *Avaxhome* dubbed it "one of Allan Dwan's unqualified masterpieces."[4] And also in 2010, Fernando F. Croce noted in *Slant Magazine* that the "deceptively modest *Silver Lode* has a dynamism and ingenuity that outclass the stolidity of many more established features" and that it is "the sort of work that separates the artists from the artisans."[5]

Amid all this praise, two words that strike a special chord are "deceptively modest." As a low-budget "quickie" without major stars, *Silver Lode* nevertheless possesses enormous vitality, complexity, and richness. In 77 short minutes, it shows us much. And in terms of its hard-edged tone, wrongly-accused-man theme, largely dark view of human behavior (especially when the chips are down), and bitter ironies, it is vintage western noir that—according to many of its admirers—surpasses even the much more widely acclaimed *High Noon*.

Staying in the Game

"There will never again be a movie career like Allan Dwan's," wrote Peter Bogdanovich at the beginning of his 1971 book about Dwan's life and career, *The Last Pioneer*.[6] And anyone who knows anything about Dwan will readily agree.

Born in Toronto in 1885, Dwan soon moved first to Detroit and then to Chicago with his family. At 18, he entered Notre Dame University, where he played football and graduated four years later with a degree in electrical engineering. Curiously, this led him to a job as an "illuminating engineer," and his expertise working on the mercury vapor arc light brought him to Chicago's Essanay Film Manufacturing Company in 1909, where he became enthralled with the movies Essanay was making. Learning that the company, hungry for ideas, was willing to pay $25 apiece for short stories he had written in college, Dwan happily accommodated. Soon he was a story editor. Then, just 16 months later, when a director's drinking put a production at risk, the actors in the film urged Dwan to step in and take over. Dwan, who knew nothing about directing at the time, simply asked the actors, "What do I do? What does a director do?"[7] They pointed him to a director's chair and a megaphone, and his career proceeded from there.

Dwan's most successful directing years, of course, were during the silent period when he directed or supervised—by his own estimate—nearly 1800 films, mostly shorts; received rapturous praise for many of his big-star, big-budget features; and—ever the engineer—solved many baffling technical problems. (He is credited, among other innovations, with inventing the "dolly shot," today a standard film technique that helps to give greater movement and energy to scenes.) What's particularly unfortunate, however, is that roughly two-thirds of Dwan's silent films are now lost, making it difficult for film historians to evaluate his overall contribution to the art.

What's also unfortunate is that, after 1929, Dwan was forced to toil mostly on low-budget, fast-turnaround projects. It's fascinating to imagine what might have been if he had received more "prestige" assignments or simply made some different career choices. As film historian Ronald Bowers has written: "The artistic disparity of his 70-odd sound films fails to adequately represent this technically innovative, unpretentious, avid storyteller, and his career will surely undergo considerable re-evaluation as the study of film history progresses."[8]

It's fascinating, too, that, instead of simply quitting, Dwan chose to stay in a tough game for three decades more. As Bogdanovich observed: "Only a man of inherent modesty ... could have survived with such good spirit and without cynicism his years of inferior projects and crippling limitations. It has been his curse, as well as his particular glory, that he would prefer to shoot almost any old thing that came up rather than wait for just the right project; it was more fun that way, and since he ... never had any pretensions, he would rather exercise his craft than not be out there at all."[9]

In 1954, now long typecast as a director of low-budget genre films, Dwan—nearing 70—enjoyed a minor renaissance that allowed him to go out on a somewhat high note. Independent producer Benedict Bogaeus asked him to direct a western called *Silver Lode*, and, after a few initial skirmishes, the two settled down to work on nine additional films together over the next four years for RKO, 20th Century–Fox, and Columbia. The results—as was typical of Dwan's career—were uneven, but, in addition to *Silver Lode*, there were several bright spots. One was the chance for Dwan to work with the great Barbara Stanwyck on two films, including the 1954 proto-feminist western *Cattle Queen of Montana*. Another was the more traditional 1954 western *Tennessee's Partner* with John Payne, Ronald Reagan, and Rhonda Fleming. Based on a Brett Harte story, this is, among the director's later films, probably his most personal and affecting. It was also, according to several sources, among his favorites. Still another was the chance to work on nearly all of these films with the very talented cinematographer John Alton. The winner of an Academy Award a few years earlier for his work on the lavish color musical *An American In Paris* (1951), Alton is revered in certain quarters today for his starkly dramatic black-and-white compositions in such classic noirs as Anthony Mann's *Raw Deal* (1948) and Joseph H. Lewis' *The Big Combo* (1955).

After *Most Dangerous Man Alive*, Dwan, who at 73 was still in demand, quietly walked away from filmmaking. "It's just a business that I stood as long as I could," he said later in life, "and I got out of it when I couldn't stand it any more."[10] Dwan lived a characteristically quiet, modest retirement, occasionally accepting interviews with film scholars mostly interested in the silent era, until his death at 96 in late 1981. One highlight during this time was his appearance, as a talking head, in several episodes of the 13-part 1980 documentary series *Hollywood: The Silent Years* directed by Kevin Brownlow and David Gill. Well into his 90s when interviewed, Dwan shared many intriguing stories and insights about the time. Some 70 years after he had begun in the film business, he was still in the game.

Since Dwan's films are so varied and his filmmaking style was so straightforward and understated, it has been difficult for many film historians to characterize his work. Of the appraisals, perhaps the best comes, again, from Bogdanovich. "If there is no unifying theme nor imposing visual style to Dwan's work," he noted (when Dwan was still alive), "it is certainly not devoid of personality and character. His approach to material has always been pragmatic and his camerawork expressive but unadorned, in the most classical American tradition. The mischievous, occasionally even wicked humor that runs through many of his films is that of a man amused by the pomposity and pretensions of the world, though he is equally tolerant of our most frivolous behavior; never one to judge his characters, he still cannot resist deflating them. Yet, throughout his career, the lives of simple people have most often inspired his finest movies, from the open enthusiasm of Douglas Fairbanks to the uncomplicated cowboys of his last films."[11]

"A moment ago you wanted to kill me": Silver Lode

The film *Silver Lode* begins with a curious juxtaposition. It is the 4th of July in the town of Silver Lode, and several children are playing in the street with fireworks. But, almost immediately, they must clear the way for four ominous looking men (perhaps the real fireworks) who are riding into town. One of them, presumably the leader, asks two women where he can find a man named Dan Ballard. As soon as he passes, one of the women says: "That man's eyes—frightening."

The man, who we soon learn is a U.S. marshal named Fred McCarty (Dan Duryea), finds Ballard (John Payne) at the home of Rose Evans (Lizabeth Scott) and her family. Ballard and Rose are about to be married. McCarty announces that he has a warrant for Ballard's arrest—the charge, murder. McCarty claims Ballard shot his brother in the back and then made off with the brother's $20,000. Ballard denies this, but McCarty represents the law. With Ballard faced with the decision to continue with the wedding or to postpone it, McCarty snidely suggests that that choice is up to him. "It's your wedding, Ballard," he says with great relish. "Or should I say 'funeral.'" Ballard decides to postpone the ceremony so he can clear himself.

After the local judge upholds McCarty's warrant, Ballard bargains for time to somehow discredit McCarty, whom he suspects is a fraud, and to prove his innocence. At first, most of the townspeople are solidly behind Ballard, but one by one they begin to question their faith in him. McCarty is, after all, a duly authorized federal officer.

With an assist from Dolly (Dolores Moran), a local saloon girl who's also Ballard's old flame, Ballard gets one of McCarty's men, Johnson (Harry Carey, Jr.), to admit that McCarty is indeed a fraud. Soon, however, Ballard's efforts to solve his problem without bloodshed start unraveling. Several gunfights follow, and Ballard and McCarty ultimately face off in the bell tower in the local church. At this point, the fleeing Ballard has no gun. News comes exonerating Ballard and exposing McCarty, but the vengeful McCarty will have none of it and shoots to kill Ballard. Finally, one of his bullets—perhaps his last—hits the bell and ricochets straight back into McCarty's heart. He falls dead, and an awed local minister declares it "an act of God!"

The townspeople apologize to Ballard for having doubted him, but he can only respond with revulsion. "You're sorry," he says bitterly. "A moment ago you wanted to kill me. You forced me to kill to defend myself, to save my own life. You wouldn't believe me. You wouldn't believe what I said. A man's life can hang in the balance ... and you're sorry."

He then finds Rose, one of the few people in town who had always stood by him, and they walk away from the crowd together.

—⁂—

It is obvious that *Silver Lode* was influenced by the enormously successful *High Noon*, which premiered two years before, and similarities between the

Rose and Dan (Lizabeth Scott and John Payne) must postpone their wedding plans when a U.S. marshal comes to town to arrest Dan for murder and robbery in Dwan's 1954 *Silver Lode*. As Dan tries to prove his innocence, more and more of the townspeople begin to doubt him.

two films abound. Many of these involve the story's main thrust and structure: a good man's wedding day is marred as bad men come to town after him in a tale told in virtual real time—both nightmares in broad daylight. At first, the townspeople rally around the threatened man, but, when the going gets tough, the people, one by one, find reasons not to support him. With the exception of two women who believe in him (his old flame and his new beloved), he must face the threat alone. When he ultimately prevails, the townspeople come back to him, but by this time he is disgusted with them. Another striking similarity is that both films are also not-so-subtle critiques of the 1950s Congressional investigations (often called "witch hunts") of Senator Joseph McCarthy and others designed to stir up anti–Communist hysteria in the U.S. and of the public's fickle and fearful response—its tendency to initially side with, then to turn against, a threatened person. To make this point unmistakable in *Silver Lode*, the villain, posing as a duly authorized federal marshal is even named McCarty.

Because *High Noon* came first and *Silver Lode* does have some B-picture limitations, there has been a tendency to dismiss the latter film as a pale imitation of a bona fide masterpiece. But, when we look closely at both films, a somewhat different picture emerges. While *High Noon* has many memorable elements from Gary Cooper and Katy Jurado's fine acting performances to Tex Ritter's entrancing rendition of "Do Not Forsake Me, Oh My Darlin'," *Silver Lode* has its share of strengths that make it distinctive and in certain ways superior to the more widely acclaimed film.

First, *Silver Lode* conveys its anti–McCarthy message with much greater clarity and power. Although an anti–McCarthy message is woven into *High Noon*, the film is also—if not mainly—a story about summoning the courage to face an imposing (perhaps life-threatening) adversary alone. The McCarthy threat is suggested, but this story thread is not developed adequately enough to make the allegory sufficiently compelling. On the other hand, *Silver Lode* does a much better job of making—and developing—the anti–McCarthy statement. Not only is the villain (not-so-subtly) named McCarty, but he poses as a representative of the federal government, presents trumped-up accusations against an innocent person to further his own interests, and is relentless in his efforts to intimidate everyone else who might stand in his way. (All of this occurs, of course, on the 4th of July, the day Americans celebrate their liberation from tyrants.) The connection is not as specific or clear in *High Noon*. A wonderful finishing touch is the development in the bell tower shootout, when McCarty, shooting at the persecuted and now unarmed Ballard, hits the bell instead, and the bullet ricochets and goes straight through McCarty's heart, killing him. It's a subtle—and brilliant—way to suggest that the efforts of Senator McCarthy and his compatriots would inevitably be self-defeating and lead to their own undoing.

Second, by making its point more directly, *Silver Lode* both keeps the action moving (essential for a genre film such as a western) and avoids the pretenses of *High Noon*. "It [*Silver Lode*] isn't a self-consciously 'serious' message film," notes *Cinema Talk*. "Instead, the ideology seems to come from the story playing out, rather than being jammed into its wiring.... Dwan doesn't dwell on his social commentary. It's there and it's easy to read, but he hasn't turned away from the genre. In a way, it makes the allegory more powerful: he hasn't sacrificed any action to reinforce the message."[12]

Third, while John Payne's Dan Ballard doesn't have quite the gravitas of Gary Cooper's Will Kane in *High Noon*, Dan Duryea's excellent turn as Fred McCarty gives *Silver Lode* a dimension *High Noon* lacks—a good bad guy. A superb villain in countless crime noirs as well as westerns, Duryea gives his character many facets. At different times, his McCarty is ruthless, arrogant, impatient, manipulative, sadistic, lecherous, darkly humorous, and endlessly suspicious. If Payne's Ballard is simply solid, Duryea's McCarty is a complicated and endlessly engaging figure.

Fourth, while *High Noon* is essentially grim and humorless, Dwan—in his characteristic fashion—leavens the darkness of *Silver Lode* with lots of humor that often pokes fun at human pomposity and other foibles. Early on, we meet a lawyer who can't resist speaking before the local judge in ridiculously overblown language. His line "Who among us is without a blot on his escutcheon?" is very funny. Later, we hear a father who—despite all the serious things that are occurring—declares his displeasure that his son won't get the chance to deliver the 4th of July speech he's prepared. And throughout the film, Dolores Moran's Dolly—one of the smartest characters in the story—fires off funny, often cutting one-liners to other characters. For example, at one point when the local telegraph operator complains to her about "frying my brains out in the hot sun fixing wire," she doesn't miss a beat, responding, "Oh, your brains were fried before that." Although this humor isn't essential to the story, it is a good complement to the more serious action and a way of giving added dimension and nuance to the world being portrayed.

Finally, especially for a low-budget "quickie," *Silver Lode* was made with great care and craftsmanship. Many of the scenes have a dynamic, vibrant quality about them. The final chase scenes, where Ballard is using every trick in the book to stay alive, are good examples. Ballard and the camera are both moving constantly, and, in the process, we see the town of Silver Lode—and the ruined 4th of July festivities—from all kinds of different, and intriguing points of view. Enhancing Dwan's inventive staging is John Alton's beautiful cinematography, which—although in color—often suggests, with elegantly rendered shadows and other dark images (as in the stable scenes), the frightening noir world that Ballard has fallen into. And adding to the mood is a fine musical score by veteran composer Roy Webb, whose other credits include work on such classic noirs as *Notorious*, *The Locket*, and *Out of the Past*. The dark, ominous musical theme that follows McCarty and his henchmen throughout the film is especially effective. *Silver Lode* may have been made quickly and on a small budget, but it was made with the kind of thoughtfulness and respect for the subject matter that often doesn't go into major productions.

"What might have been if...?"

If there were ever a fitting epitaph for Allan Dwan, it may very well be that eternal question: "What might have been if...?" Considering both his enormous output of high-quality work during the 1910s and 1920s and the enormous promise that he showed entering Hollywood's Golden Age in the early 1930s, we have to wonder what he would have achieved if he had made some different business decisions, worked with different producers, and/or been pickier about scripts and projects. Certainly, by 1929, he was considered just as accomplished—if not more so—than directing contemporaries such as Frank Capra, John Ford, Raoul Walsh, William Wellman, and others. And he clearly was capable of adapting to changes in the industry and growing as an artist; the parade had by no means passed him by. But, as the careers of these other directors flourished, his mostly persevered in the shadows of the low-budget netherworld. Yes, what might have been *if* Dwan had received that career-changing opportunity that would, in turn, have led to better scripts, bigger budgets, and—perhaps—far greater commercial and critical success? No one who ever worked with him doubted that he was just as talented and committed to quality as other directors whose careers far eclipsed his.

In a smaller way, too, we can make a similar point in relation to Dwan's late minor-masterpiece, *Silver Lode*. Although the director made several other westerns during the 1950s, none is as noir-ish in storyline or tone as this is. That's our loss, because it would have been interesting to see what else Dwan might have done with the noir western form—where else he might have been able to take it. In *Silver Lode*, he seamlessly blends the noir "wrongly accused man" theme with a critique of McCarthyism, commentary on the fickleness of the mob, some witty humor, and some riveting action to create a very artful and satisfying entertainment. *Silver Lode* is clearly a noir western, but among dark westerns it has a sensibility all its own—a sensibility we can easily trace back to the main creative force behind it, the ever-inventive Allan Dwan.

9

Helping the Western to Grow Up
The Complex, Shaded Characters in Delmer Daves' *3:10 to Yuma* and *The Hanging Tree*

"Every new mining camp's gotta have its hanging tree. It makes folks feel respectable."—*The Hanging Tree*

If we count an appearance he made at age 11 in a 1915 silent film called *A Christmas Memory,* Delmer Daves (1904–1977) had a 50-year Hollywood film career as a bit actor, prop boy, screenwriter, producer, and—most significantly—director. He received his first directing assignment in 1943 and between then and 1965 made 24 films in different genres from westerns to war stories, noirs, adventure stories, and romantic melodramas. While he was responsible for highly regarded war films such as 1945's *Pride of the Marines* and edgy, suspenseful noirs such as 1947's *The Red House* and *Dark Passage,* he is best known today for his westerns. He made eight of them, all during the 1950s, and in the process he exerted an enormous influence on the genre. His very first, 1950's *Broken Arrow,* continues to receive widespread praise for its respectful, sympathetic treatment of Native Americans, something that was almost non-existent in westerns at the time. As the decade progressed, his westerns also dug more deeply into the human psyche, often blurring the traditional western stereotypes of good guys, bad guys, virtuous women, and barroom "hussies" and giving western fans more complex and shaded characters that, as such, were more identifiable and compelling. He was instrumental in helping to make the western more authentic emotionally, in helping the genre to grow up.

Part of Daves' contribution was to give many of his stories a darker, more

9. Helping the Western to Grow Up

noir-like edge. Most of his western heroes, for example, are survivors of traumatic events and have the emotional scars to prove it—scars that influence their views of the world and the ways they interact with it. The communities of people the heroes interact with also have their dark sides. In a few of his westerns, groups with respectable intentions can—with a twist here and there—quickly turn bloodthirsty. In several of his westerns, racism—especially toward Native Americans and Hispanics—is a prominent theme. And, in all of his westerns, the scope—like most noirs—remains small and contained. Daves was not as interested in vast, sweeping epics as many of his peers were. As the critics like to say, he worked on a smaller canvas, focusing intently on the internal and external struggles of a handful of individuals trying to survive in a usually harsh world.

After receiving a law degree from Stanford, Delmer Daves chose to work in the movies, first as a writer, then as a director, then sometimes as a writer-director-producer. Today, his best-remembered work is his series of intelligent, adult 1950s westerns.

If we wanted to, we could probably find enough noir content in five or six of Daves' westerns to qualify them for this book. His 1956 film *Jubal*, for example, has been called "Othello on the range."[1] Mirroring the Shakespeare tragedy, it features a sensitive hero thrust into the middle of a tricky domestic situation that involves an insecure older rancher, his beautiful young wife, and a conniving ranch hand who's bent on exploiting the rancher's inability to manage that "green-eyed monster," jealousy. *The Last Wagon* (also 1956) features a traumatized white hero who uses "Comanche justice" to avenge the deaths of his Comanche wife and two sons. And his *The Badlanders* (1958) is actually a remake of the 1950 noir classic, John Huston's *The Asphalt Jungle*.

Among Daves' westerns, however, two of the most noir-like both in their sensibility and style are also two of the best. The first is, along with *Broken Arrow*, perhaps Daves' most famous film—1957's *3:10 to Yuma*. Made in black and white when most westerns, including even the lowest of the low-budget efforts, were being made in color, it could have easily been re-imagined as a late 1940s or early 1950s crime noir. It has, in fact, most of the key noir ingredients—bleak town settings; claustrophobic interior scenes; odd, anxiety-provoking camera angles; taut, edgy dialogue; nerve-racking suspense; and a strong sense of identification between hero and villain. The second, 1959's *The Hanging Tree*, while not as well known, is no less fascinating. Its hero is a man living with a past trauma who can be alternately kind or cruel and who, even though he struggles with it, remains cold and aloof even from those who offer him friendship or affection. The film also features one of the most chilling sequences in any Daves film—scenes of a large raucous crowd's celebration of a gold strike that, with very little provocation, turns into a crazed lynch mob.

"The Honest Man of the Western"

Despite his early flirtation with film as a bit player in *A Christmas Memory*, the young Delmer Daves was determined to study law. But, while a student at Stanford University, he took a summer job as a prop boy on the 1923 silent epic, *The Covered Wagon*. Although he did finish his law degree, he eventually relocated in Hollywood full time and found work in various capacities. Before long, he was once again playing bit parts. Then, by the early 1930s, he was getting screenwriting credits in such Dick Powell-Ruby Keeler musicals as 1934's *Dames* and *Flirtation Walk*. The writing assignments kept coming, and by the early 1940s he had several major credits under his belt, including 1936's *The Petrified Forest* with Bette Davis and Humphrey Bogart, 1939's *Love Affair* with Charles Boyer and Irene Dunne, and 1942's *You Were Never Lovelier* with Fred Astaire and Rita Hayworth. As Hollywood lore goes, one of his talents as a dialogue writer during this time was his ability to construct dialogue for the actress Kay Francis that never included the letter "r." This was to compensate for a speech impediment she had that pronounced each "r" as if it were a "w."

Daves' first directing effort (a film he also scripted) was the crisp 1943 war adventure *Destination Tokyo*, but perhaps his major breakthrough was 1945's *Pride of the Marines*, a moving story about a "man's man" Marine (wonderfully played by John Garfield) who must undergo a grueling rehabilitation from war injuries and, in the process, learns to overcome his own bitterness and live with his disability. The August 1945 *New York Times* review praised the film for its ability to treat the difficult subject matter "with uncommon compassion, understanding and dignity, as well as with absorbing human interest."[2]

Soon Daves was deep into the strange, tortured world of noir, writing and directing the 1947 films *The Red House* with Edward G. Robinson and *Dark Passage* with Bogart and Bacall. Far from a big hit when it was released, *The Red House* (a story about a mysterious farmer and his dark secret) has since become a favorite of many noir enthusiasts including director Martin Scorsese. *Dark Passage* is an experimental film that exploits the use of the point of view camera for the first third of the story. It remains a fascinating, although largely self-conscious, curiosity.

Taking his cue from other noted noir directors such as André de Toth and Anthony Mann, Daves soon moved into westerns and, in 1950, made one of his most admired, *Broken Arrow*. Based on actual events—the negotiations that eventually led to a peace treaty between the U.S. government and the Apaches in the 1870s—the heart of the film is the relationship between former U.S. Army scout Tom Jeffords (James Stewart) and Apache chief Cochise (Jeff Chandler). Although white actors played most of the Apaches (clearly not a break from traditional Hollywood practice) and characters were romanticized, the treatment of Cochise and other Native Americans was generally quite sympathetic for a western at the time. They were portrayed with intelligence and great sensitivity, as people who are as wary and fearful of the white settlers as the whites are of them. To give viewers a more complete sense of "Apache-ness," the dialogue—when actors are supposed to be speaking the Apache language—often has a lovely poetic quality to it. When Cochise approaches a young Apache woman in a healing ritual, for example, he tells her: "I have old wounds." To this, the woman replies: "Yes, but each scar is a mark of love for your people. The path of your people is stretched long behind you, and you are the head and you are the heart and you are the blood.... You will be well."

After a string of forgettable films (mostly action-adventure stories) in the early 1950s, Daves returned to the western mid-decade, making six between 1956 and 1959 and, as was his habit, often writing the scripts for them as well. While these films are all different, they all share several characteristics: a tight, in-depth focus on a small number of characters; an interest in the duality of human nature; and, for the most part, an absence of typical western stereotypes. Sometimes in these films, Daves' ability to see beyond the stereotypes was quite innovative and influential. One example is *3:10 to Yuma* with its charming, immensely likable villain and its stolid, plodding hero who is, in many ways, envious of his adversary. Another is 1958's *Cowboy*. As film historian Patricia King Hanson writes: "Although ostensibly a comic western, *Cowboy* had an underlying anti-macho theme ahead of its time. In the beginning of the film the main characters, played by Glenn Ford and Jack Lemmon, are opposites: Ford a traditional 'he-man' cowboy, and Lemmon a tenderfoot. By the end of the film both characters become aware of the opposite sides of their own natures. At least a decade before the theme became popular, *Cowboy* showed that men's hard and soft sides could co-exist and could make entertaining subject matter for a motion picture."[3]

In 1959, Daves' career took still another turn, moving from westerns to a series of youth-oriented romantic melodramas (all featuring Troy Donahue) in the early 1960s, the 1963 family drama *Spencer's Mountain* (which inspired the long-running television series, *The Waltons*), and a couple of additional offerings. While they are not considered Daves' best work, it can be a mistake to write these films off altogether. As Hanson notes about them, "Daves's writing and direction make the work much better than its subject matter would suggest. Like his contemporary Douglas Sirk, whose films have been criticized in terms similar to those directed at Daves, his films are actually richer than general critical opinion would seem to indicate."[4]

After his poorly received *The Battle of Villa Florita* in 1965, Daves retired from filmmaking. He lived quietly in Southern California until his death in 1977.

While Daves was active as both a writer and a director for more than 30 years, contributed to several classic 1930s films as a writer, wrote and directed respected noirs, and made an impression with his early 1960s "young love" films, his 1950s westerns are his most personal and most distinctive films. As writer Brian Garfield notes in his survey of American westerns, "Daves is in fact the author of an amazingly diverse oeuvre. It is as if he intended to create a vast tableau chronicling the evolution of the West, focusing not on glamorous, legendary figures and events, but rather on more humble, modest, and particularized dramas. His *mise en scene* is similarly varied, though its modest self-effacement has led to ill-considered charges of aesthetic paucity. Daves's very considerable strengths and virtues are best summed up by one French critic's description of him as 'the honest man of the western.'"[5]

"You must need money awful bad to do this": 3:10 to Yuma

Based on the 1953 short story "Three-Ten to Yuma" by the great western-turned-crime fiction writer Elmore Leonard, Daves' *3:10 to Yuma* is, along with Budd Boetticher's *The Tall T*, one of the first of the writer's many stories and novels to be adapted to film. And today, after numerous critically acclaimed adaptations of Leonard's work including—among others—1967's *Hombre*, 1995's *Get Shorty*, 1998's *Out of Sight*, 1997's *Jackie Brown*, and 2007's remake of *3:10 to Yuma*, it remains one of the best.

The film begins with a stagecoach robbery orchestrated by the notorious Ben Wade (Glenn Ford) and his gang of about a dozen hardened bad men. When the driver of the stage resists, Wade shoots him dead without a second thought.

On a nearby hill witnessing the events are Dan Evans (Van Heflin)—a rancher struggling to keep his small spread afloat despite a three-year drought—and his two young sons. The boys want their father to do something to help those being robbed, but, unarmed and far outnumbered, he can't.

The action now shifts to nearby Bisbee, Arizona, where Wade and his men visit a saloon and Wade, with great bravado, tells Emmy (Felicia Farr), a barmaid, that they *witnessed* a robbery and murder. She alerts the marshal (Ford Rainey), who assembles a posse. The marshal is uneasy about these 12 strangers and waits until they leave town before he and the posse head to the coach. Unknown to the marshal, however, Wade stays, telling his right-hand man that he'll catch up with his men later. He then returns to the saloon and charms Emmy into bed.

After their interlude, Wade, knowing that he will soon be leaving for good, asks Emmy if she has any regrets, but, in a curious bit of reflection, she tells him that she is not the least bit unhappy. "I ain't complainin'," she says wistfully. "I got something to remember. It's funny. Some men you can see every day for 10 years and you never notice. Some men you see once and they're with you the rest of your life."

Hearing that Wade may still be in town, the posse, along with Dan Evans, returns and captures him. Knowing that Wade's gang will soon be back for him, the marshal hatches a scheme to sneak Wade into nearby Contention City, where he can board the 3:10 train to Yuma the next day, be tried for his crimes, and be imprisoned in the penitentiary there. At first, Dan doesn't want to participate, but, when Mr. Butterfield (Robert Emhardt), the owner of the stage line, offers him $200, he agrees because he desperately needs the money to keep his ranch going. As all the men leave to carry out this plan, Emmy stands alone in the middle of town and watches Wade and everyone else disappear into the dust created by the stage and their horses.

Knowing that Wade's gang is watching the posse's every move, the first part of the marshal's plan is to secretly move Wade from the stage carrying him to Dan's ranch and send the stage on as a decoy. Dan and another deputy

Rancher turned law enforcer Dan Evans (Van Heflin, right) is determined to get cagey outlaw Ben Wade (Glenn Ford) on the train at the appointed time in Daves' 1957 masterpiece *3:10 to Yuma*. Throughout this film, the extended use of confined, often-claustrophobic interiors, a standard feature of noir crime dramas, helps to intensify the drama.

9. Helping the Western to Grow Up 157

who's also the town drunk, Alex Potter (Henry Jones), will then sneak Wade to Contention City under cover of night.

At the Evans ranch, Wade dines with Dan, his sons, and his wife, Alice (Leora Dana). Again, he uses his charms on a woman he sees as vulnerable, and—because Dan lacks Wade's personal charm and money—he becomes jealous.

He has to put aside his feelings, however, because he and Potter have to take Wade to Contention City. Before the three leave that night, the ever-confident Wade tells Alice: "I hope I can send him [Dan] back to you all right."

The next morning, they arrive and—with Butterfield's help—Dan puts Wade into a hotel room, the bridal suite. The plan is for Dan to guard Wade while Potter acts as lookout.

With a tired, anxious Dan all to himself in the confined room, the clever, calculating Wade begins to probe for soft spots. "You must need money awful bad to do this," he begins.

"Maybe I do," Dan says.

Wade then starts offering Dan large amounts of money, spurring Dan to tell him: "Do me a favor, will you? Don't talk to me for a while."

But Wade keeps probing, keeps trying to get under his skin. Knowing how much Dan loves his wife, he says: "I'll tell you one thing though, Dan. I'd treat her a whole lot better than you do. I'd feed her better. I'd get her real pretty dresses she'd be real happy wearing. I wouldn't make her work so hard, Dan. I bet she was a real beautiful girl before she met you."

At this, Dan becomes furious, but he maintains control, saying repeatedly that he is committed to putting Wade on the 3:10 to Yuma.

Knowing that Wade's gang will certainly catch up with them, Dan also asks Butterfield to round up some men to help. Butterfield obliges. But, when Wade's gang returns, the men, sensing the futility of the situation, refuse to participate. Potter is then shot and hanged in the hotel lobby as an example. Alice now comes to see Dan, professes her love, and begs him not to go through with this plan. Dan, however, feels that this is something he just has to do—not just for the money or her but for himself.

Then, even Butterfield, who has steadfastly supported the effort, sees the hopelessness of the situation and tells Dan he won't accompany him to the train station. Deeply disappointed, Dan asks Butterfield to get Alice out of town as soon as possible.

About 3:00, the walk to the train station begins. Using Wade as his "human shield," Dan makes it all the way to the station. But the gang catches them. One of its members tells Wade to crouch down so they can get a clean shot at Dan. But surprisingly, Wade doesn't. Instead, he jumps on the train with Dan.

As the train leaves Wade's gang behind, Dan seems stunned by this turn of events, but Wade says with characteristic bravado, "I've broken out of Yuma before."

Alongside the tracks, Dan sees Alice standing on her buckboard with Butterfield standing near her. She beams with relief and pride. Then, in a final touch, it begins to rain. The drought that had been haunting Dan may now be over as well.

Like *Silver Lode* and several other westerns made during the 1950s, *3:10 to Yuma* owes a debt to Fred Zinnemann's 1952 western, *High Noon*. Similar to the Zinnemann film, it's about a man who—even after just about everyone else abandons him—still summons the courage to face the bad guys head on, do the right thing, defy the odds, and prevail. Most of it takes place in a very compressed period of time, with repeated shots of timepieces playing an essential part in heightening the tension and suspense. And it even has a very memorable theme song that's played to great effect as the story unfolds and pays off handsomely in the film's finale.

But *3:10 to Yuma* is clearly its own film, one that is notable for its complex, non-stereotypical characters; rich black-and-white visual design; and noir-ish style and sensibility. In many ways, it's a very intriguing blend of its two principal authors, Leonard and Daves, mixing Leonard's well-defined characters, grim situations, and sharp, stark dialogue with Daves' talent for realizing small, narrowly focused western dramas filled with high stakes and deep feeling for the characters.

In fact, perhaps the film's most fascinating element might just be its many original, well-developed characters, none of which fully conforms to the western stereotypes audiences were used to seeing in 1957.

The first of these is Ben Wade, ostensibly the villain. Wade is certainly not the first interesting bad guy to appear in a western, but, in 1957, he may very well have been the *most* fascinating one to date. In fact, his closest competitor at the time may be another character originated by Leonard, Frank Usher (Richard Boone), who appears in Budd Boetticher's *The Tall T* (also 1957). Both Wade and Usher are more than just bad men; they are individuals who think not only about themselves but also about those around them. Each has a distinctive point of view, a sense of irony about the odd situations each finds himself in, and (even though it's often twisted) great sensitivity for those around him. Each is also envious of things in life that the hero possesses that he lacks—things such as a ranch, a loving wife and family, or the good will of his community. Two facets, however, set them apart. First, Wade has a great deal more charm, especially with women. For Emmy, he is irresistible, and, as she declares, even though she has known him very briefly, she will remember him for the rest of her life. Second, Wade, by the end of the story, connects so strongly with Dan Evans that—instead of letting his gang kill Dan—he sacrifices his freedom (at least for a while) to spare Dan's life. He is a dynamic character who undergoes a major change—something new for a villain in a western.

Writing for Turner Classic Movies, Rob Nixon also suggests that Ben Wade is even more. "It may be reasonably posited that Wade is actually the central character of the piece, despite being the villain," says Nixon. "Instead of being merely the obstacle to the hero's mission, he is in many ways the force that prods Van Heflin's Dan Evans into a higher moral duty and toward taking greater risks for what is ultimately right."[6]

As western heroes go, Dan Evans is also quite different. Far from the strong, silent, supremely self-confident type, he is a struggling rancher who feels that he's let his wife and sons down—that he's been a failure as a family man and provider. He's also envious of Wade, especially of his money and his charm, things he can't give his wife. In addition, he struggles with committing to the posse that plans to take Wade to Contention City. Initially, he doesn't want to get involved. Later, he agrees to help simply for the money. Finally, he follows through on the commitment not for the money but because he sees this course of action as something he must do to reclaim his own self-respect. He, too, is a dynamic character who grows and changes as the story unfolds. An interesting catalyst in his change, incidentally, is Alex Potter, who is eager to prove his worth as part of the posse and meets a sad end. As Dan tells Alice: "The town drunk gave his life because be believed that people should be able to live in decency and peace together. Do you think I can do less?"

The women in the story are not the ordinary western females, either. Particularly intriguing is Emmy, whose small but key role both helps to illustrate Wade's great charisma and is in its own right quite touching and moving. Her wonderful short speech about his sticking with her for the rest of her life is nothing less than poetry. Alice, too, is not simply the loyal, steadfast wife we've seen in many westerns. At first, she seems annoyed by Dan's defeatist attitude. Later, she regrets pushing him into taking action when she sees that his activism might very well lead to his death. As Wade and Evans are counterpoints to each other, each having specific strengths and conveying different worldviews, so too are Emmy and Alice. Alice might have a good, dutiful man by her side for many years, for example, but will she ever have the sublime but fleeting moment that Emmy has with the very seductive—and dangerous—Ben Wade?

Many of the smaller, character roles have something special about them as well. Butterfield is more than simply the cowardly capitalist stereotype we often see in westerns. He is sincere about doing the right thing, but he is also a realist. When he feels that staying the course will probably result in his death, he backs down but feels great shame and guilt about doing so. Potter is more than the stereotypical town drunk, too, and, in his poignant efforts to prove himself, he presages Dean Martin's memorable "Dude" character in Hawks' *Rio Bravo* two years later. Even Wade's number-one henchman (Richard Jaeckel) has a quirky sense of humor and a fondness for telling others misleading stories to achieve his ends. In one scene, for example, he has a humorous exchange with a naïve bartender when he talks about tracking down his runaway wife and wondering why she left because he was usually a good husband who "never hit her too hard."

In addition, the actors who portrayed these characters all invested a great deal in their roles. Particularly good is Glenn Ford, an extremely likable actor who almost always played good guys in films. Ford apparently lobbied hard to be cast against type in this film, and Columbia Pictures' decision to oblige him paid off in a big way. He took his good looks, charm, intelligence, wit, and all the other "winning" attributes he usually brought to his heroic roles and twisted them around to great effect. It's clear, too, that he's having great fun playing Ben Wade. Van Heflin does an excellent job of fleshing out Dan Evan as well, making an essentially colorless character quite engaging and sometimes riveting. In the other key roles—Felicia Farr's Emmy, Leora Dana's Alice, Robert Empardt's Butterfield, Henry Jones' Potter, and Richard Jaeckel's henchman—the actors all put something special into what they were doing, and the effort shows. This is one of those rare westerns (before or since) where not merely one or two but most of the key characters rise well above the stereotypes, and, along with the film's writing and direction, the actors deserve much of the credit for this film's effectiveness.

Just as the film's complex characters are more reminiscent of a noir crime drama than a traditional western, its visual design is clearly and consciously noir. When nearly all westerns at this time were shot in lush Technicolor, Daves and his cinematographer, Charles Lawton, made the bold decision to shoot in black and white in order to emphasize the bleakness of the time and place and the starkness of the choices the characters, especially Dan Evans, must make. To underscore the impact of the drought on his ranch (and his life),

Daves and Lawton even used special red filters to make the Arizona landscape seem even more parched and arid than it actually was. In addition, there are curious noir touches such as the sharp, sword-like fence posts Evans and Wade pass by on their walk to the train near the film's end, images suggesting that the situation is fraught with danger. The camera placement, especially in the lobby of the hotel where Evans holds Wade, is also very noir-like, many shots coming from odd, extreme angles to heighten viewer anxiety. And perhaps the most noir-like visual touch of all is the claustrophobic nature of the small hotel room where Evans holds Wade captive. A facet of *3:10 to Yuma* that has inspired some writers to call it a "chamber western,"[7] this extreme spatial confinement—the antithesis of the expansive use of space we see in most westerns—dramatizes not only how Wade but *both* men are trapped by this situation.

Over the years, some critics have viewed Ben Wade's unexpected change of heart at the end of the story as weakness of the film. It's true that *3:10 to Yuma* would have been more uncompromising as a noir if Wade hadn't changed. But the change is also consistent with Wade's personal code, something that's been well established. Evans saved Wade's life earlier in the story. So, by Wade's estimation, he owes Evans one. Besides, as we learn, sparing Evans isn't such a big deal in Wade's mind, because he will most likely bust out of Yuma, anyway.

"*3:10 to Yuma* is affecting and exciting because its director, Delmer Daves…[has] imbued it with a deep respect for the implicit promise of its story and with a skill for invention at once simple and daring," film writer Blake Lucas has noted.[8] And it's difficult to argue. The film is built around a strong plot and complex, thoughtfully conceived characters—solid foundations that allow Daves, Lawton, and others to tell the story directly and boldly—no frills, just thrills. In an era of great noir-ish westerns, this spare, unpretentious effort is a standout.

"A man with frail hope": The Hanging Tree

Filmed near Yakima, Washington, in the summer of 1958 and released in February of 1959, *The Hanging Tree* is the last of Daves' eight westerns. Considered a modest commercial and critical success in its day, it has, over the years, gradually attracted a small but fervent following of admirers. In 2012, for example, film writer Glenn Erickson called it a "wonderment."[9] In its *Companion to the Western*, the British Film Institute has also noted: "This is Daves' most complex and ambitious film and certainly his finest western…. [I]t is a brooding, romantic, opaque work of great dramatic intensity and breathtaking visual beauty."[10]

Whether or not we fully agree with these assessments, *The Hanging Tree* is nevertheless a very moving film—one that takes us deep inside its leading character; probes how past personal trauma can affect present behavior; explores the dark, avaricious sides of people; considers the horrors of the mob mentality; and—in the end—certainly makes a strong and lasting impression on viewers. From a directorial perspective, it has often been praised for its imaginative and dynamic use of space, exploiting the outdoor locales near Yakima to build tension and fuel audience anxiety. This is a fascinating departure in approach from Daves' films such as *3:10 to Yuma* and *The Badlanders*, which largely depend on very confined settings (a hotel room and a cave) to achieve similar results.

The film begins with an exodus of people heading to what we learn to be a new mining camp in Montana called Skull Creek. One of them is Dr. Joe Frail (Gary Cooper). As several of the travelers pass the outskirts of the camp, they notice a grim-looking hanging tree and one says: "Every new mining camp's gotta have its hanging tree. It makes folks feel respectable." Frail then passes it and, before moving on, gives it a serious looking over.

Once in town, Frail buys a nearby cabin to set up his medical practice and soon afterwards rescues a young man named Rune (Ben Piazza) from a sure trip to the hanging tree after he tries to steal gold from a claim and is wounded. Frail removes a bullet from Rune's chest, but doesn't like the young man's attitude and threatens to expose Rune unless he becomes Frail's indentured servant "maybe forever." Rune doesn't like this one bit but has no real choice but to comply.

Soon a stagecoach is robbed and overturned near town. The driver and a male passenger are killed, but the passenger's adult daughter is missing and may have survived. People in town form a search party, and the woman, Elizabeth Mahler (Maria Schell), is discovered by Frenchy (Karl Malden), a loud, crude man with a fierce appetite for everything from gold to women.

Burned, blinded, and dehydrated, all from overexposure, Elizabeth is brought to a house next to Frail's so he can oversee her recovery. As Elizabeth's burns heal, she becomes increasingly fond of Frail and Rune.

Noticing that she is quite beautiful, Frenchy sneaks in one day and tries to kiss her against her wishes. Seeing this, Frail chases him out, pursues him, beats him up, and threatens to kill him if he ever tries anything like that again. Gradually, Frail takes not just a protective but also a controlling attitude over her, suggesting that Skull Creek is no place for her and that she should leave.

9. Helping the Western to Grow Up

Daves' last western, 1959's *The Hanging Tree* stars Gary Cooper as Dr. Joe Frail, a mysterious man with a dark past, who ultimately finds love with Elizabeth (Maria Schell), a woman he nurses back to health after she is injured. While ultimately redemptive, the film has many noir-ish elements, including a very disturbing depiction of mob violence.

In time, Elizabeth regains her sight and begins to express romantic feelings for Frail. Coldly, though, he rejects her overtures. Frustrated and annoyed by his controlling nature, she leaves Frail and—declaring Skull Creek her new home—decides to team with Rune and Frenchy on a gold claim. To fund their effort, she pawns a family heirloom. Unknown to her, however, it is virtually worthless. Frail finds out and tells the pawnbroker to let her believe it is valuable and to give her whatever she needs to work the claim. Frail will supply the funding secretly. So, even though she believes she has escaped Frail's control, he—effectively—is still in charge.

Eventually, though, she finds out about Frail's secret funding and asks Frail why he can't respond to her affection. He reveals that his wife had once had an affair with his own brother. He found them together, both dead in an apparent murder-suicide. In a rage, he burned down their house with their bodies in it. He tells Elizabeth he is "not allowed to forget." And we learn why he has chosen the name "Frail," because, as he had once remarked, "it suited a man with frail hope."

After this—and just as a discouraged Frenchy is about to call it quits with their claim—Elizabeth, Frenchy, and Rune all strike it rich, finding a "glory hole" of gold under a tree stump. They ride into town in triumph, Frenchy freely tossing pieces of gold all about them. The celebration, however, quickly turns into drunkenness and then to a riot. Frenchy takes advantage of the commotion to make advances on Elizabeth. She rejects him, sparking a brutal physical assault and attempted rape. Again, Frail catches Frenchy, and this time he shoots him in self-defense. By now, the mob is also very excited (some members in their enthusiasm even setting buildings on fire), and one character with a grudge against Frail incites the mob to lynch him for killing Frenchy. Now, in a frenzied fury, the mob takes him to the hanging tree and strings him up. Rune and Elizabeth rush in carrying their gold and the deed to the claim. Elizabeth offers everything to the townsfolk if they will let Frail live. As the mob members fight each other to grab the gold and the deed, the lynching becomes less important and the crowd moves away from the hanging tree.

Frail is deeply touched by what Elizabeth has done, and, as Rune takes the noose off, Frail asks Elizabeth to come to him.

In many respects, *The Hanging Tree* is more like a traditional 1950s western than a noir. Its heroine is good and true. Its villain has few, if any, redeeming qualities. It's brimming with rough, churning energy. And it's filmed in vibrant color against a vast, sprawling landscape.

From the first shots, however, when we notice the name on the main character's black doctor's bag, "Frail," we sense that what we'll be seeing is, at least in some respects, different from a traditional western. One of the key narrative characteristics of film noir is its emphasis on the ambivalence and alienation of principal characters in an uncertain, sometimes threatening world. And, perhaps more fully than any character in a Daves western, Dr. Joe Frail—the man "with frail hope"—fits this description. On one hand, Frail is very competent and kind. In addition to his work as a doctor, he shows his considerable skills as everything from a gunman and fist fighter to a gambler and businessman. He's intelligent, shrewd, and exceedingly able. He also has a big heart, once even lending a poor family his own cow to help feed a malnourished girl with milk. On the other hand, he has a dark side. After he removes the bullet from Rune, for example, he treats the young man very harshly—forcing him into indentured servitude, perhaps indefinitely. And, after he nurses Elizabeth back to health, he coldly rejects her great warmth and affection. We learn, of course, that one reason for his cold, distant, and sometimes harsh behavior is the traumatic event—finding his brother and adulterous wife dead from a murder-suicide—that's about as noir-ish a memory as they come. It's curious, too, how Frail's good and dark sides sometimes co-mingle. One of the most interesting examples in the film is—after he rejects Elizabeth's affections—when he secretly funds her gold mining efforts. This is a conflicted, emotionally scarred man, one who is capable of caring deeply but also one who is anxious and fearful about again bearing the intense personal pain that can come when love goes wrong.

In addition to the Frail character, *The Hanging Tree* has other intriguing noir attributes worth examining.

Certainly, one is the film's dark view of human nature, showing how a community that seeks out a doctor to heal its members one day can quickly, and viciously, be ready to hang him the next. We see this of course in the film's bizarre, disturbing mob sequence. The celebration of a gold strike spurs some overly enthusiastic people to start burning parts of the camp. Some people respond as a volunteer fire brigade, while others—whipped up in the hysteria and hearing that Frail has killed Frenchy—immediately want to lynch him. Then, only after Elizabeth offers the townspeople both all the gold she has and her claim, do they stop the lynching. There are no apologies or even embarrassed expressions on their faces. As film writer Leonard Quart notes: "The film's view of human nature is pretty dark; the men in the camp are ... an easily manipulated, uncontrolled mob that only can be diverted from murder by avarice—in the form of gold coins offered them."[11] Glenn Erickson takes this a step farther, suggesting that "one could, I suppose, interpret the movie's town as a representation of America as a lawless madhouse full of greedy, reckless maniacs."[12]

Another noir attribute is the film's clever and very original use of its Washington state landscapes—especially a cliff overlooking Skull Creek—to heighten anxiety and suspense. More often—and much like Daves does during the hotel lobby and room scenes in *3:10 to Yuma*—noir films focus on small, confined settings and unusually high or low camera angles to create a similar effect. In *The Hanging Tree*, the land itself is dangerous. One scene that, in its own way, is particularly noir-ish is when a still-blind Elizabeth runs out of the house where she is recovering and right to the edge of the cliff overlooking Skull Creek. Here, she hears the raucous sounds of the people and the town, and stops, confused, disoriented, and quite frightened. It's a terrifying moment for her, and one that also suggests other fears she is experiencing at this point in the story. Another scene is when men searching for Elizabeth have found the wreckage of the stagecoach. The leader of the group instructs the men about their next steps. But what's disturbing here is the camera placement, emphasizing neither the leader nor the men but instead the vastness of the territory they need to cover and the difficulty—if not impossibility—of the job they have before them. While praising other aspects of the film, the 1959 *Variety* review noted that "the main contribution comes from the director" and his ability to exploit "the natural splendor of the Washington location."[13] Also praising the imaginative use of locations, Erickson has called this Daves' "best all-around film as a director."[14]

As with *3:10 to Yuma* and most of Daves' other westerns, two other major strengths of *The Hanging Tree* are the characterizations and the performances Daves was able to get from the actors. Joe Frail is a very complicated character filled with numerous quirks and contradictions, and Gary Cooper (in one of his last roles) invests a great deal in him. Frail isn't merely a collection of attributes but a real, credible person. The character of Elizabeth could have easily become overly sentimentalized, but Maria Schell does something very special with her. Erickson even goes as far as to call the role and the portrayal "transcendent," making Elizabeth "one of the most soulful and vibrant women in American westerns."[15] Frenchy is clearly a brute and a narcissist, but Karl Malden gives him a good measure of humor along with other ordinary, identifiable characteristics. Quart has praised Malden's "strong performance," as one that "turns Frenchy into a recognizable, odious human being rather than a one-dimensional villain."[16]

While there is a great deal of darkness and savagery in *The Hanging Tree*, part of the film's power lies in its very moving ending. Both Elizabeth and Frail are able to heal themselves of their own literal and figurative blindness—to see things around them in a new and more life-affirming way. And all of this comes together wonderfully in the final moments. "The film's ending is sublime, almost Biblical in its purity," Erickson writes. "What will redeem a man who no longer believes in love or trust? Cooper and Schell make us believe one of the best-earned romantic finishes in the era of the classic Big-Sky 50s western."[17]

―⚞―

While Daves' films such as *Broken Arrow* and *3:10 to Yuma* are still very much part of the continuing conversation about classic Hollywood films in general and notable 1950s westerns in particular, Daves himself and several of his other fine films (both westerns and non-westerns) have been unfairly left out. Part of the reason again is that—like Henry King, Allan Dwan, and others—Daves had a simple, direct, unpretentious directorial style that did not draw sufficient attention to itself and was deemed inferior to the more obvious, flamboyant styles of some other directors. Again, too, this is a great pity. Certainly in his westerns (and often in his other films as well) there is a specific and recognizable sensibility behind them—a worldview, if you will. For Daves, the characters and their personal struggles in a wild and often hard land—not directorial flourishes—were what mattered, and he examined these characters with intelligence, maturity, and unusual sensitivity. In fact, we might even be so bold as to call him the great humanist of the 1950s western—one who not only brought more complex, shaded characters and other noir touches to the genre but who also helped to take it to new levels of maturity. All those who made (and continue to make) westerns after Daves, owe him a considerable debt.

10

"They're going to kill us, Mrs. Mims"
Horror and Absurdity Ride Together in Budd Boetticher's *The Tall T* and *Ride Lonesome*

"Fancy runnin' into you in all this empty."—*Ride Lonesome*

Among the directors of 1950s Hollywood westerns, Budd Boetticher (1916–2001) had a special knack for bringing together the best of the old and new genre styles. On one hand, his most memorable films—a handful he made with actor Randolph Scott in the late 1950s—pay eloquent tribute to the traditional western. Their quiet, earnest, stoic heroes (all played by Scott—perhaps the ultimate strong, silent type) look the evildoers straight in the eye without even the hint of a flinch. Their females are usually good, true women who just need the right man. Their landscapes are often grand and picturesque. And, while not always simple, their morality is usually clear: we know who's good, who's not, and who falls in between. On the other hand, these films are anything but traditional westerns. The heroes, even as they stare down the evildoers, develop curious, complex, and ever-evolving relationships with them. In the few films in which the good woman and the hero ultimately get together, a sense of loneliness and loss still hovers over the proceedings; there is never a clear-cut happy ending. The landscapes, which can sometimes appear grand and picturesque, more often look bare, bleak, and unforgiving—the tall, smooth, stately rocks that frame the characters seeming as lonely as the people. These films are not noir in the strictest sense; there is no doomed hero, femme fatale, or nightmarish expressionistic dreamscape. But an unmistakable stream of noir flows through them. These are clearly not westerns in which communities of hearty settlers pull together to "civilize" the wild places and build the great nation. They are stark tales of survival or revenge in a grim world where everyone is ultimately alone; human existence is unsparing and frequently brutal; the universe is indifferent; and, if you're clever enough or lucky enough to still be alive by story's end, your reward is more of the same.

To help make this bleak, brutal world not only bearable but also more complex and highly entertaining, Boetticher adds another ingredient to his mix—an underlying layer of noir-ish absurdity. While these films are dark, they are also very funny in a grim, ironic way. As terrible things that cause death and suffering occur (or are recalled), we often can't help but smile with gallows-humor detachment. "They're going to kill us, Mrs. Mims," one character tells another in one of these Boetticher films. It's a chilling comment that's undercut by a woman's odd, funny-sounding name—just the kind of juxtaposition the director loved to give us again and again. Numerous film critics have likened these films to the existentialist-influenced "theater of the absurd" popular in the 1950s and 1960s, and their point is well taken. The films seem to have more of an affinity with the darkly humorous plays of Samuel Beckett or early Tom Stoppard than they do with classic western masters. As film historian Jim Kitses has noted about Boetticher: "The world [in these films] is finally a sad and funny place, life a tough, amusing game that can never be won but must be played."[1]

In addition, these films are drenched in noir duality. In them, everything and its opposite not only exist together but are also fused together in odd, intriguing, and darkly ironic ways. Their spare, barren landscapes, for example, are both bleakly empty and brimming with beauty. In certain respects, they serve as the Technicolor western equivalents to the ominous but also gorgeous cityscapes we see in well-photographed black-and-white crime noirs. Good and evil characters not only co-exist, but can also strongly identify with one other, suggesting that the capacities for both good and evil reside within all of us. Often, they even share similar attributes and aspirations, identifying closely with each other the way noir heroes and villains much like the Teresa Wright and Joseph Cotton characters in Hitchcock's *Shadow of a Doubt* (1943) or the Robert Mitchum and Kirk Douglas characters in Tourneur's *Out of the Past* (1947). Victory and defeat are connected, too. In each film, the hero prevails, but ultimately how satisfying is the triumph (if we can even call it that)? And all this occurs in a world, of course, where the horrors of life and the absurdly comic also ride side by side.

Of the seven westerns Boetticher directed between 1956 and 1960, four are often cited as standouts: *7 Men from Now* (1956), *The Tall T* (1957), *Ride Lonesome* (1959), and *Comanche Station* (1960). This chapter focuses on two,

The Tall T and *Ride Lonesome*, both because they are superb films and because they have interesting noir components we don't often see in Boetticher's other films. *The Tall T*, for example, shares many similarities with noir hostage dramas such as André de Toth's *Crime Wave* (1954), and *Ride Lonesome* has elements of noir revenge/redemption stories such as Fred Zinnemann's *Act of Violence* (1948).

"The last of the old Hollywood two-fisted directors"

In a 2005 article that pieced together several interviews he had conducted with Boetticher in the late 1980s and early 1990s, film writer Sean Axmaker labeled Boetticher "the last of the old Hollywood two-fisted directors."[2] It's a colorful description, and an apt one. Many classic-era directors made films that were larger than life. Boetticher might be one of the few directors whose life, in many respects, was larger than his films.

Adopted as an infant, he was named Oscar after his adoptive father, a wealthy Indiana hardware retailer who young Oscar grew to truly dislike. In fact, in a filmed interview late in his life, Boetticher said that one of the happiest days in his life was when he learned that he was adopted—and not genetically connected to his parents.[3] After attending a military academy, young Oscar went to Ohio State University, where he excelled

Initially, Budd Boetticher wanted to be a bullfighter. Then, after coming to Hollywood in the 1940s as a consultant for a film about bull fighting, he moved to directing genre films, primarily westerns. Many consider his best works to be a series of late–1950s westerns he made with actor Randolph Scott.

in both football and boxing. And, when he had finished school, he set out for Mexico, where he quickly learned the art of bullfighting and became a respected matador—a professional choice that also horrified his mother.

There are several differing accounts of how young Oscar made the transition from bullfighting to the movies. One—which Boetticher himself liked to tell—involved his giving Darryl Zanuck, 20th Century–Fox's powerful studio chief, a lesson in bullfighting to show the mogul that he indeed knew his stuff.[4] But, regardless of how he got there, Boetticher, because of his bullfighting experience, was hired as a technical advisor for 20th Century–Fox's 1940 romance involving a bullfighter, Rouben Mamoulian's *Blood and Sand*. This led to other studio jobs and, in 1944, to his first credited directing assignment, *One Mysterious Night*, a low-budget crime film. For the next seven years, he made more than 15 films, mostly undistinguished, low-budget film noirs.

Then, in 1951, Boetticher had a breakthrough. The film wasn't a noir or a western but a very personal story, which Boetticher wrote himself, based on his bullfighting experiences in Mexico. Eventually titled *The Bullfighter and the Lady*, the film wasn't bankrolled by a major studio but by the actor John Wayne, who was just beginning what would eventually become Batjac, his own independent film production company. Although Boetticher was outraged when—without his permission—Wayne brought in John Ford to edit the film, Boetticher still received an Academy Award nomination for Best Original Story. (Later in Boetticher's life, the cuts were restored.)

After directing a variety of genre films in the early 1950s, including a couple of under-rated westerns, *Horizons West* (1952) with Robert Ryan and *The Man from the Alamo* (1953) with Glenn Ford, Boetticher—by now fed up working for film studios—had an acrimonious parting with his employer at the time, Universal International. Again, he was at loose ends.

And again, John Wayne gave him a much-needed break. This chapter in Boetticher's life began when Wayne showed him an original script for a western titled *7 Men from Now*. It was by Burt Kennedy, a radio writer and part-time bit player aching to write for films. After reading just 35 pages, Boetticher told Wayne that he loved it and absolutely wanted to direct the film. With Wayne committed to John Ford's *The Searchers* at the time and unable to play the lead, they turned to another western film icon, Randolph Scott. Boetticher, Kennedy, and Scott had great fun working together when filming the story, and, after the film proved to be a success, they decided to continue working together. They brought Scott's long-time business partner, producer Harry Joe Brown, into the mix and created their own semi-autonomous production company. Combining Scott's first name and Brown's last, the company eventually became known as Ranown Pictures, and the five films the four men made together (with numerous other contributors, of course) over the next few years—now often referred to as the Ranown Cycle—cemented Boetticher's own renown.

Of the five films, the foursome was fully involved in three—*The Tall T*, *Ride Lonesome*, and *Comanche Station*—and, along with *7 Men from Now*, all are widely hailed to be western masterpieces.

Among Boetticher and Scott's films, these four are distinctive for several reasons.

One is the writing. Wayne once told Burt Kennedy that his work on western scripts was like "writing Broadway in Arizona."[5] It's a wonderful comment, suggesting that Kennedy could bring the sophisticated, witty dialogue of an accomplished Broadway playwright to the land of sagebrush and saddle sores. It's also an accurate appraisal; Kennedy could write sharp, crackling dialogue that often suggests much more than was actually being said while also fitting his often-rustic characters like a glove. In turn, actors loved working with his lines. In fact, Scott preferred to call Kennedy's dialogue "lyrics." Just a few examples of his fresh, vivid use of colloquial language include: "Fancy runnin' into you in all this empty," "Help me get safe away," "I full intend to do it," "We'll night at the river bed," "I did him a hurt once," and "This country's nowhere for a woman without she's got a man." It's telling that the two Ranown films that don't receive nearly as much attention today, *Decision at Sundown* (1958) and *Buchanan Rides Alone* (1959), are the two that Kennedy wasn't involved with (except to do some script rewrites on *Buchanan*). It's also intriguing that, after his work with Boetticher, Kennedy's work both as a writer and then as a director was generally unexceptional. Kennedy often said that he and Boetticher developed the scripts for these films together, so maybe this is a classic case of a synergistic relationship. Feeding off each other, with each making complementary contributions to the process, the two might have been able to do something together that neither could quite pull off alone.

To complement the excellent dialogue, there's the tight, highly effective, and sometimes just plain beautiful minimalist visual style of the films. All of them were made on shoestring budgets, and each was shot in less than three weeks. Boetticher often noted that limited resources helped to impose great discipline on the production teams, and everything about these films reflects this discipline. Every visual image and movement is clear and precise. There's never the feeling that anything—even the slightest gesture or twitch—is wasted. This style is also refreshingly unpretentious. We never feel (as we often do in some later dark westerns) that the filmmakers are trying too hard to say something profound. Each story is just what it is—and nothing more. Finally, these films can sometimes be breathtakingly beautiful in their sparseness and simplicity. Shot mostly in the stark Alabama Hills near Lone Pine, California, on the eastern side of the southern Sierra Nevada mountain range, the compositions are filled with arresting shapes and colors (which often reflect other elements in the story). Along with Boetticher, cinematographer Charles Lawton also deserves enthusiastic kudos for his work on three of these films.

Still another strength is the fine acting—something audiences didn't always see in low-budget 1950s westerns. After *7 Men from Now*, the lead roles were written specifically for Scott, who was keenly aware of his limited range. These roles accommodated his abilities quite well, and he rose to the occasion, delivering—particularly in *7 Men from Now* and *The Tall T*—perhaps the best work of his career. To compensate for Scott's limitations as well as to stay within his limited budgets, Boetticher, who had a great eye for up-and-coming (and less costly) talent, cast marvelous young actors in the villainous roles. Just a few of these "up-and-comers" to get career breaks in these films include Lee Marvin, Richard Boone, Henry Silva, Pernell Roberts, and James Coburn—all of whom went on to highly successful acting careers.

Finally, one component of these films that people rarely discuss is the music, especially the scores of Heinz Roemheld for *The Tall T* and *Ride Lonesome*. Both complement the action and heighten the mood extremely well. In *The Tall T* particularly, the music shifts beautifully at one point to accommodate a major shift in the film's tone and, throughout the story, is highly effective.

Today, filmmakers and critics rave about these four films, but they were not big deals in their time. They played as second features in double bills, received little critical attention, and—while they made modest amounts of money—were quickly forgotten.

After making a low-budget gangster film, *The Rise and Fall of Legs Diamond*, in 1960, Boetticher again felt that it was time for a change. Always a bullfighter at heart, he headed back to Mexico to make a film starring the legendary matador, Carlos Arruza. The next seven years, which Boetticher discussed in a memoir titled *When in Disgrace*, could be the inspiration for several very dark noir films. The story includes an affair with a Mexican actress that cost him his marriage, a near-fatal illness, time spent in both jail and a mental hospital, countless financial setbacks in his efforts to make his film, and then finally the accidental deaths of both Arruza and most of Boetticher's film crew in an automobile crash. The film, *Arruza* (1972), was eventually completed. But, for Boetticher, the 1960s was truly the decade from hell.

Returning to Hollywood, he tried to restart his directing career in 1969 but found that there was little interest in him. He was only in his mid-50s but, for all intents and purposes, his career as a director was over.

Eventually, however, interest in his films—especially the late 1950s westerns—grew, and Boetticher was frequently invited to film festivals and interviewed by film writers and historians. He lived quietly in Southern California with his wife Mary, whom he married in 1970, and he died in 2001 at age 85.

"I sure don't know why I like you, Brennan": The Tall T

In 2000, the year before both Boetticher and Kennedy died, the Library of Congress selected *The Tall T* for preservation in the U.S. Library of Congress's National Film Registry. Each year, 25 U.S. films are chosen for this honor, and, so far, *The Tall T* is the only film that either Boetticher or Kennedy played a major role in developing that's made this list. Within Boetticher's small but passionate following, it could also be the most revered.

Part of the reason for this film's staying power might also be the contributions of two additional people. One is the great western and then crime fiction writer Elmore Leonard, whose short story, *The Captives*, is the basis for the film's screenplay. Leonard's work has many assets. Among them are a wonderful ear for dialogue and a special genius for creating villains. When it came to putting words in the mouths of evil or just shifty characters, Leonard could have been Burt Kennedy's mentor and inspiration. With Leonard's villains, however, it isn't just what they say but who they are. While capable of great evil, many of them don't see themselves as evil at all—just regular guys who've had to resort to crime simply because they've gotten some tough breaks in life. In fact, they have regular dreams—such as finding a good woman to marry or a nice ranch to settle down on—dreams that, at least in their cases, are nothing less than delusional. The other contributor is the fine actor Richard Boone. Best known today for playing Paladin, the tough but refined hero of the highly successful television western series *Have Gun—Will Travel* (1957–1963), Boone also shined as a villain in numerous films from the 1950s to the 1970s. In *The Tall T*, his character, Frank Usher, is one of his most complex and compelling bad-guy roles and (with the possible exception of Lee Marvin in *7 Men from Now*) possibly the best villain in all of Boetticher's films. In fact, we can even take this a step further. While Scott's Pat Brennan is officially the

10. "They're going to kill us, Mrs. Mims"

hero of *The Tall T*, the character that drives most of the action; possesses the most captivating mix of humanity, vanity, greed, and evil; and triggers his own doom—the true noir hero—is Boone's Usher.

―⁂―

The story of *The Tall T* begins, as stories often do in Boetticher films, with a lone rider (Scott) riding toward us as the opening credits are shown on the screen. He arrives at a stagecoach way station, passing through on his way to a town called Contention, and we learn that his name is Pat Brennan. After a friendly chat with the station manager and his son (for whom Brennan promises to bring back some cherry candy), he moves on. Then, after he buys the candy in town, he visits his old boss and, in a bet, loses his horse. On the way back to the way station where he plans to borrow another horse, he hitches a ride on a stagecoach driven by his crusty, humorous pal Rintoon (Arthur Hunnicutt) and carrying a pair of middle-age honeymooners, Willard and Doretta

Captive Pat Brennan (Randolph Scott) stays alive only because he intrigues outlaw leader Frank Usher (Richard Boone) in Boetticher's *The Tall T* (1957). But, as the number of his sharp comments grows, Brennan sorely tries Usher's patience.

Mims (John Hubbard and Maureen O'Sullivan). We've already learned that Doretta's father is the richest man in the area and that Mims has married Doretta for her money.

Up until this point the tone of the film has been light, almost comical. But, once the stage reaches the way station, everything changes dramatically. There is no sign of the stationmaster or his son. Instead, three outlaws greet the stage—Chink (Henry Silva), Billy Jack (Skip Homeier), and their leader, Frank Usher—all itching to rob it. They've already murdered the stationmaster and the boy, and, when Rintoon goes for his shotgun, they make quick work of him, too.

Just as quickly, they find out that this is the wrong stage; the one with the money will be coming along later. Eager to save his own skin, the cowardly Mims tells the outlaws about his wife's rich father and suggests that holding her for ransom could result in more money for them—if, of course, they let Mims and Doretta go free.

Frank sees right through Mims, but he likes the idea and sets it into motion, telling Billy Jack to escort Mims back to Contention to tell Doretta's father what's happened and to demand $50,000. Despite Chink's urging, Frank also spares Brennan—for the moment, at least. He likes Brennan's courage, integrity, intelligence, and basic decency. These are qualities he sees (or wants to see) in himself, and he'd like to know more about this man.

The group relocates at a hideout that's basically a campsite and a small cave. The next day, Mims and Billy Jack return, saying Doretta's father has agreed to the ransom terms but needs some time to collect the money. When he's heard about the plan for the drop-off, Frank tells Mims he's free to go. Still the coward, Mims begins to leave without even saying goodbye to Doretta. Disgusted, Frank simply says: "Bust him, Chink." And, with that, his henchman eagerly swings into action, shooting Mims as he rides away.

Though Doretta later admits that she cared little for Mims, she's shocked and horrified by his death. Brennan, however, encourages her to get a grip. "They're going to kill us, Mrs. Mims," he tells her later. "Think about that for a while." He also tells her that the only way they have a chance of survival is to work together and look for any opportunity that may present itself. Then, unexpectedly, he kisses her.

The next morning, when Frank rides out to pick up the ransom money, Brennan sees his chance to strike back. Working with Doretta, he kills first Billy Jack and then Chink.

When Frank returns, Brennan surprises him from behind. Frank has no choice but to toss down his gun and the money. But, he knows he has one card left. Sensing that Brennan will not shoot him from behind, he keeps his back to Brennan, slowing walks to his horse, mounts, and rides off. Safely out of range, however, his greed and ego get the best of him. He pulls a rifle out of his saddlebags and comes back firing. Brennan shoots him.

As Brennan and Doretta begin their journey back to Contention, she is again distraught. He looks at her sympathetically and says: "Come on, now, it's going to be a nice day." As they walk side by side, she shyly puts her arm around him, and, much more assertively, he returns the favor.

"The basic deception in the films of the Ranown cycle, and the key to their dramatic structure," Jim Kitses has written, "is that the Randolph Scott figure is the hero only in a technical sense: it is the villain who is our true hero."[6] While this statement is debatable in films such as *Ride Lonesome* (where the Scott character both drives the story's action and undergoes a major personal change), it certainly applies to *The Tall T*. Here, Scott's Brennan is mainly a static character who (after the film's first 20 minutes) mostly responds to events that have been thrust upon him. Even Doretta, who eventually develops some courage and self-esteem, is more dynamic. Here, the true hero isn't Brennan but Frank, and he's about as noir-ish as they come.

We never learn exactly how or why Frank turned bad. We only know that, according to him, he was once a respected man back in Wyoming. We know that he can't go back, either, because, as Frank says, "there are those who'd rather see me hang." From what we see in *The Tall T*, Frank also shows no desire to mend his evil ways. He plans a stagecoach robbery, holds a woman for ransom, and is responsible for killing four people, including a young boy who only wants some store-bought candy. As he watches Doretta sob after he's ordered her husband killed, he can only ask: "What do you suppose is the matter with her?" He even has a sadistic side, taking great pleasure in watching Doretta burn her hand when she touches an unexpectedly hot coffee pot or Brennan bump his head on a low overhang and responding with strangely uproarious laughter. On paper, this is one bad man.

But he is also a man of great complexity, and, as the story unfolds, we see many sides of him.

First, he is lonely and craves conversation with Brennan, the only character he considers worthy of his friendship. While he knows there is a certain risk to keeping Brennan alive, he is willing to take the chance both because it represents a rare opportunity for real companionship and because his vanity permits it. (Frank senses Brennan's capabilities immediately but underrates them—or perhaps overrates his own.) The great irony in all of this is that this desire for someone of decency, integrity, and emotional depth to talk to proves to be Frank's undoing. If he had only taken Chink's advice to "bust" Brennan early on, he would have easily prevailed.

Second, Frank has a curiously exalted view of himself. From his perspective, he's not an ordinary outlaw who's only interested in money, loose women, and drink the way "animals" (as Frank calls them) such as Chink and Billy Jack are. He sees himself as a clear cut above them (morally as well as intellectually), and one reason he gives is that he "never tripped a hammer on a man" in his life, instead leaving the dirty work to "young guns." In addition, Frank has a noble dream. He is fascinated that Brennan has his own ranch and asks him to talk about it. "I'm going to have me a place someday," Frank responds after hearing Brennan's description. "I've thought about it. I've thought about it a lot. A man should have something of his own, something to belong to, to be proud of." All this suggests, of course, that Frank is profoundly deluded. He's certainly not the moral superior of Chink or Billy Jack, and there's absolutely no way he's ever going to have that dream ranch. But, for his own peace of mind, he needs to think this way. Although he's not a good man, he yearns to be one.

Third, there are moments when Frank shows great sensitivity. A few occur during his conversations with Brennan when he shows genuine interest in him and even admits to liking him. Another is when he brings a meal to a sleeping Doretta in the cave. Although he doesn't need to, he gently puts her plate down, sets a coffee cup to one side to be sure it won't spill, and covers Doretta's shoulder with her blanket. In terms of understanding Frank, this is one of the more interesting moments in the film. Is he longing for a connection with a woman the way he longs for mature conversation with Brennan? Is he acknowledging the suffering Doretta has been through and showing empathy for her? Or, as part of his own desire to identify with Brennan, is he emulating him— doing essentially what Brennan would do if he'd brought in the meal?

The Tall T has several noir-ish elements in addition to the Frank character, of course. Chink, for example, is the kind of sociopathic henchman we see often in noir. The dynamic of the captor taking a liking to the captives is reminiscent of numerous hostage noirs such as de Toth's *Crime Wave*. In addition, the darkness and starkness of the settings (such as the inside of the cave); the grisly violence (well illustrated in Billy Jack's death); and the simply worded, highly evocative, "hard-boiled" dialogue (e.g., "Bust him, Chink") all combine to give the film a highly noir-ish look, sound, and feel. But the critical noir element in *The Tall T* is Frank, a complex bad man with many familiar human qualities whose humanity—not lack of it—ultimately leads to his downfall.

"I did him a hurt once": Ride Lonesome

One of the criticisms of Boetticher's four most acclaimed late 1950s westerns is that they are all essentially the same story. It's as though—numerous film writers have contended—he and Kennedy simply made the same movie over and over. There is definitely a great deal that's repeated. Since all the films were shot in and around the Alabama Hills near Lone Pine, we see many of the same settings again and again. We hear many of the same lines of dialogue from film to film, too, such as "Some things a man can't ride around," and to change the subject of a conversation, "You make good coffee." And we see similar bits of storytelling business such as the key villains wearing some combination of red and turquoise clothing and the heroes using the same tricks to defeat the villains.

But to say that it's all basically the same misses the point, too. In some cases, the repetitions are there for specific reasons. In *The Tall T*, for example, the Scott character says, "Some things a man can't ride around" to express his decision to face the villain. Then, in *Ride Lonesome*, one of the dubious supporting characters uses the same line as he prepares to confront the Scott character. It's curious—perhaps to emphasize an affinity the two characters share. And it's clearly deliberate. Also, in *Comanche Station*, Boetticher and Kennedy show a hanging tree that figures prominently in *Ride Lonesome*. It's not necessary to the action at all; it's as if they simply want to pay homage to the previous film.

In a broader sense, too, the stories are very different. While *The Tall T* is primarily a hostage thriller, for example, *7 Men from Now* is mainly a revenge/love story, *Ride Lonesome* a revenge/redemption drama with lots of comic relief, and *Comanche Station* a road picture often complicated by poor relations with the Native American characters.

Revenge is also part of what gives *Ride Lonesome* some key characteristics of noir, specifically noir revenge dramas such as Zinnemann's *Act of Violence*, in which something horrible has taken place before the action starts and an obsessed hero first seeks payback and then ultimately finds some peace. Unlike *The Tall T*, where the villain drives the action, the clear hero here is the Scott character, Brigade. Not only does he put his plan for vengeance into motion and carry it out, but he is also much more dynamic than Brennan in *The Tall T*—he changes in a fundamental way.

In true Boetticher style, *Ride Lonesome* begins with the credits rolling as the Scott character rides alone through the Alabama Hills. In this story, his initial action is all business. The rider's name is Brigade, and he is closing in on Billy John (James Best), who's wanted in Santa Cruz for shooting a man in the back. When they meet, we learn that the Scott character is not a law officer but a bounty hunter who intends to bring Billy John back to Santa Cruz for the reward. Unknown to him, however, Billy John has compatriots hiding in the rocks. He threatens to have one of them kill Brigade, but Brigade is undeterred, saying that, no matter what happens, he'll kill Billy John first. Knowing he means it, Billy John backs down, telling his friends in the rocks to let his outlaw brother Frank (Lee Van Cleef) know what's happened and to ask Frank to come after them. Hearing this, the others gallop away, leaving Billy John alone with Brigade. Brigade cuffs him, and they ride off.

They come upon a stagecoach way station, where they meet a couple of shady characters, Boone and his friend Whit (Pernell Roberts and James Coburn), and the stationmaster's wife, Carrie Lane (Karen Steele). Boone and Whit, we learn, also have an interest in bringing in Billy John. For them, his return means amnesty—the chance to have past offenses pardoned and to start a new life on Boone's ranch. But to get amnesty it would have to be the two of them—and not Brigade—who turn in Billy John. They know that Brigade won't agree to this and that a reckoning is inevitable, but—for the time being, at least—they join up with him. We also learn that Indians have killed Carrie's husband, the stationmaster. So, with no other option available to her, she joins the four men on the journey to Santa Cruz.

Along the way, though, Boone senses that bringing Billy John in might not be Brigade's true purpose. Brigade, he observes, is taking a roundabout way in, making it easy for someone else—namely Billy John's brother Frank—to catch up with them.

We see Frank and his gang in pursuit. Frank also figures out what Brigade is up to. "It ain't the money Brigade wants, not the money at all," he tells one of his gang members. "I did him a hurt once. Long ago—so long I 'most forgot." Frank realizes that he, not Billy John, is the one Brigade wants and that Brigade is simply using Billy John as bait to force a confrontation. He even knows where Brigade plans that confrontation to take place.

10. *"They're going to kill us, Mrs. Mims"*

Bounty hunter Ben Brigade (Randolph Scott) must earn the trust of widow Carrie Lane (Karen Steele) as he also brings in a prisoner in Boetticher's *Ride Lonesome* (1959). Along the way, Brigade must also deal with a host of shady characters, including the prisoner's older brother, who may be Brigade's real target.

Soon the pieces in this puzzle begin to fall together. Brigade and the others in his group all arrive at a clearing dominated by an ominous hanging tree. They stop to camp for the night. Boone and Whit discuss how they will confront Brigade. And, in a rare display of personal revelation, Brigade tells Carrie about his plan to lure Frank to this place. Several years before—to get back at Brigade for sending him to jail—Frank did that "hurt" he "'most forgot" about—he kidnapped Brigade's wife, took her to this spot, and hanged her from this tree. Now—Brigade tells Carrie—he will have his revenge.

The next day, as Frank and his gang ride into the clearing, Brigade and Billy John are there to meet them. Brigade has his rifle, and Billy John is sitting, hands tied on a horse underneath the tree with a noose around his neck. Brigade taunts Frank, saying that, if he wants Billy, he'll have to come get him. Frank charges and starts shooting. Billy's horse bolts and he is left swinging on the rope. Brigade kills Frank. Then he shoots Billy's rope, enabling Billy to fall down and live. With Boone and Whit covering Brigade, the others in Frank's gang gallop away.

Although Boone has come to like and admire Brigade, he fears that he still must have his reckoning with him. He prepares, but—quite unexpectedly—Brigade tells him that, since he doesn't need Billy John anymore, he and Whit can have him and get their amnesty. And here, the group parts ways. Boone, Whit, Carrie, and Billy John all ride to Santa Cruz. Brigade stays behind and—as if to exorcise a personal demon—burns the hanging tree. The film's final shot—of Brigade looking up at the tree in flames—is one of the most riveting moments in all of Boetticher's westerns, one that stays with us long after we see it.

While the villain is a major character, a formidable adversary, and essentially the true noir hero in *The Tall T*, *Ride Lonesome* is an entirely different story. Here, the main villain (also named Frank) is little more than peripheral (he has only two real scenes); two characters often referred to as villains, Boone and Whit, are mainly likeable rogues who really don't pose a major threat to the Scott character; and another bad man, Billy John, is little more than a hapless pawn in the proceedings. Here, the principal emphasis is not on a villain but on a hero bent on getting his revenge.

In a sense, Scott plays a dual role with Brigade. On one hand, he's a traditional western hero similar to dozens Scott had played in previous films—the strong, silent type out to right a wrong. On the other hand, Brigade is right out of a noir film—a traumatized man obsessed with carrying out a dark plan, a normally law-abiding individual now willing to go around the law.

A close noir counterpart is Robert Ryan's Joe Parkson in Fred Zinnemann's *Act of Violence* (1948). In that film, Parkson is World War II veteran enraged by his commanding officer's cowardice and the deaths of fellow soldiers that resulted from it. He returns after the war determined to kill the officer and, after events unfold, eventually finds some emotional peace.

In *Ride Lonesome*, Brigade follows a similar trajectory. Enraged by the hanging of his wife, Brigade blames himself for allowing this to happen. Another curious similarity is the length of time between the original evil and the revenge: both Brigade and Joe Parkson have let their rage smolder for years and, in both cases, it has taken a toll on their psyches. Another similarity is vigilantism. In both stories, the initial wrongdoing was clearly against the law and the person who did the wrong should face the legal consequences. But, most likely because it is so deeply personal, the revenge is handled *outside* the law—the avenger must see to it himself. Still another similarity is that both do achieve some sense of personal peace when the conflicts are eventually resolved. The memorable burning tree scene at the end of *Ride Lonesome* certainly illustrates this: Brigade has finally exorcised his personal demons and, after many years, he can move on.

In exacting his revenge, Brigade also exhibits some of the sadism we see in *The Tall T*'s villain, Frank Usher. The scene when he has put Billy John under the hanging tree illustrates this quite clearly. Both Billy John and his brother Frank are squirming with tension, and Brigade seems to be enjoying it. He wants these two bad men to suffer.

In addition to Brigade's vengeance-obsessed character, *Ride Lonesome* has a good share of other noir elements. Among them are the music by Heinz Roemheld, which, from the film's first moments, creates genuine noir anxiety; the horrific act of Frank's hanging Brigade's wife (which, thank goodness, we never see in flashback); and some wonderfully noir-ish night shooting such as the scene when we first see Frank and his gang all in silhouette. But, as with *The Tall T*, the main noir ingredient in this Boetticher western is the darkness that resides within the character driving the story's main action.

—⚡—

For Budd Boetticher, the creative stars aligned for only a short time. During that four-year period in the late 1950s, he found creative partners and working circumstances that complemented his own challenging personality and made four low-budget westerns that are both masterpieces of their kind and serve as the cornerstone of his filmmaking legacy.

Yet, while this time of great creative output was short, the influence of this handful of films has been lasting. In watching *Budd Boetticher: A Man Can Do That*, a documentary Turner Classic Movies produced in 2008, for example, it's interesting to see Clint Eastwood sitting side by side with Quentin Tarantino—two very different people representing two very different generations of filmmakers—and to hear both rhapsodize over Boetticher's storytelling craftsmanship; ironic wit; and dark, noir-ish take on the world. In the same documentary, it's also intriguing to see other filmmakers as diverse as Martin Scorsese, Taylor Hackford, Peter Bogdanovich, and Robert Towne all chiming in with enthusiastic praise for the director.[7] Although Boetticher's westerns had a relatively minor impact on the film world in the late 1950s, this kind of testimony affirms that their stature has not only grown substantially over the decades since then but will likely continue to grow.

11

Darkness in Shinbone
Noir Is Busting Out All Over in John Ford's *The Man Who Shot Liberty Valance*

> "Cold-blooded murder—but I can live with it...." —*The Man Who Shot Liberty Valance*

Unlike most of the other directors whose westerns have been discussed in this book, John Ford (1894–1973) is clearly a widely recognized name— easily one of the best known, most honored, and most highly revered in all of film. In his day, Ford received a record four Academy Awards for directing his feature films and another two for his World War II documentaries—an achievement that remains unmatched today. When he died, several newspaper obituaries hailed him as the greatest director of the sound era. Over the years, scores of fellow filmmakers from Ingmar Bergman and Akira Kurosawa to Martin Scorsese and Steven Spielberg have all enthusiastically praised his work. Bergman, for example, once called Ford, "the best director in the world,"[1] and Spielberg has said that he will not start a new project without first looking at two or three Ford films for inspiration.[2] Today, although many of the well-known directors of Hollywood's classic era have fallen out of favor, critical acceptance and popular interest in Ford remain high. In 2012, for example, the British Film Institute's once-a-decade *Sight and Sound Magazine* poll of critics worldwide voted Ford's 1956 film *The Searchers* one of the 10 "greatest films of all time." That same year, a Dublin-based group called John Ford Ireland launched an annual Ford symposium, which brings together scholars and film enthusiasts from all around the world for a four-day Ford love fest each June. And, with the possible exceptions of Alfred Hitchcock and perhaps one or two additional directors, more books have been written about Ford and his work than about any other filmmaker.

One curious tidbit about Ford's work is that, while he is best known today for his string of great post-war westerns from *My Darling Clementine* (1946) to *The Man Who Shot Liberty Valance* (1962), these were all largely dismissed by the Academy of Motion Pictures Arts and Sciences and other film awards groups. We can suggest several reasons for this. One, of course, is the Academy's long-standing condescension toward the genre. Another might be Ford's subtlety as an artist. Many of his later westerns are much more complex thematically and artistically than many viewers first realized, and, simply put, it's taken decades for people to come to fully appreciate their intricacies and richness.

Another curious tidbit is that, unlike most of the other major Hollywood directors working the late 1940s and 1950s, Ford is hardly, if ever, associated with classic noir films. It's not difficult to understand why, either. In the noir heyday years of 1949 and 1950, for example, when Hitchcock was making *Strangers on a Train*, Fritz Lang *House by the River*, and Billy Wilder *Sunset Boulevard*, Ford was at work on *She Wore a Yellow Ribbon*, *Wagon Master* and *Rio Grande*, three films that are light years away from anything even remotely noir—crime drama or western.

Shown here in 1962, the year *The Man Who Shot Liberty Valance* was released, an aging John Ford was still breaking new ground in the western, a genre he had begun working in nearly 50 years earlier.

Yet audience attitudes had changed as a result of the war, and Ford, who had seen his share of grim wartime action in both the Pacific and in Europe, had changed as well. While his work would never be heavily noir-ish and would always reflect his strong personality and very personal worldview, darker noir influences did seep in. The first evidence of this is his characterization of Doc Holliday in his 1946 masterpiece *My Darling Clementine*. Ford's Holliday, played by Victor Mature, is a fascinating psychological study of an already-troubled man haunted by the very real prospect of an impending early death. We see the noir influence again in the characterization of Ethan Edwards in *The Searchers*. Brilliantly portrayed by John Wayne, Ethan shares many characteristics with the kind of noir anti-hero we might see an actor such as Robert Ryan play: he's tormented by profound personal losses, obsessive, vengeful, and deeply racist. And *Sergeant Rutledge*, Ford's 1960 western about the court martial of an African American cavalryman, has several noir elements, ranging from its treatment of dark subjects such as racial prejudice, murder, and rape to its occasionally eerie, highly expressionistic flashbacks.

While we see noir shadings in Ford westerns before 1962, none of these films is nearly as noir-ish in both sensibility and style as a film that—oddly—most people don't think of as a noir western: *The Man Who Shot Liberty Valance*. There is a sadness, pessimism, and sense of determinism that permeates this film that is in stark contrast to the unbridled exuberance and optimism of Ford westerns dating all the way back to his early silent films and continuing certainly as late as 1950's *Wagon Master*. *Valance*'s visual style—initially off-putting to people who were, by 1962, used to expansive, beautifully shot Technicolor Ford films such as *She Wore a Yellow Ribbon* and *The Searchers*—is also a departure. In *Valance*, there are no expansive landscapes, and there is not even Technicolor. Instead, we see confining, sometimes claustrophobic interiors or exterior town scenes, many set at night, and all shot in ominous, shadow-laden black and white.

The Man Who Shot Liberty Valance is much more than a typical noir western, of course. It is a multi-tiered exploration of what occurs when a somewhat primitive society makes the difficult but inevitable transition to a supposedly more "civilized" one. And, along the way, it asks many probing questions. Who wins in this transition, for example, and who loses? Is a more civilized society really better than the society it is replacing? And what roles do education and communications media play in the transition process? Do they exist to make citizens better critical thinkers and to keep them well informed about the vital issues of the day? Or are they really there simply to reinforce the existing order by instilling conformity and ensuring lockstep loyalty? Of special note too is the film's ambiguity: it's drenched in it. The big questions the film asks are never neatly answered. If anything, these questions simply lead to more curiosity and more questions. So much is open-ended, up in the air, unresolved. In the end, this film is extraordinarily rich in ideas, perhaps Ford's densest work as well as the summation of thinking he began to articulate in his first silent westerns and then cultivated throughout his long career.

While *Valance* is much more than a noir, however, it is also, in many respects, very much a noir. While several of Ford's other post-war westerns have pronounced noir shadings, none takes us to the dark side as fully or deeply as this film does.

"Pappy"

In a 2013 interview, Vince Gilligan, the main creative force behind the landmark cable TV series *Breaking Bad*, made a point of singling out one classic era American director for his influence on the show. The director's name was John Ford.[3] Hearing this, a good number of film buffs may have harkened back to Orson Welles' famous remark more than 40 years before. When asked whom he looked to for guidance, the always-provocative Welles said, "The old masters, by which I mean John Ford, John Ford, and John Ford."[4]

It's difficult to imagine not only American westerns but also much of contemporary American film without John Ford. The silent film master D.W. Griffith may have given us the rudiments of great visual-kinetic storytelling with his genius for seamlessly mixing close-ups, long-shots, tracking shots, intimate scenes, and scenes of great scope and grandeur, but Ford (who, incidentally, once played a Ku Klux Klansman in Griffith's seminal 1915 film *Birth of a Nation*) brought the American experience into focus in a way no one else had ever done. Add to that—he did it with a poet's eye and ear. Visually, his compositions are often stunning in their form, but Ford never simply went for the visual effect for its own sake. His images always suggest and reinforce meaning: they tell us things about the story we are seeing and the characters in it. Aurally, the words and accompanying music in his films can be pure poetry. In fact, he was a master at mixing the language of ordinary people and simple folk tunes with his visual images to create high art. There has never been anyone else like him.

Today, he is probably best known as the old man John Wayne called "Pappy" who made westerns in Utah's Monument Valley, but he had been busy in films since he was a young man of 20—more than 30 years before *My Darling Clementine* kicked off his spectacular post-war run with westerns.

Born John Martin Feeney in Portland, Maine, in 1894, he changed his last name to Ford after he moved to Hollywood in 1914 to join his older brother Francis, who had already established himself as a film actor, director, and writer under the name Francis Ford. By 1917, young John was directing his own films, often westerns for the young Universal Motion Picture Manufacturing Company, and often starring silent star Harry Carey, Sr., who taught his young director much about filmmaking. Moving to Fox in 1921, Ford soon conceived and directed one of the first great western epics, 1924's *The Iron Horse*, a story of the building of the Transcontinental Railroad that deftly balanced an intimate personal story with the great rush of historical events.

After winning a directing Oscar for his 1935 film about the Irish Revolution, *The Informer*, Ford became a dominant force in American filmmaking just prior to World War II, receiving three consecutive directing Oscar nominations for 1939's *Stagecoach*, 1940's *The Grapes of Wrath*, and 1941's *How Green Was My Valley*, and winning the latter two. Immediately after the war, his drama *They Were Expendable*, a story about the early dark days of the War in the Pacific and a film historian and director Peter Bogdanovich has called "probably the finest U.S. war picture,"[5] was released.

Immediately after this, Ford, during his final 20 years as a working director, focused his attention more toward westerns. There were other career highlights during this time, of course. He received his record fourth directing Oscar for his contemporary Irish tale, 1952's *The Quiet Man*, and he directed both Ava Gardner and Grace Kelly to well-deserved Oscar nominations for their work in his under-appreciated 1953 adventure-drama *Mogambo*. But the westerns—often starring John Wayne—accounted for 13 of the 26 feature films he completed as well as for most of his major popular and critical successes. Of these, the ones that film fans are probably most familiar with today are 1948's *Fort Apache*, 1949's *She Wore a Yellow Ribbon*, and 1950's *Rio Grande* (the three films often called his "Cavalry trilogy," even though they don't really make up a trilogy), 1950's *Wagon Master*, *The Searchers*, and *The Man Who Shot Liberty Valance*.

Along the way, he also made some duds, but even his weaker films have fine moments. While receiving negative-to-mixed reviews, for example, his 1961 western *Two Rode Together* includes a four-minute single shot of characters played by James Stewart and Richard Widmark cagily sizing each other up as they talk about ordinary things while sitting on a river bank—a scene that Martin Scorsese claims was so thrilling to watch that it inspired him to become a filmmaker.[6]

While Ford's post-war westerns take on numerous themes, a few of these seem to find their way into film after film. One is the subject of discrimination (racial, religious, or class-driven) and the need to overcome our own personal prejudices and come together as a human community. Another is the transition from a primitive society to a more "civilized" one. What's gained and what's lost when this occurs? We see this question asked in films from *My Darling Clementine* through *The Searchers* and to *Liberty Valance*. It's a question Ford had no easy answers to, and his intentional ambiguities are part of what makes these such powerful and intriguing films.

After filming his last western, the 1964 epic *Cheyenne Autumn*, Ford completed only one feature film, the sadly under-appreciated 1966 drama *7 Women*. Although he wanted to continue working, he found—that after *7 Women's* failure at the box office and his advancing age (he was 72)—he could no longer get work. During the seven years before his death in 1973, he moved into the role of crusty elder statesman, giving interviews (in which he sometimes told tall tales about his life), participating in a documentary about his work, and receiving numerous honors, including the very first American Film Institute Lifetime Achievement Award in 1973.

On August 31, 1973, as Ford lay dying, a Catholic priest was called to administer the last rites. According to Ford's son Patrick, the priest kept talking, and Ford, never a fan of too much talk in his films, opened his eyes one last time and said: "Cut!" And that, according to Patrick, was Ford's last word.[7]

For people who wish to learn more about Ford and his work, there are dozens of books to choose from as well as literally thousands of articles, blogs, and other pieces. Among the biographies, the most frequently praised is Joseph McBride's wonderful 2001 book *Searching For John Ford*. Among the studies of his films, an excellent choice is Tag Gallagher's very insightful 1986 book *John Ford: The Man and His Films*. And among the documentaries, perhaps the best is Peter Bogdanovich's *Directed by John Ford* (2006), a fascinating two hours that weaves shots of Ford's films together with archival interviews with Ford, John Wayne, Henry Fonda, James Stewart, and others with more contemporary interviews with such filmmakers as Spielberg, Scorsese, and Eastwood.

"This is the West, sir": The Man Who Shot Liberty Valance

As *The Man Who Shot Liberty Valance* opens, it is about 1910.

A living American legend, Senator Ransom Stoddard (James Stewart) and his wife Hallie (Vera Miles) come by train to the Western town of Shinbone. They are returning to pay their respects to Tom Doniphon (John Wayne), an old friend who has just died. Maxwell Scott (Carleton Young), an ambitious newspaper editor, pressures Stoddard into telling his story. Who was this Tom Doniphon? Why is his death important enough to warrant a visit from a national leader of such stature?

Stoddard, as if releasing himself from a great burden, begins to talk, and the film fades to flashback.

Decades before, when Stoddard first arrives in Shinbone as a young lawyer fresh from the East, the notorious Liberty Valance (Lee Marvin) robs the stage he is riding on, brutally beats him, and leaves him for dead. Tom finds him and takes him to his girlfriend, Hallie, to be nursed.

Young Ranse becomes active in Shinbone, working first in a restaurant and then for a crusading newspaper editor, Dutton Peabody (Edmond O'Brien),

As his henchman Reese (Lee Van Cleef) looks on, Liberty Valance (Lee Marvin) faces adversaries Ransom Stoddard (James Stewart) and Tom Doniphon (John Wayne) in Ford's 1962 *The Man Who Shot Liberty Valance*. The film, one of the director's last, is filled with noir-ish shadings, both visual and psychological.

starting a law practice, and even teaching school. Yet the menacing, chaotic presence of Valance looms. The local law officer, Link Appleyard (Andy Devine), is—according to Ranse's account—a cowardly, doddering fool who is of absolutely no help. The only person who's not afraid of Valance is Tom, but he has plans of his own to work his ranch and to marry Hallie. He's content to stay out of the way—that is, unless Valance threatens him personally.

Then destiny intervenes. Angered by Valance, a totally outmatched Ranse faces the outlaw in a showdown in the street at night. The shots are fired, and, amazingly, Valance is the one who falls. Ranse is immediately christened "the man who shot Liberty Valance," is hailed as a hero, leads the campaign for statehood, and becomes a successful politician and eventually a major figure in American politics. Hallie, as we know from the first moments of the story, has gone with him and long been Mrs. Stoddard. Unknown at first to Ranse and Hallie, however, is that he had help. Along with his hired hand Pompey (Woody Strode), Tom was waiting in an alley with a Winchester. It was his bullet, fired simultaneously, that killed Valance, and, because his act wasn't self-defense, no one must know. So, Ranse and Hallie go off together, both living with the unsettling reality that the act that built Ranse's reputation, his shooting of Valance, is a lie. Saddened by the loss of Hallie, Tom withdraws to lead what apparently is a lonely, empty life.

We return to 1910. Now that Tom is dead, Ranse—even though it may cost him dearly—finally reveals the truth. When he does, however, it's not what his listeners want to hear. In one of Ford's most famous moments, newspaperman Scott refuses to print the truth because it would be too devastating to the people who've believed in Stoddard all these years. "This is the West, sir," he says. "When the legend becomes fact, print the legend."

As they ride away from Shinbone on the train, Ranse must also come to grips with another difficult realization—that, despite all the years he and Hallie have been together, she has never stopped loving Tom. In fact, she may have always loved Tom more than she'd ever loved him. The sadness is overwhelming.

Meanwhile, a train conductor assures Ranse that the train's engineer is taking all the necessary steps to get him back to Washington, D.C., as soon as possible. Then, before returning to his other duties, he adds: "Nothing's too good for the man who shot Liberty Valance."

—m—

When *The Man Who Shot Liberty Valance* was released in April 1962, it was an instant hit. Audiences loved it and critical praise came from all quarters for its ironic, bittersweet story about the "civilizing" of a more primitive world; its razor-sharp dialogue; its intriguing, perplexing ambiguities; and its standout acting performances from such pros as John Wayne, James Stewart, Vera Miles, Edmond O'Brien and (at his most charismatically evil) Lee Marvin.

But the praise was by no means universal or without reservations. The *New York Times* reviewer, for example, criticized the film for its "obvious, overlong, and garrulous anticlimax."[8] Others felt that the actors, particularly the 54-year-old Wayne and 53-year-old Stewart, were too old for their roles. And others—long accustomed to lots of sentiment and optimism from Ford— found the film's downbeat, often-pessimistic tone disconcerting. Of all the criticisms, however, perhaps the most pointed were aimed at the film's visual design. Simply put, people didn't know what to make of it. By 1962, audiences expected a John Ford western to include glorious sundrenched Southwestern locales shot in sumptuous Technicolor. But this film wasn't shot anywhere near the wide-open spaces of Monument Valley, Moab, or other familiar Ford haunts. Instead, most of the shooting took place on western sets at Paramount Studios; many of these scenes were set at night and have a murky, uneasy, claustrophobic quality about them; and—a good decade after color had become the dominant photographic medium for westerns—it was shot in old-fashioned black and white. Completely gone is the sumptuous "Ford look" of such western classics as *She Wore a Yellow Ribbon* (1949) and *The Searchers* (1956). In its place, darkness and ominous black shadows seem to be everywhere. Cinematographer William Clothier and others involved with the production wanted to photograph it in color, but Ford insisted both on black and white and staging it the way he wanted, and, when the reviews started pouring in, he took his share of hits, critics calling the film everything from visually dull to downright ugly.[9]

According to several accounts, Ford insisted on black and white because he felt that the scenes in which we see the shooting of Liberty Valance could not have been as credibly conveyed in color. But, in a television interview he made during the 1980s, Lee Marvin suggested that Ford's thinking was much broader than this—that the fundamental design was for a black and white film shot largely in confining settings.[10] And in *Ride, Boldly Ride*, their study of the American western, Mary Lea Bandy and Kevin Stoehr contend that the decisions both for black and white and for the confined town settings were probably made because Ford meant for us to focus exclusively on the tragedy and its characters and ideas "so its protagonists cannot escape into the depth of the landscape."[11]

While it's irresistible to speculate about *why* Ford chose the visual design he did, this might not be a productive or even necessary activity. The fact is *that* Ford chose this approach, and the result—regardless of what his intentions were—is perhaps the most noir-like film he ever made. Not only in the film's visual design but also in its philosophical point of view and narrative structure, noir is busting out all over.

Let's consider the film's point of view first. The great director of Italian "spaghetti westerns," Sergio Leone, has called *Valance* his favorite Ford film because, as Leone put it, "it was the only film where he [Ford] learned about something called pessimism."[12] While the wording of Leone's quote might not be ideal, the basic idea is there. For John Ford, whose films often brim with sentiment and optimism, *Valance* is a major departure. Rather than "cynical," as some people have called it, this is a very sad and pessimistic film. Three basically good people—Tom, Ranse, and Hallie—all have big dreams, and, in each case, the dream is either tarnished or shattered altogether. Tom's dream of marrying Hallie never materializes. Ranse helps to "civilize" the West but at the expense of his integrity. And Hallie settles into a passionless marriage, never finding the happiness she might have had with Tom. An added tragic irony is when Ranse, at great risk to his own reputation, "confesses" and sets the record straight, newspaperman Maxwell Scott won't let him. For the good of the country, Scott surmises, the people must have their heroes and disturbing truths must be suppressed. So, for Ranse, there is no catharsis; he (and for that matter Hallie) must continue to live the lie. At the very end of the film, Hallie mentions Ranse's achievements and asks, "Aren't you proud?" Ranse doesn't answer, suggesting that—because his entire career has been based on a lie—he isn't. There's also the point suggested elsewhere in the film that the "civilized" West might not be as wonderful as Ranse, Hallie, and others had once envisioned it could be—that something vital and essential, something Tom so roughly and eloquently represented, had to be sacrificed for the transition to occur.

Many noir films are about flawed dreams gone bad—the dreams of pulling off the brilliant heist, getting away with murder, starting a new life after a jail break, or perhaps finding true love with a femme fatale. And usually these dreams fit the fairly narrow worldviews of the noir anti-hero protagonists. In *Valance*, the dreams are also flawed, but they are (befitting the main characters) larger, more expansive, and far less venal. Here, as in other Ford films such as *How Green Was My Valley*, well-meaning people make choices that—while it's not their intention—lead to more suffering than anyone bargained for. Tom gives up all hope of ever marrying Hallie. Hallie marries Ranse. Ranse must live with the realization that Tom has always been—and will probably always be—Hallie's great love. Add to this—all three must live with the lie about who really shot Liberty

Valance. Add to all of this—there's the undercurrent in the film that the "great dream," the dream of bringing the "blessings of civilization" to the "untamed West" is not as idyllic as originally imagined, that in fact something vital has been taken out of the equation. If that's not sufficiently noir, then nothing is. In terms of its point of view, this is a very dark story.

To underscore this dark perspective, Ford relies heavily both on a noirish narrative structure and a noir-ish visual design.

The narrative structure, of course, is classic noir flashback with voice-over narration. The story begins and ends with the older Ranse and Hallie's return to Shinbone to pay their respects to the recently departed Tom. The visit gives Ranse the opportunity to tell the central story the way it should be told—to come clean, as it were. Occasionally throughout, we also hear Ranse's voice-over. The film even offers another very noir-ish flourish (harkening back to films such as 1946's *The Locket*) when Tom tells Ranse what really happened the night Liberty Valance was shot—a flashback within a flashback.

This structure accomplishes several things. First, it helps to build curiosity and suspense around Ranse, Hallie, and Tom. How, for example, did this very prominent man, Ranse, emerge from the backwater of Shinbone? Why is Hallie, when we first see her, so distracted and devastated? Why doesn't anyone in Shinbone know who Tom is anymore? Second, this structure allows us to question the veracity of Ranse's account. Is it really the truth? Or is it slanted and at times self-serving? Throughout we're given hints that it is at least colored. One very telling clue is the characterization of law officer Link Appleyard. In the flashback, he's portrayed as fool and a bumbler. But, in the real-time scenes, he comes across as a thoughtful, sensitive man who is nobody's fool and who even seems far more in tune with Hallie's feelings than Ranse is. It's curious, too, that his first name, "Link," may suggest a connection between current and past stories. And third, the flashback structure also underscores a very noir-like determinism. Because the critical events and decisions in these people's lives have already occurred—and occurred decades before— their destinies have been set. Tom is already dead, and Ranse and Hallie are nearing the end of their lives. Their pasts have helped define them, and to a large extent both Ranse and Hallie remain prisoners of those pasts. Ironically, when Ranse makes the very courageous choice to tell the real story (or at least his version of events), he finds that, for the good of the nation, it will be suppressed. And a few minutes later, the film ends with its famous last line, emphasizing that Ranse and Hallie will—because there doesn't seem to be any other way out—go on living the lie.

The film's visual design is heavily noir-ish as well. Not only is it filmed in black and white, which was highly unusual for a 1962 western, of course, but the abundance of darkness is highly unusual for any kind of western except for a noir-ish one. Many exterior scenes, for example, are set at night, and many of these are darkly lit streets and alleys. Occasionally, interiors, such as the newspaper office before Liberty Valance and his thugs brutalize Dutton Peabody, are also set in darkness. And in every case, a sense of both mystery and anxiety is heightened—a very noir-like practice. Ford uses dark shadows in very noir-ish ways as well. In several scenes, for example, black shadows beside characters clearly suggest the dark thoughts that might be swirling around in their heads. Finally, it's quite intriguing how many scenes in the film show light filtering through windows and casting lattice-like shadows over characters. We see this over and over again—in the funeral parlor, in the streets of Shinbone at night, in the schoolroom, in the room adjacent to statehood convention, and so on. Not only do these shadows suggest a claustrophobic environment, but they also suggest entrapment—as if the characters are somehow caged, somehow imprisoned in this world. It's a very popular noir device, one employed in numerous films to suggest prison bars or another, similar kind of entrapment. And it dramatically underscores the noir-ish theme of determinism we see throughout the film—that, to some extent at least, these characters are all trapped by their past choices as well.

"It is our misfortune as film critics that we must discuss a film one-thing-at-a-time when on the screen so many things are happening and reverberating at the same time," critic Andrew Sarris once wrote.[13]

When we consider a film as rich in content and complex in design as *The Man Who Shot Liberty Valance*, this statement resonates all the more deeply. Every moment in this film offers us at least two and usually more things to think about: what's being said, how it's being said, what's left unsaid, why it's left unsaid, what we see, how the whole frame is composed, how our senses are responding to the visuals, what's led to this moment in the story, what will come after it, and so on. This is partially why it's unfair to pigeonhole *Valance* as simply a noir western; it is about many things. But in both its sensibility and style, it is also deeply noir-ish—a film about dreams gone awry, living with moral compromise, and the futility of trying to free ourselves from our pasts as well a film that reinforces these themes narratively with a flashback story structure and visually with black-and-white cinematography, dark shadows, claustrophobic settings, and many of other noir trappings.

Conclusion
Ride On, Dark Cowboy

The movie western—to use Tom Doniphon's appraisal of Ransom Stoddard in *The Man Who Shot Liberty Valance*—is "a persistent cuss." At various times since the early 1900s, numerous people have declared it dead and buried. Then, almost as soon as they do, a new crop of westerns begins to sprout, fueled by the fertile soil of a proud tradition and offering audiences something that's both different from the past and pertinent to the present.

This happens, of course, because many of us have embraced westerns as our foundation myths in roughly the same way that the ancient Greeks cherished their Trojan War stories or the British are still drawn to their Arthurian legends. We love seeing these western stories told and retold, often with new embellishments that may speak to contemporary concerns or preoccupations.

In the more than half-century since the films featured in this book were first released, the western form has undergone many permutations. It's intriguing, for example, to imagine just what Sam Fuller and Delmer Daves would have to say about the 21st century remakes of their respective films, *I Shot Jesse James* and *3:10 to Yuma*. And it's even more fun to imagine what John Ford or William Wellman—neither of whom was ever shy about using salty language—would have to say about Jon Favreau's quirky cross-genre experiment *Cowboys and Aliens* (2011).

Yet one element that has remained a prominent part of the western genre has been its noir-ish sensibility and style. In fact, noir, which peacefully coexisted with traditional westerns during the late 1940s and throughout the 1950s, has effectively taken over. In the 21st century alone, a sizable majority of the significant westerns from Andrew Dominik's 2007 *The Assassination of Jesse James by the Coward Robert Ford* to Paul Michael Thomas' 2007 *There*

Will Be Blood, to David Milch's 2004–06 HBO series *Deadwood* are filled with dark themes and noir-ish visual designs to go with them. Reflecting not only our largely pessimistic times, but also our desire for a less idealized, more accurate depiction of human nature, these 21st century tales have certainly turned the mythical West into a much darker place then it was, say, in 1939 when the ever-smiling Gene Autry first sang "Back in the Saddle Again."

It's curious, too, that as the noir style and sensibility have spread into science fiction, action, superhero, and other film genres, variations of western noir dark cowboys—even more than typical crime noir anti-heroes—have also become prominent (if not dominant) in those genres. As previously mentioned, perhaps one of the foremost examples of this since 2000 has been Christopher Nolan's Batman trilogy (2005's *Batman Begins*, 2008's *The Dark Knight,* and 2012's *The Dark Knight Rises*) with Christian Bale as the gloomy superhero. But countless other examples from the Wolverine character (played by Hugh Jackman) in the X-Men films to Walter White (played by Bryan Cranston) in AMC's *Breaking Bad* series (2008–13) abound. Whether it's in a fantasy Gotham City or present-day Albuquerque (where *Breaking Bad* is set), the dark cowboy still rides. (Instead of on a horse, it might be in the Batplane or in Walter White's mobile meth lab, but he still rides.)

What's ahead for the dark cowboy and the noir western? Very likely, it will be more of what we see today both in film and on cable TV channels that specialize in edgy original programming—occasional stories set in the "Wild West" along with stories set in the present, future, or elsewhere in the past that are effectively noir westerns. Judging by the kinds of film and TV entertainments audiences have flocked to over the last couple of decades, our fascination with noir-ish stories and their shaded, morally ambiguous anti-heroes has greatly increased. And, if anything, this fascination will continue to grow.

Yes, the dark cowboy—and the western myths he evokes—will be with us for a long time.

Fifty Additional Noir-ish Postwar Westerns Worth Seeing

Here is a list of films made between 1946 and 1962, which readers curious about continuing their study of the noir western might consider seeing. Not all of them are masterpieces. In fact, some, such as King Vidor's *Duel in the Sun*, leave *much* to be desired. But all do have a sufficient amount of noir content in them, and most are also available on DVD.

Again, this list is highly subjective and no doubt leaves out noir westerns that many readers might find equally or more deserving of inclusion.

Finally, this list does not include many westerns made between 1946 and 1962, which, while they may be excellent films—some even masterpieces—in their own right, have comparatively little noir-ish content. Examples here range from Stevens' *Shane* (1952), to Hawks' *Rio Bravo* (1959), to Peckinpah's *Ride the High Country* (1962).

1. *Duel in the Sun* (1946) King Vidor (with Gregory Peck and Jennifer Jones) Forbidden, destructive passions explode in this overwrought epic that critics quickly nicknamed "Lust in the Dust."
2. *My Darling Clementine* (1946) John Ford (with Henry Fonda and Victor Mature) Wyatt Earp and a brooding, self-destructive Doc Holliday form an uneasy alliance and eventually have it out with the brutal Clantons at the OK Corral.
3. *Red River* (1948) Howard Hawks (with John Wayne and Montgomery Clift) John Wayne goes to the dark side as he loses control over his men during a do-or-die cattle drive.
4. *The Man from Colorado* (1948) Henry Levin (with Glenn Ford, William Holden, and Ellen Drew) After the Civil War, a Union officer who has become addicted to killing becomes a federal judge and continues right on with his addiction.
5. *Station West* (1948) Sidney Lanfield (with Dick Powell and Jane Greer) Sparks fly between a military intelligence officer operating undercover and a sultry saloon singer with serious secrets of her own.
6. *Lust for Gold* (1949) S. Sylvan Simon (with Glenn Ford and Ida Lupino)

A late 1800s story about the legendary Lost Dutchman Gold Mine is framed by a modern story, both involving that eternal lust for gold.

7. *Rimfire* (1949) B. Reeves Eason (with James Millican) An undercover army agent investigating the thefts of army gold shipments must look into stories of a gambler's ghost terrorizing the local town.

8. *Roughshod* (1949) Mark Robson (with Gloria Grahame and Robert Sterling) Two traveling brothers help four stranded saloon girls while trying to avoid an escaped convict, who has vowed to kill one of the brothers.

9. *The Walking Hills* (1949) John Sturges (with Randolph Scott) A group, in which several members have unresolved conflicts, take off in search of a legendary lost wagon filled with gold. When they find it, they learn that it's empty. Or is it?

10. *Winchester 73* (1950) Anthony Mann (with James Stewart, Stephen McNally, Shelley Winters, and Dan Duryea) After one son kills his father, the other son seeks vengeance. In the meantime, both lust after a classic Winchester 73 rifle.

11. *The Furies* (1950) Anthony Mann (with Barbara Stanwyck, Walter Huston, Judith Anderson, and Gilbert Roland) There's a great noir look and feel plus lots of neurotic behavior and shades of Greek tragedy in this drama about a very dysfunctional family that runs a ranching empire.

12. *Rawhide* (1951) Henry Hathaway (with Tyrone Power and Susan Hayward) A man new to the stagecoach business must defend a remote way station from four robbers who've taken it over.

13. *The Secret of Convict Lake* (1951) Michael Gordon (with Glenn Ford and Gene Tierney) A convict escapes from prison to kill the man who framed him, but, after he meets the man's beautiful future wife, he has second thoughts.

14. *Rancho Notorious* (1952) Fritz Lang (with Marlene Dietrich, Arthur Kennedy, and Mel Ferrer) A rancher, seeking to avenge his fiancée's murder, winds up at Chuck-a-Luck, a ranch set up to hide criminals, and finds himself in over his head.

15. *High Noon* (1952) Fred Zinnemann (with Gary Cooper, Grace Kelly, and Thomas Mitchell) Bad men come back to get even with the marshal who put their leader in prison, but the marshal can't find any townspeople to help him.

16. *The Lawless Breed* (1952) Raoul Walsh (with Rock Hudson and Julia Adams) After his release from prison, outlaw John Wesley Hardin tells the story of what got him there.

17. *Bend of the River* (1952) Anthony Mann (with James Stewart and Arthur Kennedy) A former gunman keeps his dark secret to himself as he helps a wagon train of people hoping to settle in Oregon.

18. *Last of the Comanches* (1953) André de Toth (with Broderick Crawford and Barbara Hale) The survivors of a massacred cavalry troop and a motley group of stagecoach passengers try to survive a Comanche attack at a desert ruin.

19. *Ride Clear of Diablo* (1954) Jesse Hibbs (with Audie Murphy and Dan Duryea) A tenderfoot railroad surveyor goes after rustlers who killed his father and brother.

20. *Garden of Evil* (1954) Henry Hathaway (with Gary Cooper, Susan Hayward, and Richard Widmark) Three Americans stuck in rural Mexico agree to help a woman rescue her husband, who is trapped in a cave in Apache territory.

21. *The Bounty Hunter* (1954) André de Toth (with Randolph Scott) A bounty hunter arrives in Twin Forks in search of three men involved in a violent train robbery, and his presence raises tensions among the townspeople.

22. *Johnny Guitar* (1954) Nicholas Ray (with Joan Crawford, Sterling Hayden, Mercedes McCambridge, and Ward Bond) A favorite among critics today, this self-conscious revisionist western features ultra-strong women characters and passive, compliant men. Western regular Bond seems utterly lost in the proceedings.

23. *The Far Country* (1954) Anthony Mann (with James Stewart and Walter Brennan) The dark cowboy goes north as a cattleman leads a drive to the Canadian city of Dawson and must deal with a devious, dishonest lawman.

24. *The Man from Laramie* (1955) Anthony Mann (with James Stewart, Arthur Kennedy, and Donald Crisp) A stranger from Laramie comes to town to avenge his brother's murder and must tangle with both the troubled son of a prominent rancher and the rancher's double-dealing foreman.

25. *A Lawless Street* (1955) Joseph H. Lewis (with Randolph Scott and Angela Lansbury) When he attempts to run a gang of criminals out of town, a marshal must come to grips with unpleasant realities from his past.

26. *The Violent Men* (1955) Ralph Mate (with Barbara Stanwyck and Glenn Ford) An ex–Union officer uses his military experience to defend his ranch against another rancher's bullying tactics as his brother carries on with the other rancher's wayward wife.

27. *A Man Alone* (1955) Ray Milland (with Milland, Mary Murphy, and Ward Bond) A man, who comes upon a stagecoach after it has been robbed and all the passengers killed, reports the crime and then is accused of perpetrating it.

28. *The Indian Fighter* (1955) André de Toth (with Kirk Douglas and Elsa Martinelli) Leading a wagon train through hostile Indian country, a man becomes involved with a Sioux chief's daughter in this film noted for its more progressive attitudes toward Native Americans.

29. *The Searchers* (1956) John Ford (with John Wayne, Jeffrey Hunter, Ward Bond, and Vera Miles) Wayne goes to the dark side again as the racist Ethan Edwards who spends years obsessively searching for his niece, Debbie, who's been kidnapped and raised by the Comanche.

30. *The Last Wagon* (1956) Delmer Daves (with Richard Widmark and Felicia Farr) After their wagon train is attacked by Comanches, the few who've survive must entrust their lives to Comanche Todd, a white man who has lived as a Comanche most of his life.

31. *Tribute to a Bad Man* (1956) Robert Wise (with James Cagney) A hard-as-nails horse rancher runs his spread with an iron hand and shows rustlers no mercy whatever.

32. *Jubal* (1956) Delmer Daves (with Glenn Ford, Ernest Borgnine, and Rod Steiger) Nicknamed "Othello on the Range," that "green-eyed monster" jealousy rears its ugly head in Wyoming as rancher's wife lusts after the handsome new ranch foreman.

33. *7 Men from Now* (1956) Budd Boetticher (with Randolph Scott, Gail Russell, and Lee Marvin) An ex-lawman out to avenge his wife's murder helps a married

couple unfamiliar with western life, developing a strong attraction to the wife along the way.

34. *Backlash* (1956) John Sturges (with Richard Widmark and Donna Reed) Seeking a man he feels could have prevented his father's death by going for help instead of running away with a stash of gold during an Apache ambush, Jim Slater stumbles into a no-holds-barred range war.

35. *Run of the Arrow* (1957) Sam Fuller (with Rod Steiger) A Confederate veteran who goes west, takes a Sioux wife, and denounces the U.S., must make a momentous decision when the Sioux and the U.S. Cavalry head into battle.

36. *Valerie* (1957) Gerd Oswald (with Sterling Hayden, Anita Ekberg, and Anthony Steel) A man tried for critically wounding his wife and killing her parents explains the series of events that drove him to violence.

37. *Black Patch* (1957) Allen Miner (with George Montgomery) A town marshal accused of killing an old friend, who has apparently robbed a bank, must prove his innocence and face a young man with a fast gun who wants to do him in.

38. *The Halliday Brand* (1957) Joseph H. Lewis (with Joseph Cotton) A son plans to destroy his father, a manipulative town sheriff, who purposely let his daughter's lover be lynched.

39. *The Left Handed Gun* (1958) Arthur Penn (with Paul Newman) When his kind, considerate boss is killed by rival cattlemen, a hot-headed young man vows revenge.

40. *The Badlanders* (1958) Delmer Daves (with Alan Ladd and Ernest Borgnine) In this remake of the 1950 noir, *The Asphalt Jungle*, two men, just released from Yuma Prison, seek revenge against a swindler by plotting a clever gold-mine robbery.

41. *The Fiend Who Walked the West* (1958) Gordon Douglas (with Robert Evans, Hugh O'Brian, and Linda Cristal) In this remake of the 1947 noir, *Kiss of Death*, a convict gets involved with a psychotic, homicidal inmate who, after he gets out of jail, terrorizes the first man's wife and kills his friends.

42. *No Name on the Bullet* (1958) Jack Arnold (with Audie Murphy) A professional killer comes to town, and, because no one knows who he has come to kill, everyone is worried.

43. *Gunman's Walk* (1958) Phil Karlson (with Van Heflin and Tab Hunter) A prominent rancher goes to great lengths to protect his wild, irresponsible son ... until the son goes too far.

44. *The Big Country* (1958) William Wyler (with Gregory Peck, Jean Simmons, Charlton Heston, and Burl Ives) A very "green" Easterner comes west, where he becomes involved in a feud between two families fighting over valuable land.

45. *Terror in a Texas Town* (1958) Joseph L. Lewis (with Sterling Hayden) A son avenges his father's killing in a showdown involving a harpoon gun.

46. *Face of a Fugitive* (1959) Paul Wendkos (with Fred MacMurray and James Coburn) A man wrongly accused of murder escapes and settles in a U.S.-Mexico border town, but his pursuers are after him.

47. *Last Train from Gun Hill* (1959) John Sturges (with Kirk Douglas and Anthony Quinn) A marshal, whose wife has been brutally raped and murdered, tries to bring the son of an old friend to justice for committing the heinous acts.

48. *Sergeant Rutledge* (1960) John Ford (with Jeffrey Hunter, Woody Strode, and Constance Towers) As an African American cavalryman faces rape and murder charges in a court martial, witnesses recount crucial past events in eerie, dreamlike flashbacks.

49. *Comanche Station* (1960) Budd Boetticher (with Randolph Scott) After a mysterious stranger ransoms a white woman from Comanches, they journey back to her husband and son.

50. *One-Eyed Jacks* (1961) Marlon Brando (with Brando and Karl Malden) A bank robber takes the stolen gold while leaving his partner to be captured. Years later, the partner escapes from prison and comes looking for revenge.

Chapter Notes

Introduction

1. Necrometrics.com, "Source List and Detailed Death Tolls for the Primary Megadeaths of the Twentieth Century," necrometrics.com.
2. Jon C. Hopwood, biography for George Stevens, imdb.com.
3. James Naremore, *More Than Night: Film Noir in Its Contexts* (Berkeley: University of California Press, 2008) p. 16.
4. Mary Lea Bandy and Kevin Stoehr, *Ride, Boldly Ride: The Evolution of the American Western* (Berkeley: University of California Press, 2012) p. 156.
5. Jake Hinkson, "A Darkness on the Plains: 8 Classic Western Noir Films," CriminalElement.com, April 23, 2013.

Chapter 1

1. William Wellman, Jr., Commentary for *The Ox-Bow Incident* DVD, 20th Century–Fox Home Entertainment, 2003.
2. Ibid.
3. Bosley Crowther, "*The Ox-Bow Incident*," *New York Times*, May 10, 1943.
4. Toshi Fugiwara, "*The Ox-Bow Incident* (1943)," *La Furia Umana*.
5. Notation on www.clinteastwood.org/forums.
6. Fugiwara.
7. Ibid.
8. Josh Anderson, "Westward Wellman," *Senses of Cinema*, July 2013.
9. Paul Tatara, "*Track of the Cat* (1954)," Turner Classic Movies website.
10. Dennis Schwartz, *Ozus' World Movie Reviews*, December 24, 2005.
11. Tatara.
12. Ibid.
13. Anderson.

Chapter 2

1. Raoul Walsh, *Each Man in His Time* (New York: Farrar, Straus, Giroux, 1974) p. 17.
2. Marilyn Ann Moss, *Raoul Walsh: The True Adventures of Hollywood's Legendary Director* (Lexington: University of Kentucky Press, 2011) p. 2.
3. Tag Gallagher, "Raoul Walsh," *Senses of Cinema*, July 2002.
4. "Raoul Walsh: A Man in His Time," short-subject documentary (Cloverland, 2013).
5. Ibid.
6. Bosley Crowther, "*Pursued*," *New York Times*, March 8, 1947.
7. Moss, p. 269.
8. James S. Rich, "*Pursued* (1947)," *DVD Talk*, September 4, 2012.
9. Moss, p. 270.
10. Ibid.
11. Ibid, p. 283.
12. Frank Miller, "*Colorado Territory* (1949)," Turner Classic Movies website.
13. Ibid.
14. Ibid.
15. "Raoul Walsh," imdb.com.

Chapter 3

1. Fred Camper, "Harsh Master: Films by Andre deToth," *Chicago Reader*, October 2, 1997.

2. Rick Lyman, "André de Toth, Director of Noted 3-D Film, Is Dead," *New York Times*, November 1, 2002.
3. Ibid.
4. Adrian Danks, "Driftin': In Tribute to André de Toth," *Senses of Cinema*, March 2003.
5. Alain Silver, "André de Toth (1913–2002): An Interview," *Senses of Cinema*, March 2003. (Originally published in *Film Noir Reader 3* on February 12, 2001.)
6. Martin Scorsese, Foreword to *Fragments* by André de Toth (London: Faber and Faber, 1994), p. vii.
7. Silver.
8. A. W. "*Ramrod*, Fast-Moving Western With Veronica Lake, Joel McCrea Opens at the Globe," *New York Times*, June 30, 1947.
9. Rick Thompson, "André de Toth, Luke Short, *Ramrod*: style, source, genre" *Senses of Cinema*, March 2003.
10. Bertrand Tavernier, Preface to *Fragments* by André de Toth (London: Faber and Faber, 1994) p. xiii.
11. Camper.
12. Ibid.
13. Tristan, "*Day of the Outlaw*," *The Library of Babel*, September 12, 2012.
14. Camper.
15. Glenn Erickson, "*Day of the Outlaw*," *DVD Savant*, June 8, 2008.
16. Tristan.
17. Erickson.
18. Ibid.
19. Tavernier, p. x.
20. Camper.
21. Tavernier, p. xv.

Chapter 4

1. Rob Nixon, "*Blood on the Moon* (1948)," Turner Classic Movies website.
2. Eric Schaefer, "Nicholas Musuraca," www.filmreference.com.
3. "Nicolas Musuraca Biography," imdb.com.
4. Schaefer.
5. Ibid.
6. Ibid.
7. Craig Butler, "*Blood on the Moon*," AllMovie.com.
8. Nixon.
9. Ibid.
10. Butler.

Chapter 5

1. Anonymous, "*Forty Guns* (1957)," Turner Classic Movies website.
2. Glenn Erickson, "The First Films of Samuel Fuller: *I Shot Jesse James, The Baron of Arizona*, and *The Steel Helmet*," *DVD Savant*, August 14, 2007.
3. Lisa Dombrowski, *The Films of Samuel Fuller: "If You Die, I'll Kill You"* (Middletown, CT: Wesleyan University Press, 2008), p. 108.
4. Ibid., p. 8.
5. Ibid., p. 9.
6. Bret Wood, "*I Shot Jesse James* (1949)," Turner Classic Movies website.
7. Dombrowski, p.19.
8. Ibid., p. 107.
9. Tony Williams, "*Forty Guns*," *Senses of Cinema*, October 2005.
10. Chris Barsanti, "*Forty Guns* Movie Review," *Contact Music*, November 1, 2005.
11. The Playlist Staff, "The Essentials: The Best 5 Sam Fuller Films," *IndieWire*, August 10, 2012.
12. Anonymous, "*Forty Guns* (1957)," Turner Classic Movies website.
13. Dombrowski, p. 203.

Chapter 6

1. "The Western Grows Up" (DVD featurette), 20th Century–Fox Home Entertainment, 2008.
2. Original theatrical trailer for *The Bravados*, 1958; available on DVD from 20th Century–Fox Home Entertainment, 2005 .
3. I.S. Mowis, "Henry King—Mini-Biography," imdb.com.
4. Gerald Mast and Bruce F. Kawin, *A Short History of the Movies*, 9th ed. (New York: Pearson Longman, 2006) p. 144.
5. Ibid.
6. Lynn Haney, *Gregory Peck: A Charmed Life* (New York: Carroll & Graf, 2003) pp. 188–189.
7. Mowis.
8. Bosley Crowther, "*The Gunfigher*," *New York Times*, June 24, 1950.
9. Mike Lorefice, "*The Gunfighter*," *RBMovieReviews*, June 15, 2003.
10. Ibid.
11. Mowis.
12. Stuart Galbraith IV, "*The Bravados*" *DVD Talk*, May 21, 2005.

Chapter 7

1. Paul Mayersberg, "Actions Speak Louder Than Words: The Films of Anthony Mann," 1967 documentary.
2. In her book *Anthony Mann*, Jeanine Basinger credits Mann with only 10 westerns, stating that his 1960 film *Cimarron* is actually an epic. Most who have written about Mann, however, include *Cimarron* among his westerns.
3. Jeanine Basinger, *Anthony Mann* (Middletown, CT: Wesleyan University Press, 2007) p. 6.
4. Ibid., p. 1.
5. Ibid.
6. Ibid., p. 9.
7. Glenn Erickson, "*Devil's Doorway*," DVD Savant, January 23, 2013.
8. Basinger, p. 90.
9. Jim Kitses, *Horizons West: Directing the Western from John Ford to Clint Eastwood* (London: BFI, 2004) p. 162.
10. Glenn Erickson, "Mann of the West," DVD Savant, May 13, 2008.
11. Kitses, p. 154.
12. Derek Malcolm, "Anthony Mann: Man of the West," *The Guardian*, March 23, 2000.
13. Basinger, p. 118.
14. Ibid., p. 119.

Chapter 8

1. Peter Bogdanovich, *Allan Dwan: The Last Pioneer* (New York: Praeger, 1971) p. 8.
2. Richard Brody, "*Silver Lode*," thenewyorker.com, retrieved February 16, 2014.
3. *Cinema Talk*, "*Silver Lode* (1954)," cinematalk.com, August 15, 2013.
4. "*Silver Lode* (1954)," avaxhome.com, November 24, 2010.
5. Fernando F. Croce, "*Silver Lode*," *Slant Magazine*, June 9, 2010.
6. Bogdanovich, p. 6.
7. Ibid., p. 17.
8. Ronald Bowers, "Allan Dwan," *International Dictionary of Films and Filmmakers*, 2001.
9. Bogdanovich, p. 13.

10. Bowers.
11. Bogdanovich, p. 13.
12. *Cinema Talk*

Chapter 9

1. Mary Lea Bandy and Kevin Stoehr, *Ride, Boldly Ride* (Berkeley: University of California Press, 2012) p. 175.
2. Bosley Crowther, "*Pride of the Marines*, Based on War Career of Al Schmid, in Which John Garfield Stars, at Strand," *New York Times*, August 25, 1945.
3. Patricia King Hanson, "Delmer Daves," FilmReference.com.
4. Ibid.
5. Brian Garfield, *Western Films: A Complete Guide* (Rawson Associates, 1981).
6. Rob Nixon, "*3:10 to Yuma* (1957)," Turner Classic Movies website.
7. Ibid.
8. Blake Lucas, *Magill's Survey of Cinema, Second Series, Volume 6* (Salem Press, 1981).
9. Glenn Erickson, "*The Hanging Tree*," DVD Savant, August 1, 2012.
10. Edward Buscombe, *The B.F.I. Companion to the Western* (London: Atheneum, 1988).
11. Leonard Quart, "From the Archives: *The Hanging Tree*." *Cineaste Magazine*, 2012.
12. Erickson.
13. Jeff Stafford, "*The Hanging Tree* (1959)," Turner Classic Movies website (*Variety* review quoted here).
14. Erickson.
15. Ibid.
16. Quart.
17. Erickson.

Chapter 10

1. Jim Kitses, *Horizons West: Directing the Western from John Ford to Clint Eastwood* (London: BFI, 2004) p. 184.
2. Sean Axmaker, "Budd Boetticher, Last of the Old Hollywood Two-Fisted Directors," *Green Cine*, December 16, 2005.
3. Bruce Ricker, director/producer, "Budd Boetticher: A Man Can Do That," Turner Classic Movies, 2008.
4. Ibid.
5. Sean Axmaker, "Burt Kennedy: Writing Broadway in Arizona," *Parallax View*, November 6, 2008.

6. Kitses, p. 181.
7. Ricker.

Chapter 11

1. Ronald Davis, *John Ford: Hollywood's Old Master* (Norman: University of Oklahoma Press, 1995).
2. Steven Spielberg, *Steven Spielberg on Watching John Ford Films*, American Film Institute Archive Video (retrieved March 15, 2013).
3. Bill Nevins, "Contemporary Western: An Interview with Vince Gilligan," IQ.com, March 27, 2013.
4. Peter Bogdanovich, *The Essentials*, Turner Classic Movies, 2005.
5. Ibid.
6. Peter Bogdanovich, *Directed by John Ford*, a Turner Classic Movies documentary, 2006.
7. Joseph McBride, *Searching for John Ford* (New York: St. Martin's Griffin, 2001) p. 720.
8. "*Man Who Shot Liberty Valance* Opens at Capitol Theatre," *New York Times*, May 24, 1962.
9. Mary Lea Bandy and Kevin Stoehr, *Ride, Boldly Ride: The Evolution of the American Western* (Berkeley: University of California Press, 2012) p. 204.
10. "Lee Marvin Interview on John Ford and John Wayne," *The Director's Series*, Ira H. Gallen Video Resources, New York (retrieved July 19, 2014).
11. Bandy and Soehr, p. 199
12. "*The Man Who Shot Liberty Valance*" (1962) Turner Classic Movies website (retrieved July 18, 2014).
13. Andrew Sarris, *The John Ford Movie Mystery* (Bloomington: Indiana University Press, 1975) p. 174.

Bibliography

Anderson, Josh. "Westward Wellman." *Senses of Cinema,* July 2013.

Axmaker, Sean. "Budd Boetticher, Last of the Old Hollywood Two-Fisted Directors." *Green Cine,* December 16, 2005.

_____. "Burt Kennedy: Writing Broadway in Arizona." *Parallax View,* November 6, 2008.

Bandy, Mary Lea, and Stoehr, Kevin. *Ride, Boldly Ride: The Evolution of the American Western.* Berkeley: University of California Press, 2012.

Barsanti, Chris. "*Forty Guns* Movie Review." *Contact Music,* November 1, 2005.

Basinger, Jeanine. *Anthony Mann.* Middletown, CT: Wesleyan University Press, 2007.

Bogdanovich, Peter. *Allan Dwan: The Last Pioneer.* New York: Praeger, 1971.

_____. *John Ford.* Berkeley: University of California Press, 1978.

Bowers, Ronald. "Allan Dwan." *International Dictionary of Films and Filmmakers,* 2001.

Brody, Richard. "*Silver Lode.*" thenewyorker.com, 2012.

Butler, Craig. "*Blood on the Moon.*" AllMovie.com.

Camper, Fred. "Harsh Master: Films by Andre deToth." *Chicago Reader,* October 2, 1997.

Croce, Fernando F. "*Silver Lode.*" *Slant Magazine,* June 9, 2010.

Crowther, Bosley. "*The Gunfigher.*" *New York Times,* June 24, 1950.

_____. "*The Ox-Bow Incident.*" *New York Times,* May 10, 1943.

_____. "*Pride of the Marines,* Based on War Career of Al Schmid, in Which John Garfield Stars, at Strand." *New York Times,* August 25, 1945.

_____. "*Pursued.*" *New York Times,* March 8, 1947.

Danks, Adrian. "Driftin': In Tribute to André de Toth*," Senses of Cinema,* March 2003.

Davis, Ronald. *John Ford: Hollywood's Old Master.* Norman: University of Oklahoma Press, 1995.

Dombrowski, Lisa. *The Films of Samuel Fuller: "If You Die, I'll Kill You."* Middletown, CT: Wesleyan University Press, 2008.

Erickson, Glenn. "*Day of the Outlaw.*" *DVD Savant,* June 8, 2008.

_____. "*Devil's Doorway.*" *DVD Savant,* January 23, 2013.

_____. "The First Films of Samuel Fuller: *I Shot Jesse James, The Baron of Arizona,* and *The Steel Helmet.*" *DVD Savant,* August 14, 2007.

_____. "*The Hanging Tree.*" *DVD Savant,* August 1, 2012.

_____. "*Mann of the West.*" *DVD Savant,* May 13, 2008.

Eyman, Scott. *Print the Legend: The Life and Times of John Ford.* Baltimore: Johns Hopkins University Press, 1999.

Fugiwara, Toshi. "*The Ox-Bow Incident* (1943)." *La Furia Umana.*

Galbraith IV, Stuart. "*The Bravados.*" *DVD Talk,* May 21, 2005.

Gallagher, Tag. *John Ford: The Man and His Films.* Berkeley: University of California Press, 1986.

_____. "Raoul Walsh." *Senses of Cinema*, July 2002.
Garfield, Brian. *Western Films: A Complete Guide*. Rawson Associates, 1981.
Haney, Lynn. *Gregory Peck: A Charmed Life*. New York: Carroll & Graf, 2003.
Hanson, Patricia King. "Delmer Daves." FilmReference.com.
Hinkson, Jake. "A Darkness on the Plains: 8 Classic Western Noir Films." CriminalElement.com, April 23, 2013.
Hirsch, Foster. *The Dark Side of the Screen: Film Noir*. Philadelphia: Da Capo Press, 1981.
Kitses, Jim. *Horizons West: Directing the Western from John Ford to Clint Eastwood*. London: BFI, 2004.
Lorefice, Mike. "*The Gunfighter*." RBMovieReviews, June 15, 2003.
Lyman, Rick. "André de Toth, Director of Noted 3-D Film, Is Dead." *New York Times*, November 1, 2002.
Maslin, Janet. "Henry King, Movie Director Known for Book Adaptations." *New York Times*, July 1, 1982.
Mast, Gerald, and Kawin, Bruce F. *A Short History of the Movies*, 9th ed. New York: Pearson Longman, 2006
McBride, Joseph. *Searching for John Ford*. New York: St. Martin's Griffin, 2001.
Miller, Frank. "*Colorado Territory* (1949)." Turner Classic Movies website.
Moss, Marilyn Ann. *Raoul Walsh: The True Adventures of Hollywood's Legendary Director*. Lexington: University of Kentucky Press, 2011.
Naremore, James. *More Than Night: Film Noir in Its Contexts*. Berkeley: University of California Press, 2008.
Nevins, Bill. "Contemporary Western: An Interview with Vince Gilligan." IQ.com, March 27, 2013
Nixon, Rob. "*3:10 to Yuma* (1957)." Turner Classic Movies website.
_____. "*Blood on the Moon* (1948)." Turner Classic Movies website.
Pippin, Robert B. *Hollywood Westerns and American Myth: The Importance of Howard Hawks and John Ford for Political Philosophy*. New Haven: Yale University Press, 2010.
Quart, Leonard. "From the Archives: *The Hanging Tree*." *Cineaste Magazine*, 2012.
Rich, James S. "*Pursued* (1947)." *DVD Talk*, September 4, 2012.
Sarris, Andrew. *The John Ford Movie Mystery*. Bloomington: Indiana University Press, 1975.
Schaefer, Eric "Nicholas Musuraca." www.filmreference.com/writersandproductionartists.
Scorsese, Martin. Foreword to *Fragments* by André de Toth. London: Faber and Faber, 1994.
Silver, Alain. "André de Toth (1913–2002): An Interview." *Senses of Cinema*, March 2003. (Originally published in *Film Noir Reader 3* on February 12, 2001.)
_____, and Ursini, James, eds. *Film Noir Reader*. Pompton Plains, NJ: Limelight Editions, 1996.
Spielberg, Steven. *Steven Spielberg on Watching John Ford Films*. American Film Institute Archive Video.
Stafford, Jeff. "*The Hanging Tree* (1959)." Turner Classic Movies website.
Tatara, Paul. "*Track of the Cat* (1954)." Turner Classic Movies website.
Tavernier, Bertrand. Preface to *Fragments* by André de Toth. London: Faber and Faber, 1994.
Thompson, Rick. "André de Toth, Luke Short, *Ramrod*: style, source, genre." *Senses of Cinema*, March 2003.
Walsh, Raoul. *Each Man in His Time*. New York: Farrar, Straus, Giroux, 1974.
Williams, Tony. "*Forty Guns*." *Senses of Cinema*, October 2005.
Wood, Bret. "*I Shot Jesse James* (1949)." Turner Classic Movies website.

Index

Academy Awards 26, 36, 42, 70, 73, 84, 99, 114, 171, 186, 189
Act of Violence 33, 170, 183
Altman, Robert 17
Alton, John 117, 139, 144, 148
The American Cinema: Directors and Directions 1929–1968 121
American Film Institute Center for Advanced Film Studies 74
An American in Paris 144
Anderson, Josh 35, 37
Anderson, Judith 46–47
Anthony Mann (2007) 117
Arruza (1972 film) 174
Arruza, Carlos 173
The Asphalt Jungle 151
The Assassination of Jesse James by the Coward Robert Ford 197
Autry, Gene 198
Avaxhome 142
Axmaker, Sean 170

Back in the Saddle Again 198
The Badlanders 151
Bandy, Mary Lea 193
Barsanti, Chris 91
Basinger, Jeanine 117, 119, 121, 128, 133, 139
Batman Trilogy 198
The Battle of Villa Florita 154
Bazin, André 13
Beggars of Life 23
Bel Geddes, Barbara 77
Bend of the River 116
Bergman, Ingmar 185
The Big Combo 144
The Big Country 18
The Big Red One 84
The Big Sleep 9
The Big Trail 41, 42

The Birth of a Nation 41, 188
The Black Angel 9
Blackton, J. Stuart 74
Blood and Sand 171
Blood on the Moon 70–80
The Body Snatcher 70, 73
Boetticher, Budd 18, 97, 168–184
Bogaeus, Benedict 143
Bogart, Humphrey 58
Bogdanovich, Peter 142, 143, 144, 189, 190
Bondi, Beulah 36
Boone, Richard 175
Border Incident 119
Bowers, Ronald 143
Bowers, William 107
Boyd, Stephen 110, 113
The Bravados 16–17, 18, 98, 107–114
Breaking Bad 188, 198
Brennan, Walter 14, 78
Brody, Richard 142
Broken Arrow 126, 150, 153
Brown, Clarence 22
Brown, Harry Joe 171
Brownlow, Kevin 144
Buchanan Rides Alone 172
Budd Boetticher: A Man Can Do That 184
Buffalo Bill 23
The Bullfighter and the Lady 171
Busch, Niven 43, 44
Butler, Craig 78, 80

The Cabinet of Dr. Caligari 9
Cagney, James 41
Cain, James M. 9
Caldwell, Erskine 120
Camper, Fred 66, 68
Capra, Frank 6, 42
The Captives 174
Carey, Harry, Sr. 189
Carousel 100

Cascade Mountains 64
Cat People 75
Cattle Queen of Montana 141, 143
Chandler, Raymond 9
Chase, Borden 116, 120, 139
Cheyenne Autumn 190
Cimarron 117, 120–121
Cinema Talk 142
Cinemark 22
Citizen Kane 8, 70
Clark, Walter Van Tilburg 22, 29, 36
Clothier, William 36, 193
Collins, Joan 113–114
Colman, Ronald 99
Colorado Territory 39, 47–53
Columbia Pictures 56
Comanche Station 16, 169, 172
Companion to the Western (British Film Institute) 161
Coonan, Dorothy 26
Cooper, Gary 56, 99, 118, 134, 147, 163, 166
The Covered Wagon 1, 152
Cowboy 153–154
Cowboys and Aliens 197
Crime Wave 58, 63, 170
The Crimson Kimono 84
Croce, Fernando 142
Crossfire 16
Crowther, Bosley 26–27, 42–43, 103
The Curse of the Cat People 73

Dachau 6
Dances with Wolves 125
A Dandy in Aspic 121
Dark Passage 150, 153
A Darkness on the Plains 18
Darwell, Jane 30
Daves, Delmer 16, 18, 97, 150–167
Day of the Outlaw 18, 55, 56, 64–69
The Day the Earth Stood Still 73
D-Day 6
Deadwood 198
Death Valley 15, 31
Decision at Sundown 172
Desilu Studios 75
Desperate 119
Destination Tokyo 152
de Toth, Andre 9, 55–69, 107
Devil's Doorway 115, 117, 120, 122–128, 130
Directed by John Ford 190
Directors Guild of America 74
Do Not Forsake Me, Oh My Darlin' 147
Dr. Broadway 119
Dombrowski, Lisa 84, 85, 86, 91, 95
Dominik, Andrew 17, 197
Double Indemnity 9, 63

Douglas, Kirk 56
Duel in the Sun 18
Duryea, Dan 148
DVD Talk 108
Dwan, Allan 18, 99, 140–149

Eastwood, Clint 17, 27, 31
El Cid 121
Erickson, Glenn 66, 67, 82, 126–127, 133, 161, 165, 166
Essanay Film Manufacturing Company 142

Fairbanks, Douglas, Sr. 24, 140
The Fall of the Roman Empire 120
The Far Country 116
Farber, Manny 84
Favreau, Jon 197
femme fatale 60, 61
film noir (defined) 9
Fleming, Victor 22
Flynn, Errol 41
Fonda, Henry 26
Forbidden Hollywood (DVD set) 22
Force of Evil 34, 132
Ford, Glenn 16, 97, 155, 160
Ford, John 6, 16, 42, 49, 97, 139, 171, 185–196
Fort Apache 189
Forty Guns 82, 90–95
Frank, Nino 9
Frisco Jenny 23
Fugiwara, Toshi 27, 30, 31
Fuller, Sam 6, 81–96
The Furies 93, 117, 122, 130, 137

Gable, Clark 41
Galbraith, Stuart 108
Gallagher, Tag 38–39, 190
Gardner, Ava 58
Garfield, Brian 154
Gentleman Jim 41
Gentleman's Agreement 98
Gill, David 144
Gilligan, Vince 188
Gish, Lillian 99, 140
Godard, Jean-Luc 82
God's Little Acre 120
Golden Globe Award 99
Gone with the Wind 7
The Grapes of Wrath 189
The Great Train Robbery 11
Griffith, D.W. 41, 42, 140, 188
Gun Crazy 94
The Gunfighter 16, 97, 98, 102–107, 110–111, 116, 120
Gunman's Chance 71

Index 213

Hammett, Dashiell 9
The Hanging Tree 15, 152, 161–166
Have Gun—Will Travel 174
Harvey, Laurence 121
Hathaway, Henry 18
Hawks, Howard 18, 97
Heflin, Van 155, 160
Hell and High Water 86
Hemingway, Ernest 9, 98
Henson, Patricia King 154
Hepburn, Katharine 6
Heroes for Sale 23
High Noon 18, 142; parallels and contrasts with *Silver Lode* 145–148, 158
High Sierra 39, 41, 47, 49, 53
Hinkson, Jake 18
Hitchcock, Alfred 185
Hollywood: The Silent Years 144
Homeier, Skip 103
Horizons West (1952 film) 171
Horizons West: Directing the Western from John Ford to Clint Eastwood (2004 book) 117
House by the River 186
House of Wax 58
How Green Was My Valley 189, 194
Howard, Leslie 7
Howe, James Wong 14, 46
Huston, John 6

I Shot Jesse James 15, 82, 84, 86–90
I Want to Live! 73
In a Lonely Place 67
In Old Chicago 99
The Indian Fighter 56
IndieWire 93
The Informer 189
Ireland, John 87, 89
The Iron Horse 12, 13, 189
The Iron Mask 140
Ives, Burl 56, 67

Jack, Harold 132
Japanese Instrument of Surrender 5
Jarmusch, Jim 82
John Ford Ireland 185
John Ford: The Man and His Work 190
Johnny Guitar 18, 93
Joyner, Courtney 40
Jubal 16, 151
Jurado, Katy 147

Kawin, Bruce F. 99
Kennedy, Arthur 116
Kennedy, Burt 171, 172, 174
The Killers 9, 47

King, Henry 15, 16, 97–114
Kitses, Jim 117, 132, 133, 169, 177
Klondike Annie 40
Korda, Alexander 57
Kurosawa, Akira 185

Lake, Veronica 14, 56, 59, 60
Lang, Fritz 6, 9, 119
The Last Frontier 120
The Last Pioneer 142
The Last Wagon 151
The Lawless Breed 39
Lawton, Charles 160–161, 173
Leave Her to Heaven 8
Leigh, Janet 131
Leonard, Elmore 154, 158, 174
Leone, Sergio 17, 82, 194
Lewis, Joseph L. 18
Lewton, Val 73
Lippert, Robert 81, 84, 86
Little Big Man 125
The Locket 74, 195
Lombard, Carole 7
London, Julie 118, 134
Lord, Jack 134
Lorefice, Mark 106
Lorre, Peter 8
Louise, Tina 56
Love Is a Many-Splendored Thing 99, 100
Lucas, Blake 161

M 9
The Magnificent Ambersons 70
Malcolm, Derek 133
Malden, Karl 105, 107, 166
The Maltese Falcon 9, 67
The Man from Laramie 116
The Man from the Alamo 171
Man of the West 117, 133–139
The Man Who Shot Liberty Valance 16, 17, 185–196, 197
Mangold, James 17
Mann, Anthony 15, 16, 115–139
Marvin, Lee 190, 193
Mast, Gerald 99
Mature, Victor 14, 97, 187
Mayo, Virginia 48, 50, 52–53
McBride, Joseph 190
McCabe and Mrs. Miller 37
McCarthy, Senator Joseph 147
McCrea, Joel 48, 50, 52, 56, 59, 60
McDonald, Joe 15, 32, 34
Meeker, Ralph 131
Men in War 120
Midnight Mary 23
Midway (Battle of) 6

Milch, David 17, 198
Mildred Pierce 9
Miles, Vera 193
Miller, Arthur C. 30, 103, 107
Miller, Frank 51, 53
Milner, Victor 117
Mitchell, Millard 107, 116, 131
Mitchum, Robert 14, 36, 43, 45, 46, 77, 78
Moab (Utah) 193
Mogambo 189
Molnar, Ferenc 57
Monument Valley 188, 193
Moran, Dolores 148
Morgan, Harry 26
Moss, Marilyn Ann 38, 46, 47
Most Dangerous Man Alive 141, 144
Mowis, I.S. 99, 101, 108
Museum of Modern Art (New York) 74
Musuraca, Nicholas 72, 73, 74–76, 77, 80
My Darling Clementine 14, 186, 187, 188, 190

The Naked Kiss 84
The Naked Spur 16, 116, 117, 128–132, 136
National Film Registry (U.S. Library of Congress) 174
Neilson, James 120
neo-noir (and representative neo-noir films) 10
New York Evening Graphic 83
New York Times 59, 114, 152–153, 193
The New Yorker 142
Night and the City 103
Night Nurse 23
Night Passage 120
Nightmare Alley 90
Nixon, Rob 159
noir western 10, (overview) 12–19
Nolan, Christopher 17, 198
None Shall Escape 57, 63, 68
Nosferatu 9
Notorious 71

O'Brien, Edmond 193
Odds Against Tomorrow 16, 73
The Odyssey 137
Ohio State University 170
One Mysterious Night 171
Operation, Burma! 41
Out of the Past 47, 72, 75, 103, 117; parallels with *Man of the West* 137–138, 169
The Ox-Bow Incident 14, 21, 22, 23, 24, 26–31, 37, 43, 45

Payne, John 146
Peck, Gregory 16, 98, 100, 107, 113

Peckinpah, Sam 17
Pickford, Jack 53
Pickford, Mary 140
Pick-Up on South Street 84
Pitfall 58, 63
Play Dirty 66
Porter, Edwin S. 11
The Postman Always Rings Twice 9
Pride of the Marines 150, 152
Promontory Summit (Utah) 13
psychological western 102, 105, 116
The Public Enemy 23
Pudovkin, V.I. 99
The Purchase Price 23
Pursued 14, 23, 39, 42–47, 53
Pushover 63

Quart, Leonard 165, 166
The Quiet Man 189

Railroaded! 119
Ramrod 14, 23, 55, 56, 58–64, 71
Rancho Notorious 93
Ranown Pictures/Ranown Cycle 172
Raw Deal 119, 125, 144
Ray, Nicholas 18
Raymond, Paula 127
The Red House 150, 153
revisionist westerns 37
Ride, Boldly Ride 193
Ride Lonesome 16, 18, 169, 170, 172
Ride the High Country 17
Rio Grande 186, 189
The Rise and Fall of Legs Diamond 173
Ritter, Tex 147
RKO 70, 71, 72, 73, 75
The Roaring Twenties 39, 47
Robbins, Tim 83
Robin Hood 140
Roemheld, Heinz 173, 183
Rolfe, Sam 132
Romola 99
Roxie Theater (San Francisco) 22
Ryan, Robert 16, 56, 67, 131, 187

Sadie Thompson 40
Safe in Hell 22
Salmi, Albert 110, 113
The Sand Pebbles 73
The Sands of Iwo Jima 141
Sarris, Andrew 84, 121, 196
Scarlett Street 9
Schaefer, Eric 72, 75
Schell, Maria 163, 166
Schwartz, Dennis 36
Scorsese, Martin 58, 82, 185, 189

Index

Scott, Lisabeth 146
Scott, Randolph 15, 56, 97, 168, 170, 175, 181
The Searchers 16, 185, 187, 189, 190, 193
Searching for John Ford 190
Selznick, David O. 21, 119
Senses of Cinema 61
Sergeant Rutledge 187
The Set-Up 70
7 Men from Now 16, 169, 171, 172
7 Women 190
Shadow of a Doubt 169
Shamroy, Leon 113
She Wore a Yellow Ribbon 186, 187, 189, 193
Sherman, Harry 59
Sherwood, Robert 140
Shock Corridor 84
Short, Luke 71
Showtime 74
Sight and Sound Magazine 185
Silva, Henry 110, 113
Silver Lode 18, 140–149, 158
Siodmak, Robert 9
Sirk, Douglas 154
Slant Magazine 142
Slattery's Hurricane 57
The Snows of Kilimanjaro 98
Sokolov 83
The Song of Bernadette 99
The Sound of Music 71, 72
Spencer's Mountain 154
Spielberg, Steven 185
Springfield Rifle 56
Stagecoach 189
Stanford University 151, 152
Stanwyck, Barbara 83, 91, 92, 95, 141
A Star Is Born 21
State Fair 99
Station West 71
The Steel Helmet 82, 84, 85
Steele, Karen 181
Stella Dallas 99
Stevens, George 6
Stewart, James 16, 97, 116–117, 128, 131, 139, 190, 193
Stoehr, Kevin 193
A Storm in Summer 74
The Strange Love of Martha Ivors 83, 94
Stranger on the Third Floor 8, 74
Strangers on the Train 186
The Strawberry Blonde 41
Sturges, John 18
Sturges, Preston 119
Suez 141
Sullivan, Barry 92

Sunset Boulevard 186
superwestern 13
Swanson, Gloria 140

T-Men 119
The Tall T 16, 169, 17, 172, 174–179
Tarantino, Quentin 82
Tarzan Escapes 21
Tatara, Paul 35
Tavernier, Bertrand 61–62, 68, 69
Taylor, Robert 124, 127–128
Temple, Shirley 7
Tennessee's Partner 143
There Will Be Blood 197–198
They Died with Their Boots On 41
They Drive by Night 39
They Were Expendable 189
Thomas, Paul Michael 197
Thompson, Rick 61
3:10 to Yuma 16, 152, 153, 154–161
The Tin Star 120
To Kill a Mockingbird 98
Tokyo Bay 5, 7
Tol'able David 99
Toland, Gregg 74
Track of the Cat 21, 23, 35–37
Transcontinental Railroad 13, 189
Tristan 66
Trosper, Guy 126, 127
Trotti, Lamar 26, 31, 35
Truffaut, François 82
Turner Classic Movies 22
Twelve O'Clock High 98, 101–102
Two Rode Together 189
The Typewriter, the Rifle, and the Movie Camera 83

Ulmer, Edgar 9
Universal Motion Picture Manufacturing Company 189

Van Cleef, Lee 110, 113, 190
Vidor, King 18

Wagon Master 106, 186, 187, 189
Walsh, Raoul 15, 38–54
Warner, Jack 36–37, 47
Warner Brothers 53
Wayne, John 41, 97, 171, 187, 188, 191, 193
Webb, Roy 71, 149
Welles, Orson 26, 73, 188
Wellman, William 14, 15, 21–37
Wellman, William, Jr. 26
West Side Story 70, 72
What Price Glory 40
When in Disgrace 173

White Heat 39, 53
The White Sister 99
Wild Boys of the Road 23
Wilder, Billy 6, 9
Williams, Tony 91
Wilson 100
Wilson, Michael Henry 40
Winchester 73 16, 116, 119–120, 137
Wings 22, 25
The Winning of Barbara Worth 99
Wise, Robert 70–80

The Wizard of Oz 7
Woolrich, Cornell 9
World War II 5
Wright, Teresa 36, 43, 45
Wyler, William 6, 18, 42

Yellow Sky 15, 23, 31–35, 37

Zanuck, Darryl 26, 82–83, 84, 100, 171
Zinnemann, Fred 18

www.ingramcontent.com/pod-product-compliance
Ingram Content Group UK Ltd.
Pitfield, Milton Keynes, MK11 3LW, UK
UKHW041955140426
5217IPUK00015B/813